Frommer's®

Hong Kong day BY day®

2nd Edition

by Graham Bond

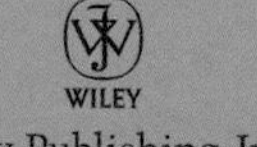

Wiley Publishing, Inc.

Contents

世紀夜總會
7/F
新輝煌
卡拉 OK
6/F

Published by:

Wiley Publishing, Inc.

111 River St.
Hoboken, NJ 07030-5774

ISBN 978-0-470-87481-3 (paper); ISBN 978-0-470-94585-8 (ebk); ISBN 978-0-470-94586-5 (ebk); ISBN 978-0-470-94587-2 (ebk)

Editor: Jamie Ehrlich
Production Editor: Heather Wilcox
Photo Editor: Richard Fox
Cartographer: Andy Dolan
Production by Wiley Indianapolis Composition Services

For information on our other products and services or to obtain technical support, please contact our Customer Care Department within the U.S. at 877/762-2974, outside the U.S. at 317/572-3993 or fax 317/572-4002.

Wiley also publishes its books in a variety of electronic formats. Some content that appears in print may not be available in electronic formats.

Manufactured in China

5 4 3 2 1

A Note from the Editorial Director

Organizing your time. That's what this guide is all about.

Other guides give you long lists of things to see and do and then expect you to fit the pieces together. The Day by Day guides are different. These guides tell you the best of everything, and then they show you how to see it *in the smartest, most time-efficient way*. Our authors have designed detailed itineraries organized by time, neighborhood, or special interest. And each tour comes with a bulleted map that takes you from stop to stop.

Hoping to wander Hong Kong's narrow streets in search of some of the best market shopping in the world? Planning to experience Cantonese culture or explore the lingering British colonial influence? Whatever your interest or schedule, the Day by Days give you the smartest routes to follow. Not only do we take you to the top attractions, hotels, and restaurants, but we also help you access those special moments that locals get to experience—those "finds" that turn tourists into travelers.

The Day by Days are also your top choice if you're looking for one complete guide for all your travel needs. The best hotels and restaurants for every budget, the greatest shopping values, the wildest nightlife—it's all here.

Why should you trust our judgment? Because our authors personally visit each place they write about. They're an independent lot who say what they think and would never include places they wouldn't recommend to their best friends. They're also open to suggestions from readers. If you'd like to contact them, please send your comments our way at feedback@frommers.com, and we'll pass them on.

Enjoy your Day by Day guide—the most helpful travel companion you can buy. And have the trip of a lifetime.

Warm regards,

Kelly Regan

Kelly Regan, Editorial Director
Frommer's Travel Guides

About the Author

Graham Bond began his career as a reporter in the British press before moving to China in 2003. He worked as deputy editor of the travel magazine *Asia and Away* until 2006 when he relocated to Guangdong, just across the mainland border from Hong Kong. From there, he has contributed China material to a range of international publications, including the (London) *Times,* the *South China Morning Post,* and the *Australian.* He is also the author of *Frommer's Shanghai Day by Day.*

Acknowledgments

Thanks to everyone in Hong Kong who helped me with the book, and to my friends and family for their support.

An Additional Note

Please be advised that travel information is subject to change at any time—and this is especially true of prices. We therefore suggest that you write or call ahead for confirmation when making your travel plans. The authors, editors, and publisher cannot be held responsible for the experiences of readers while traveling. Your safety is important to us, however, so we encourage you to stay alert and be aware of your surroundings.

Star Ratings, Icons & Abbreviations

Every hotel, restaurant, and attraction listing in this guide has been ranked for quality, value, service, amenities, and special features using a **star-rating system.** Hotels, restaurants, attractions, shopping, and nightlife are rated on a scale of zero stars (recommended) to three stars (exceptional). In addition to the star-rating system, we also use a **kids icon** to point out the best bets for families. Within each tour, we recommend cafes, bars, or restaurants where you can take a break. Each of these stops appears in a shaded box marked with a coffee-cup-shaped bullet.

The following **abbreviations** are used for credit cards:

AE	American Express	DISC	Discover	V	Visa
DC	Diners Club	MC	MasterCard		

Travel Resources at Frommers.com

Frommer's travel resources don't end with this guide. Frommer's website, **www.frommers.com**, has travel information on more than 4,000 destinations. We update features regularly, giving you access to the most current trip-planning information and the best airfare, lodging, and car-rental bargains. You can also listen to podcasts, connect with other Frommers.com members through our active reader forums, share your travel photos, read blogs from guidebook editors and fellow travelers, and much more.

A Note on Prices

In the "Take a Break" and "Best Bets" sections of this book, we have used a system of dollar signs to show a range of costs for 1 night in a hotel (the price of a double-occupancy room) or the cost of an entree at a restaurant. Use the following table to decipher the dollar signs:

Cost	Hotels	Restaurants
$	under $100	under $10
$$	$100–$200	$10–$20
$$$	$200–$300	$20–$30
$$$$	$300–$400	$30–$40
$$$$$	over $400	over $40

How to Contact Us

In researching this book, we discovered many wonderful places—hotels, restaurants, shops, and more. We're sure you'll find others. Please tell us about them, so we can share the information with your fellow travelers in upcoming editions. If you were disappointed with a recommendation, we'd love to know that, too. Please write to:

Frommer's Hong Kong Day by Day, 2nd Edition
Wiley Publishing, Inc. • 111 River St. • Hoboken, NJ 07030-5774

10 Favorite **Moments**

10 Favorite **Moments**

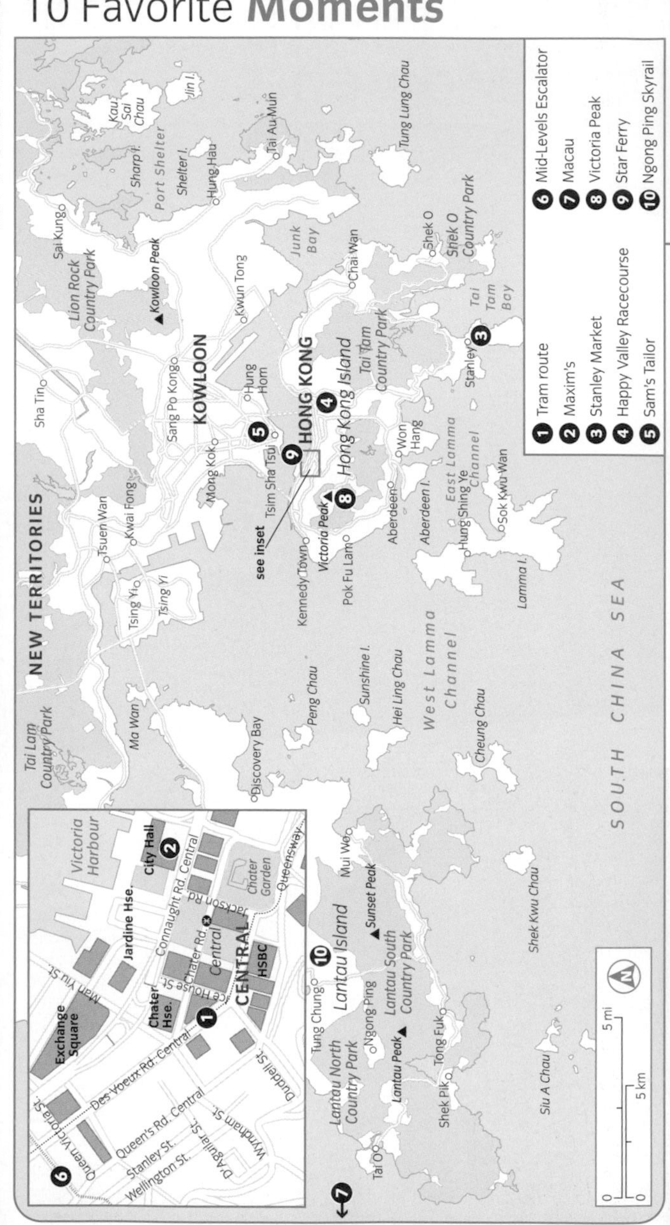

Previous page: The Hong Kong skyline from Victoria Peak.

Hong Kong might have remained a sleepy fishing village had the Chinese not ceded control to the British at the end of the First Opium War in 1842. Instead it grew into one of Asia's most vibrant trading and cultural centers. Even under British rule, which ended in 1997, Hong Kong maintained its distinctly Chinese charm. The skyscrapers that sprouted beside the South China Sea loomed large over smoky temples and busy fish markets. Today the city offers a harmonious blend of East and West, tradition and modernity, colonial influence and Chinese culture.

❶ **Take a nostalgia trip on the trams.** The double-decker trams that have been rattling along the northern edge of the island since 1904 are the ideal perch from which to observe Hong Kong street life. Locals use the trams to get around, but at only $HK2 a ride, they also offer a great value tour of Hong Kong Island's urban jungle, passing dazzling skyscrapers and crumbling apartment blocks. *See p 152.*

❷ **Start your day with dim sum at Maxim's Palace.** Dim sum are like Chinese tapas—bite-sized morsels, often served direct from the steam-basket for breakfast or lunch. Head to Maxim's Palace, one of the few places where dim sum is still delivered to diners on trolleys. You can choose from hundreds of dishes, but highlights are the squid tentacles, soup dumplings *(xiao long bao)*, and barbecued pork buns *(char siu bau)*. *See p 87.*

A tram stop at night in Central.

❸ **Hike to Stanley.** The market has made Stanley a popular tourist destination, but the journey there is an equal part of the appeal. I suggest walking across the steep "Twins," the two hills that form a gateway to the north. The hike is challenging, but you'll be rewarded with glorious views. The free-spending need not hold back on purchases; you can take the bus back. *See p 70.*

❹ **Play the ponies.** Gambling has a place alongside dining and shopping as being one of those rare activities that draws people from *every* sector of Hong Kong society. Join the throngs at Happy Valley on a Wednesday night or Sha Tin on a Saturday or Sunday, and you'll feel like a local in no time. *See p 110.*

❺ **Get custom fit.** Over the years, Hong Kong and China's huge textile industry has seen high-quality, inexpensive, personalized tailoring services flourish. If you've never had a suit, dress, or shirt tailor-made before, Hong Kong's Tsim Sha Tsui is the place to indulge—try Sam's for the best of the best. *See p 66.*

❻ **Ride the Mid-Levels escalator in the morning.** Most visitors use the Mid-Levels escalator at night, when

The Star Ferry affords panoramic views of Hong Kong Island.

they're on their way to the restaurants, bars, and shops in Central and Soho. But to get a sense of just how manic a city Hong Kong can be, take a ride on the escalator during the morning commute (6–10am) when they only run downhill. *See p 8.*

❼ **Get away to Macau.** Despite its proximity to Hong Kong, Macau has a totally distinct charm. You can sample authentic Portuguese food, enjoy well-preserved colonial architecture, go bungee-jumping, gamble in the world's biggest and busiest casinos, and still be in bed by midnight thanks to the regular, high-speed ferry service. *See p 128.*

❽ **Walk on the Peak.** Victoria Peak is the highest point on Hong Kong Island. Instead of heading to the highly commercialized observation platform, take a stroll along Harlech and Lugard roads. The views are jaw-dropping and the scattered mansions offer insight into the Peak's significance as a repository of wealth and power. *See p 7.*

❾ **Cross Victoria Harbour the old-fashioned way.** Riding the Star Ferry is arguably Hong Kong's defining experience. The panoramic view of Hong Kong Island is stunning, but the real appeal is the maritime ambience. The ludicrously cheap fare is the deal-clincher. *See p 7.*

❿ **Soar above the mountains of Lantau.** At 5.7km (3½ miles) in length, the Ngong Ping Skyrail is the world's longest cableway, and one of the most spectacular too. Lantau's mountainous landscape is negotiated at steep angles, and the new glass-floor cabins enhance the thrill. *See p 15.* ●

Ngong Ping cable car crossing the Lantau Trail on Lantau Island.

1 The Best **Full-Day Tours**

The Best in **One Day**

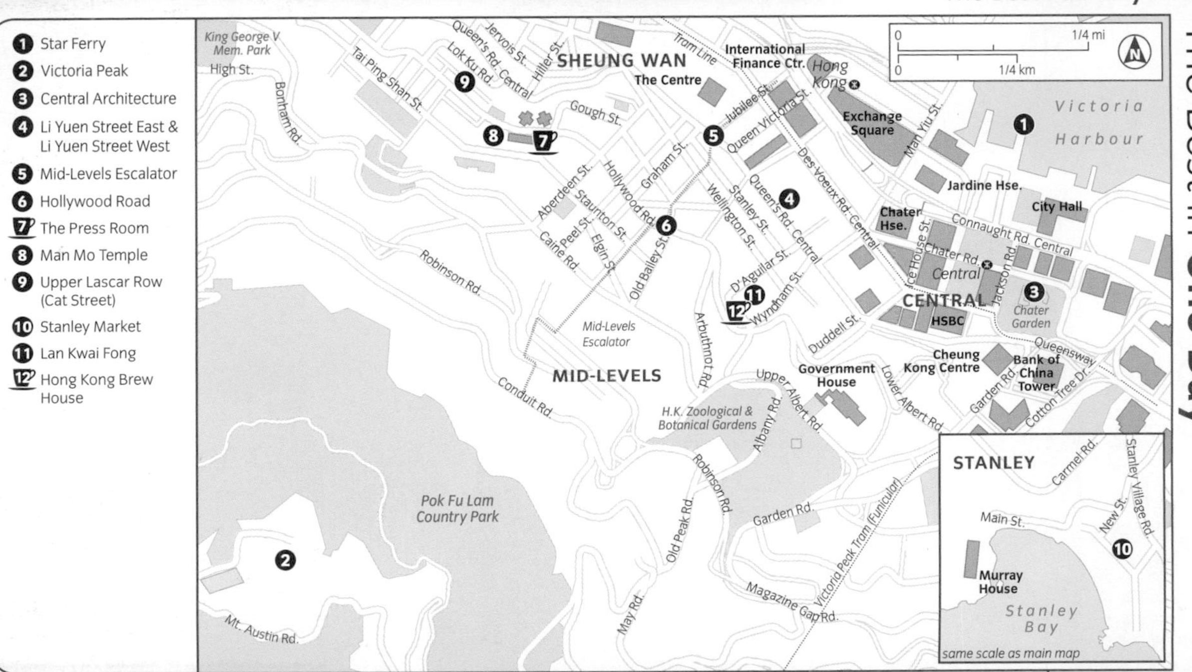

Previous page: Buddhist monks pray at the Po Lin Monastery.

Hong Kong may be geographically small, but seeing it all in 1 day is tough. If that's all you've got, I suggest you enjoy a quick ride on the Star Ferry (regardless of which side of the harbor you're staying on) before focusing on Hong Kong Island. You'll get a sense of Hong Kong's history, architecture, and East-meets-West way of life. **START: Star Ferry.**

1 ★★★ Star Ferry. From its first sailing in 1898 until the opening of the Cross Harbour Tunnel in 1972, the Star Ferry was the primary means of crossing Victoria Harbour. It remains one of the most spectacular ocean crossings in the world. Take the upper deck for a better view and bear in mind you're only on the water for about 5 minutes, so have your camera prepped in advance. *15 min. Star Ferry Pier, Central/Tsim Sha Tsui. ☎ 852/2367-7065. www.starferry.com.hk. $HK2.50 upper deck, children $HK1.50. Daily 6:30am–11:30pm. MTR: Central, exit A/Tsim Sha Tsui.*

2 ★★★ Victoria Peak. At 396m (1,299 ft.), Victoria Peak is Hong Kong's highest point—with stunning views, it's also the city's ritziest neighborhood. Take the wonderfully old-fashioned tram and enjoy the scene from the 270-degree open-air observatory. Better still, make the circular walk along nearby Harlech and Lugard roads. If it's a murky day, I recommend postponing your visit until around dusk when the lights of Central will pierce through the gloom. *2 hr. Peak Tower. ☎ 852/2849-7654. www.thepeak.com.hk. Peak Tram $HK25 adults, $HK9 kids. MTR: Central, exit J2. Bus: 15C from Central Pier Bus Terminus (near Pier 7).*

3 ★ Central Architecture. From the tram terminus, make the short walk down Garden Road to join the maze of elevated pedestrian walkways that dissects the Central district, Hong Kong's political and financial heart. Chater Garden and Statue Square are surrounded by some of Hong Kong's most famous buildings, including the colonial Legco building and the sci-fi forms of the Bank of China Tower and the Lippo Centre. The veranda at the northern edge of Chater Garden is the best spot to take in the view, while an abundance of greenery makes for a relaxing stroll below. *60 min. MTR: Central, exit J2.*

The Peak Tram runs every 10 to 15 minutes, from 7am to midnight.

A View from the Top

Don't expect an idyllic scene when disembarking the Peak Tram. Passengers exit immediately into one of two huge, adjacent malls crammed with shops, restaurants, and bars. You can get away from the melee by walking along Lugard Road, where the urban skyline looks even more stunning. As you'll see, you're still a way off from the peak, and it's possible to get extra elevation by climbing Mount Austin Road (or one of the smaller trails off Lugard Rd.) to reach Victoria Peak Gardens. The actual peak is unfortunately occupied by a telecom tower and remains off-limits. To enjoy the best of the Peak, it's critical you watch the weather. The view is among the world's finest, but smog or mountain-hugging vapor can spoil the moment.

4 ★ The Lanes (Li Yuen St. East and Li Yuen St. West). Welcome to one of Hong Kong's quintessential shopping experiences: cheap goods in incredibly tight spaces. These two parallel streets are lined with hawkers selling counterfeit designer handbags and other inexpensive goods in tiny stalls filled to the brim with merchandise. *30 min. Between Des Voeux Rd. and Queen's Rd. MTR: Central, exit C.* *See p 65.*

5 ★★★ Mid-Levels Escalator. Touted as the longest people-mover in the world, this engineering marvel runs through Mid-Levels, a yuppie neighborhood terraced into the lower part of Victoria Peak. The escalator—a combination of steps and ramps—passes through buildings and over streets lined with cheap noodle stalls and upmarket bars and galleries (Staunton St. is my favorite).You can get off wherever you like to explore. If you plan to ride up the escalator, you need to wait until after 10am—before that time it runs downhill for morning commuters. *1 hr. MTR: Central, D2.*

6 ★ Hollywood Road. Hollywood Road was the first thoroughfare in Hong Kong, built in 1844 by the British Army and named after the holly shrubs that lined it at the time. Walk east for 5 minutes (past the point where the road becomes Wyndham St.) and you'll see some of Hong Kong's most historic buildings on the south side of the road. Retrace your steps and head west. There's a great range of Chinese

Mao alarm clocks for sale along Hollywood Road.

A brass lion guards an altar at Man Mo Temple.

furniture, Tibetan rugs, ceramic sculptures, and (of course) Maoist kitsch. ⌚ *1 hr. Exit Mid-Levels escalator at Hollywood Rd. Bus: 26.*

7 ★ **The Press Room.** Once the headquarters of the English-language *South China Morning Post,* this hip, atmospheric eatery has a large window overlooking the street. It serves hearty, Asian-influenced Western cuisine, including a *fruits de mer* platter that offers some of Hong Kong's finest shellfish. *108 Hollywood Rd.* ☎ *852/2525-3444. $$$.*

8 ★★★ **Man Mo Temple.** Hong Kong Island's oldest temple was built in 1847 and became a hub for the flourishing Chinese community in Sheung Wan. It's dedicated to the gods of literature and war (Man and Mo); the grand entrance is flanked by stone lions for protection. Inside, amid statues of Man, Mo, and other gods, ashes flutter from the huge, curling incense sticks that hang from the ceiling—the smoke is intended to carry prayers to heaven—as the Buddhist faithful pray to their ancestors. ⌚ *30 min. Hollywood Rd. (near Ladder St.).* ☎ *852/2803-2916. Free admission. Daily 8am–6pm. MTR: Sheung Wan, exit A2. Bus: 26.*

9 ★ **Upper Lascar Row (Cat Street).** The nickname Cat Street comes from this area's shady past, when it was known as a market for stolen goods. In Cantonese slang, thieves are "rats," and the people who buy from them are "cats." Today's goods are legit, though not necessarily high quality. ⌚ *20 min. Upper Lascar Row. MTR: Sheung Wan, exit A2. Bus: 26.* *See p 65.*

10 ★ **Stanley Market.** If you still have plenty of daylight left, head to Stanley. The bus ride alone makes the trip worthwhile, with outstanding views of Hong Kong's steep hillsides and ocean vistas. Unfortunately, the goods at Stanley's famous market are overpriced. Wander the waterfront or visit the Hong Kong Maritime Museum in historic Murray House before returning downtown. ⌚ *3 hr. Bus: 6, 6A, 6X, or 260 from Central Exchange Square bus terminal.* *See p 65.*

11 ★★ **Lan Kwai Fong.** If you only have 1 evening, spend it at LKF. Walking up D'Aguilar Street at night is like stepping into a permanent street festival. It's frat-partyish and raucous, but undeniably fun. More-sensitive souls will prefer nearby Soho. *MTR: Central, exit D2.*

My favorite pub in LKF is the 12 **Hong Kong Brew House.** It's a cavernous place with a great beer selection and a patio out front. If you come early, you can nab a seat outside and watch the madness unfold. *33 Wyndham St.* ☎ *852/2522-5559. $.*

The Best in **Two Days**

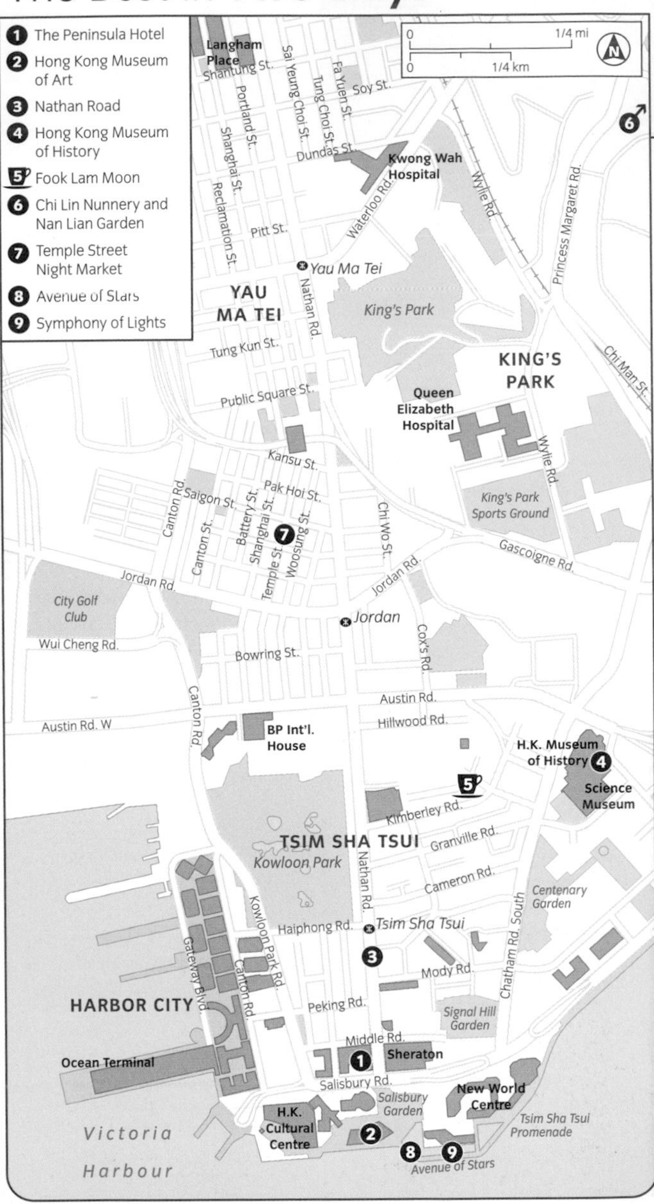

On your second day, head into the heart of Kowloon. The southern reaches of this artificially engorged peninsula are dominated by historic architecture and hulking museums, but farther north it's a riot of commercialism set against an atmospheric backdrop of crumbling tenement blocks and neon signs. **START: Tsim Sha Tsui Star Ferry Pier.**

1 ★ The Peninsula Hotel. Opened in 1928, this Hong Kong landmark is the territory's oldest existing hotel. Once located at the end of the Trans-Siberian Railway, the Peninsula quickly became a magnet for the wealthy elite; it still has a fleet of Rolls-Royces for hire. Wander inside to enjoy the colonial grandeur. For a slightly less gilded but equally swish insight into colonial Hong Kong, pop in to 1881 Heritage next door, the recently restored site of the Marine Police Headquarters. *1 hr. Salisbury Rd. ☎ 852/2920-2888. MTR: Tsim Sha Tsui, exit E.* *See p 124.*

An exhibit on Cantonese opera at the Museum of History illustrates how performers prepare for a show.

Seated Ming Dynasty Buddha at the Hong Kong Museum of Art.

2 ★★ Hong Kong Museum of Art. It's a beige monstrosity from the outside, and a bit like a high school library from within, but don't be fooled—the artwork, ranging from modern Chinese painting to Neolithic bronzes, makes this museum well worth a visit. My favorite is the permanent exhibit on the history of Hong Kong, which includes old photographs that show just how much things have changed around these parts. *2 hr. 10 Salisbury Rd. ☎ 852/2721-0116. www.hk.art.museum. Admission $HK10 adults, free for kids under 4. Free Wed. Mon–Wed, Fri 10am–6pm; Sat 10am–8pm; Thurs closed. MTR: Tsim Sha Tsui, exit E.*

Lotus pond at Chi Lin Nunnery.

3 ★ **Nathan Road.** Also known as the Golden Mile, this is Kowloon's major artery and the closest thing Hong Kong has to New York City's Fifth Avenue. The overwhelming number of neon signs alone makes it worth a stop. It's the place to come for bespoke clothing, as well as upmarket malls like iSquare and Woodhouse. For a change of pace, head into adjacent Kowloon Park, or visit the fascinating Haiphong Road Temporary Market, popular for fresh fish and meat. *1 hr. MTR: Tsim Sha Tsui, exit C1.*

4 ★★ **Hong Kong Museum of History.** This innovative museum takes you chronologically through Hong Kong's history. Exhibits include replicas of pre-British-era homes, as well as a full-size model of a streetcar of the type used in Central around 1881. You'll learn everything you need to know about the opium wars, the Japanese occupation during World War II, and the 1997 handover from the United Kingdom to China. *1 hr. 100 Chatham Rd. S. ☎ 852/2724-9042. www.lcsd.gov.hk/hkmh. Admission $HK10 adults, free for kids 3 and under. Wed free. Mon, Wed–Sat 10am–6pm; Sun 10am–7pm; closed Tues. MTR: Tsim Sha Tsui, exit B2. Bus: 5 or 5C from Star Ferry terminal.*

5 ★★ **Fook Lam Moon.** Founded in 1948, this restaurant (now part of a small chain) serves the best classic Cantonese dishes in Hong Kong, including braised shark's fin with brown sauce, goose web, roast suckling pig, and braised abalone. The decor is a bit outdated, but with food this good, who cares? *1/F, 55 Kimberley Rd. ☎ 852/2366-0286. $$.*

Shop Smart

Because so much of the Hong Kong experience involves market shopping, it's worth sharing a few insider tips. This being Asia, sizes tend to run small, but don't be dismayed if you can't find an XL—just ask, as merchants tend to keep additional sizes and colors stashed away for such occasions. And definitely don't be afraid to bargain with market vendors; it's considered a normal part of shopping here. The rule of thumb is to offer a quarter of what the seller is asking, and then try not to settle for more than half of the original price. If you're not happy with the final price, walk away. Unless you've stumbled upon a must-have antique or some truly unique jewelry, you'll likely see similar goods at the next stall you visit.

❻ ★★★ **Chi Lin Nunnery and Nan Lian Garden.** It may be brand-new, but the Nan Lian Garden and adjacent Chi Lin Nunnery offer insight into ancient China. The restive gardens were cultivated around Tang-dynasty concepts of beauty while the all-timber and highly photogenic nunnery buildings went up without the use of a single metal hinge or nail. 🕘 *90 min. MTR: Diamond Hill.* *See p 23.*

❼ ★★★ **Temple Street Night Market.** Oddly, the shopping ops are arguably the least important part of the night market's appeal. This is a fine place to try alfresco dining, Hong Kong style, at one of the *dai pai dong* stalls (head to the junction with Nanking Rd.). Cantonese opera singers sometimes hold miniconcerts on the street, and fortunetellers, many of whom speak English, will read your future for a price (again, do some bargaining). 🕘 *2 hr. Temple Street.* ☎ *852/2920-2888. MTR: Jordan, exit A.* *See p 65.*

❽ ★★★ **Avenue of Stars.** The Avenue of Stars was a $HK40-million project opened in 2004 to honor Hong Kong's film industry. It's a lot like the scene along Hollywood's Walk of Fame—there are stars for such local legends as director Wong Kar-wai and actors Jet Li and Maggie Cheung. There's also a statue of Bruce Lee. The real star, though, is the panoramic view of Hong Kong Island. 🕘 *30 min. Avenue of Stars. MTR: Tsim Sha Tsui, exit G. Star Ferry terminal in Tsim Sha Tsui.*

A fortuneteller gives a reading at the Temple Street Night Market.

❾ ★ **Symphony of Lights.** Every night at 8pm, 44 buildings on either side of the harbor participate in a massive 15-minute light-and-laser show coordinated to music. It is as unusual as it sounds, and worth checking out. You'll get the best view from the Avenue of Stars. 🕘 *15 min. Avenue of Stars. MTR: Tsim Sha Tsui, exit G. Star Ferry terminal in Tsim Sha Tsui.*

A bronze statue of kung fu film star Bruce Lee looms over the Avenue of Stars.

The Best in Three Days

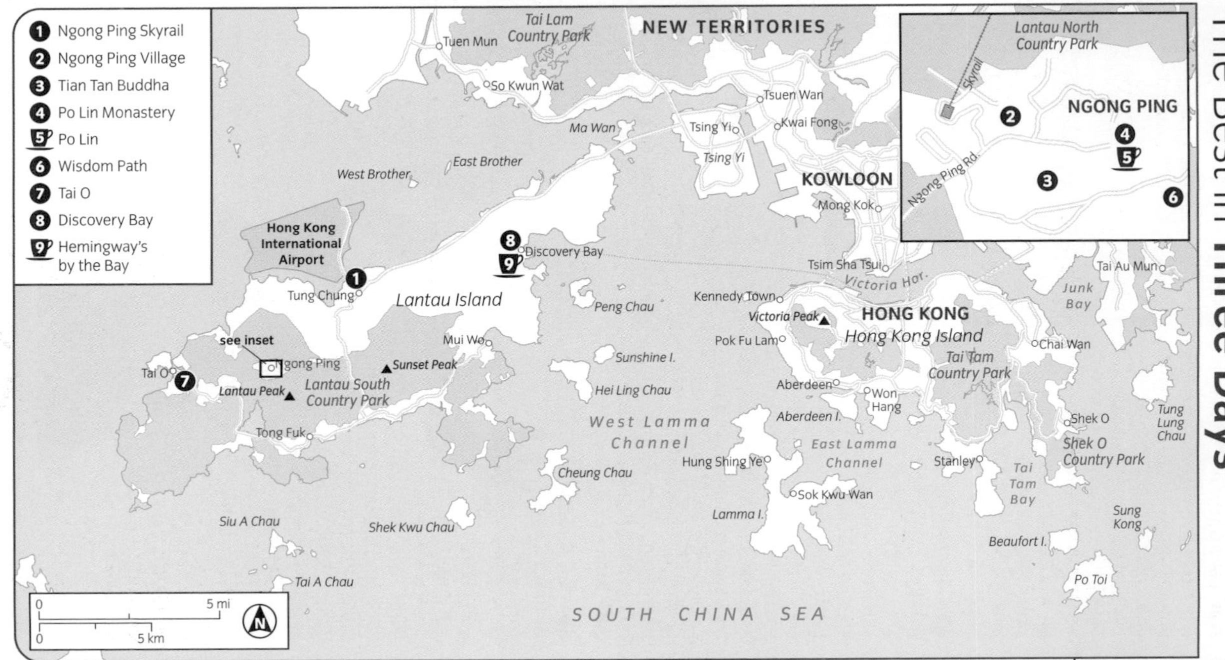

Day three is all about enjoying Hong Kong's greatest, and least appreciated, asset—its natural beauty. With its mountainous interior and craggy coastline, Lantau has long been a favorite for outdoor-types. Disneyland, Discovery Bay, and the Tian Tan ("Big") Buddha have helped to add mass-market appeal, as well as a spiritual edge. **START: Tung Chung MTR.**

1 ★★★ Ngong Ping Skyrail. The Skyrail, a 5.7km (3½-mile) cableway, was beset by problems upon opening in 2005 (including breaking down midflight). However, it's been running smoothly since 2006 and is now a thrilling experience in all the right ways. Your air-conditioned glass carriage rises up above Hong Kong International Airport and sweeps across Lantau's mountainous interior before dropping you off near the mountaintop. I highly recommend paying the extra $HK50 for a ride in the glass-bottomed crystal cabin. *30 min. Round-trip $HK107 adults, $HK54 kids 3–11. Mon–Fri 10am–6pm; Sat–Sun 9am–6.30pm. MTR: Tung Chung.*

A traditional Chinese gateway at the Ngong Ping village.

2 kids Ngong Ping Village. This replica Tang village offers a bit of Chinese culture and history in a Disneyland-style setting. A "Walking with Buddha" attraction tells the story of Siddhartha Gautama, the young prince who attained enlightenment and became the Buddha. The *Monkey's Tale Theatre* is a high-tech cartoon telling the traditional Buddhist story of the Monkey King. Best of all is a Chinese tea ceremony, which offers an inside look at this age-old custom along with a history of the role tea has played in Chinese culture. *1 hr. ☎ 852/2109-9898. Free admission to village. Admission to Walking with Buddha and Monkey's Tale Theatre each $HK36 adults, $HK18 kids. Combination ticket for both shows $HK65 adults, $HK35 kids. Mon–Fri 10am–6pm; Sat–Sun 10am–6:30pm.*

3 ★★★ Tian Tan Buddha. The blurb claims this as the world's "largest seated bronze Buddha," a slightly niche category that doesn't really do justice to its sheer, visceral impact. Built in 1993, the Buddha is 31m (102 ft.) high and weighs 250 tons. He also has a fantastic view of Lantau from 750m (2,461 ft.) above sea level, but there are

The Tian Tan Buddha looks out over the island of Lantau.

Transportation City

Hong Kong has an enviable range of public transport options, anchored by the ever-expanding MTR network which now reaches into most corners. It's no wonder many residents have never driven a car. In this book, we list MTR stops, which often require a bit of walking, as well as bus routes and ferries when necessary. While we normally recommend public transportation, taxis are relatively cheap and may be your best option if you have limited time. A prepaid Octopus card (see the "Savvy Traveler" chapter, p 147) can be used on all forms of transport, as well as in shops and leisure venues, and will save you both time and money. Be sure to pick one up.

260 steps to negotiate before you can enjoy it too. The museum inside the statue is small and unremarkable. More worthwhile is the set vegetarian lunch at the Po Lin Monastery (see below). ◷ *1 hr. Free admission to Buddha. Regular lunch $HK60; deluxe lunch $HK100. Daily 10am–6pm. Bus: 2 from Mui Wo Pier.*

❹ ★ **Po Lin Monastery.** This monastery was founded more than 100 years ago by reclusive Buddhist monks; the remaining structures date from 1921 and 1970. The largest temple at Po Lin (which means "precious lotus") has a golden roof and three bronze statues of the Buddha representing the past, present, and future. As you wander the grounds, you'll see monks going about their daily routine. ◷ *45 min. Ngong Ping.* ☎ *852/2895-5248. www.plm.org.hk/eng/home.php. Daily 10am–6pm. Bus: 2 from Mui Wo Pier.*

One of the many statues of Buddhist gods that adorn the Po Lin Monastery.

Having lunch at ❺ **Po Lin Monastery** is a real treat. You'll buy a timed ticket either at the base of the Buddha (if you're planning to visit) or at the monastery itself. I suggest opting for the regular lunch, which is served family style (big helpings of vegetables, soups, and rice are brought to the table for all to share) in a colorful dining room packed with Chinese families. You can also opt for the deluxe lunch, which is served on plates in a quieter room filled mostly with tourists. *Ngong Ping.* ☎ *852/2895-5248. $.*

❻ ★ **Wisdom Path.** The Wisdom Path, signposted from the monastery, leads to a figure eight of 38

The Wisdom Path was laid out in a figure eight to symbolize infinity.

wooden pillars engraved with quotes from the *Heart Sutra*. The *Heart Sutra* is a text read by Confucians, Buddhists, and Taoists, and it includes mantras describing the philosophies of wisdom, compassion, and enlightenment. The path is just off the 70km (43-mile) Lantau trail, and it's possible to sacrifice the next stop on your tour and hike back down to Tung Chung instead. ⌚ ***45 min. Wisdom Path, Ngong Ping. www.tourism.gov.hk/english/current/current_heart.html.***

7 ★★ **Tai O.** Located on the northwestern coast of Lantau, this fishing village is known as the "Venice of Hong Kong" thanks to its traditional stilt housing. For a small fee, you can usually catch a short fishing boat ride along the coast—if you're lucky, you may see Chinese white dolphins. If you'd rather stay on land, head for the shops, where you can pick up a jar of shrimp paste, a pungent sauce made by fermenting shrimp in spices in the sun. There are a variety of walks that can be made around the village. Check out the sign next to the bus stop for ideas. ⌚ ***3 hr. Tai O Fishing Village. MTR to Tung Chung, then bus 11.***

8 ★★ **Discovery Bay.** In stark contrast to Tai O, this ever-expanding

The Monastery & the Buddha

Po Lin Monastery was founded in 1906 by three Zen masters, Da Yue, Dun Xiu, and Yue Ming, who arrived on Lantau from Zhejiang in eastern China. Soon monks from across southern China were being drawn to the quiet beauty of the monastery. The "Big" Buddha went up on neighboring Muk Yue Peak in 1993, bringing with it an influx of visitors, though the monks don't seem to mind. As for the Buddha, he sits cross-legged (the real Buddha was said to be seated cross-legged when he achieved enlightenment) and his right hand is raised in a vow to eliminate suffering from all beings on Earth. His left hand rests on his thigh with the palm up, as a symbol of Buddha's compassion in granting happiness to all people. The icon on his chest—redolent of the Nazi swastika—represents the everlasting presence and compassion of the Buddha.

Stilt houses line the shores at the Tai O fishing village.

town has a condo/resort feel to it and now has a purpose-built outdoor dining zone which offers downtown comforts beside the sea. There are around 20 international restaurants beside a sandy strip that faces in the direction of Hong Kong Island. Disneyland provides a sideline attraction in the form of its nightly 8pm firework display. When the evening is done, it's back to Hong Kong Island by high-speed ferry. ⌚ ***2–3 hr. Discovery Bay, Lantau. Bus: DB01R from Tung Chung Citygate Bus Station. Ferries sail to Central Pier 3 24-hr.***

Caribbean-themed **9 Hemingway's by the Bay** is quintessential Discovery Bay. There's a large outdoor deck where you can enjoy exotic cocktails and Caribbean cuisine while listening to the tropical sounds of calypso and reggae. The barbecue meats are sprinkled with Jamaican and Trinidadian spices and, depending on how many of the huge selection of rums you sink, you might just end your trip to one of Asia's most populous cities believing you've found an exotic beach paradise. ***Shop G09, Block A, Discovery Bay. ☎ 852/2987-8855. $$.*** ●

Double-decker wooden trams are just one of many options for making your way around Hong Kong.

2 The Best Special-Interest Tours

Chinese Hong Kong

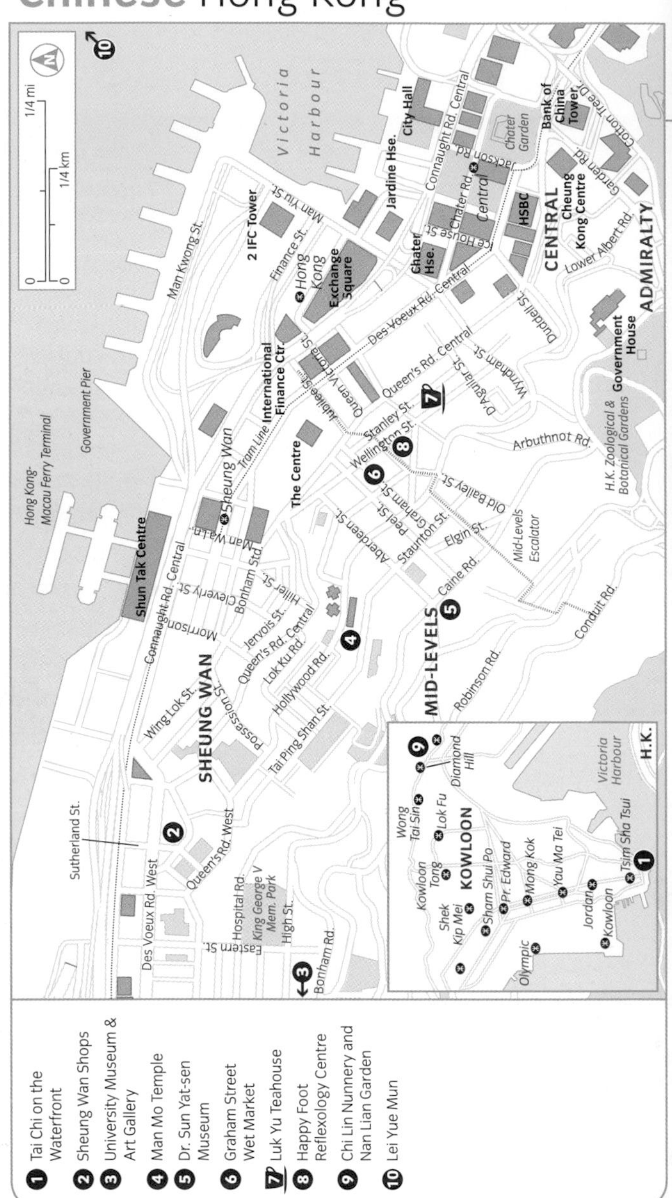

Previous page: Massive coils of incense, which can burn for weeks at a time, hang from the ceiling of the Man Mo Temple.

Hong Kong may have been raised on immigration, but at its core remains a Chinese city. That will seem obvious to anyone wandering the bustling streets of Sheung Wan, whose shops and markets are the very reason why the words "Hong Kong" translate as "fragrant harbor" in Chinese. **START: MTR to Tsim Sha Tsui.**

❶ ★★ Tai chi on the waterfront. The routines of tai chi are hugely popular with older Chinese as exercise for both mind and body. You'll see people practicing it in parks all over Hong Kong. The tourist board offers free classes for beginners in front of the Hong Kong Museum of Art between 8 and 9am on Mondays, Wednesdays, and Fridays. ⌚ *1 hr.* ☎ *852/2508-1234. www.discoverhongkong.com. No need to reserve. MTR: Tsim Sha Tsui.*

❷ Sheung Wan Shops. Family-run Chinese wholesale businesses dominate this neighborhood. Sutherland Street, just off Des Voeux Road West, is home to scores of dried seafood shops, while nearby Ko Shing Street is good for herbal medicine dealers. The stores on Queen's Road West, meanwhile, specialize in joss paper, used in ancestor-worship ceremonies. ⌚ *1 hr. MTR: Sheung Wan.*

❸ ★ University Museum & Art Gallery. Located on Hong Kong University's colonial-era campus, this museum contains Chinese antiquities, including pieces dating from the Neolithic period to China's Qing dynasty. The dazzling collection of bronze works date from the Shang dynasty (1600–1040 B.C.) while the museum also has the world's largest collection of Yuan dynasty Nestorian

Dried fish for sale along Des Voeux Road in Sheung Wan.

The Chinese consider tai chi to be exercise for the mind as well as for the body.

crosses—fascinating for their blending of the Buddhist swastika and Christian cross. *1 hr. 94 Bonham Rd. Free admission. Mon–Sat 9:30am–6pm; Sun 1:30–5:30pm. Bus: 23, 20, or 40M from Admiralty.*

4 ★★ Man Mo Temple. See p 9. *45 min. Hollywood Rd. and Ladder St. ☎ 852/2803-2916. Free admission. Daily 8am–6pm. Bus: 26.*

5 ★ Dr. Sun Yat-sen Museum. Often called the father of modern China, Sun Yat-sen helped overthrow the Qing dynasty in 1911 and end thousands of years of dynastic rule. He became the first provisional president when the Republic of China was founded in 1912 and is admired by Chinese of all political leanings. He spent his early years in Hong Kong and returned here often. This attractive museum details his life and his revolutionary struggles. *1 hr. 7 Castle Rd. Adults $HK10. Free Wed. Daily 10am–6pm, except Thurs (closed) and Sun (open till 7pm). Mid-Levels escalator. Disembark at Caine Rd. and walk west.*

A bronze statue of Sun Yat-sen stands outside the museum that bears his name.

6 ★★ Graham Street Wet Market. You'll find yourself surrounded by tanks of live fish, crustaceans, and even the occasional turtle along this narrow street. Be brave and try the Cantonese "hundred-year" eggs—chicken, duck, or quail eggs that have been soaked in a mixture of salt, lime, clay, and rice straw for several weeks. Surprisingly, these dark green eggs aren't terribly flavorful on their own (which may not be a bad thing), but they're excellent with dipping sauce. *45 min. Graham St. MTR: Central, then Mid-Levels escalator. Bus: 26.*

In addition to food and Chinese medicine, you'll find souvenirs like Cantonese opera headgear in Sheung Wan.

7 ★★★ Luk Yu Teahouse. Serving tea and dim sum since 1933, Luk Yu is considered Hong Kong's most authentic remaining teahouse, complete with ceiling fans, spittoons, and waiters who look as if they've been around since the place opened. It's always crowded with regulars—a sure sign that the food is good. The English-language menu doesn't list all of the options available, so ask your waiter for help. *24–26 Stanley St. ☎ 852/2523-5464. $$$.*

Dim Sum

Traditionally served for breakfast or lunch, dim sum is the generic name for a gamut of steamed dishes that are designed to be shared. In the past, waiters rolled the offerings past the table on a trolley for you to pick and choose. These days, it's more likely that you'll check off what you want on a paper menu. Below are some of the classic dishes you must try:

char siu bau—steamed barbecue pork buns
cheung fun—steamed rice-flour rolls with shrimp, beef, or pork
chun gun—fried spring rolls
fan guo—steamed dumplings with shrimp and bamboo shoots
fu pei gun—crispy bean-curd rolls
fung jau—fried chickens' feet
loh mei fan—sticky rice wrapped in lotus leaf
pai guat—small braised spareribs with black beans
siu mai—steamed pork and shrimp dumplings

8 ★★ Happy Foot Reflexology Centre. It's time for a very Asian remedy for tired feet: a foot massage. I recommend Happy Foot because their reflexologists are consistently excellent and the prices are reasonable (starting at $HK198 for 50 min.). The Chinese believe that when a skilled foot reflexologist goes to work, he or she is not just giving your toes a rubdown, but is specifically targeting pressure points that correspond to the rest of your body. ⌚ *1 hr. 11/F, Jade Centre, 98–102 Wellington St. (accessible off Cochrane St.) Daily 10am–midnight. MTR: Central, exit D2.*

A sign for Happy Foot Massage illustrates pressure points on the feet that correspond to the rest of the body.

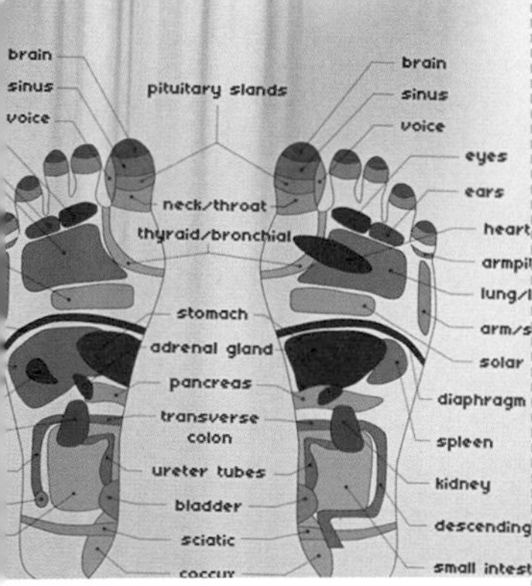

9 ★★★ Chi Lin Nunnery and Nan Lian Garden. A short MTR ride from Central, the Buddhist Chi Lin Nunnery is a palatial complex of timber prayer halls. ⌚ *90 min. MTR: Diamond Hill.* *See p 13 for more details.*

10 ★★ Lei Yue Mun. Continue a few stops along the MTR to enjoy a slice of old Hong Kong life at this charming fishing village. At its heart is a long bazaar selling a dizzying variety of seafood. Select your catch and take it, live, into one of the restaurants where it will be cooked to order. Come for sundown when it's easy to get a seat with a view, and wander the village after dark. ⌚ *2 hr. 58A Hoi Pong Rd. C. ☎ 852/2727-4628. MTR: Yao Tong.*

Hong Kong Modern Architecture

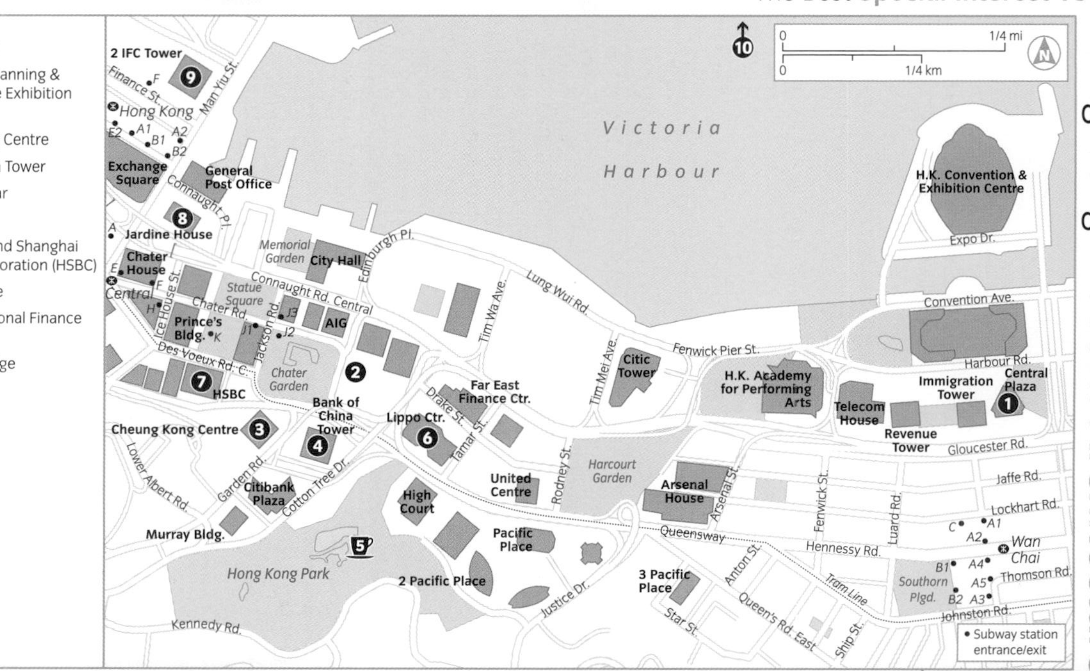

Hong Kong's mountains, inlets, and bays are pretty, but what makes them truly unique is the way they've been decorated with hulking great skyscrapers. In this town even a tenement block can be awe-inspiring in terms of its size, scale, and the amount of laundry hanging from its windows. Add in dazzling creations from the likes of Cesar Pelli and Norman Foster and you can see why architecture is one of Hong Kong's standout features. **START: MTR to Wanchai.**

❶ ★★★ **Central Plaza.** Start with a literal overview. The third-tallest building in Hong Kong, at 342m (1,122 ft.), offers the most expansive skyscraper view on Hong Kong Island from its untouristy 45th-floor observation deck. The astonishing density of skyscraper development is revealed from floor-to-ceiling windows on what is, essentially, a transit floor for office workers. ⏱ *45 min. 18 Harbour Rd. Daily 8am–8pm. MTR: Wan Chai, exit A5.*

❷ **Hong Kong Planning & Infrastructure Exhibition Gallery.** There's a bit too much technobabble for my tastes, but this gallery nevertheless provides a good introduction to architecture in Hong Kong, in particular what's in store for the future (such as the ambitious plans for developing the old Kai Tak Airport in Kowloon). Look out for the easily missable slides depicting old Hong Kong installed into the central dividing wall. ⏱ *30 min. G/F Murray Road Multi-storey Car Park, 2 Murray Rd. Free admission. Wed–Mon 10am–6pm. MTR: Central, exit J2.*

Take the escalator in Central Plaza's lobby to the elevator to the observation deck for excellent views of Hong Kong.

❸ **Cheung Kong Centre.** This 62-story building is home to many of Hong Kong's banking firms, as well as the offices of Li Ka-shing, China's richest man. As with many other high-rises here, it was designed with feng shui principles in mind—the walls are black so as to absorb the negative energy of its much criticized neighbor, the Bank of China Tower (see below). You can go inside to marvel at the 20m-high (66-ft.) lobby (which is below street level so the building's riches won't flow out) and walk to the back, where there is a lovely little garden. ⏱ *30 min. 2 Queen's Rd. MTR: Central, exit J2.*

❹ ★★ **Bank of China Tower.** Chinese-American architect I. M. Pei looked to bamboo for inspiration when designing this standout 70-story building. The tower has no internal structural columns and its weight is supported by its four corner and diagonal braces. For all its structural beauty, the building has been criticized by feng shui experts for its sharp corners, which cast negative energy on nearby government buildings. The 43rd-floor

The Bank of China building rises dramatically over the colonial-era Legislative Council Building.

viewing deck is nowhere near as open as at Central Plaza, but there are good views of the famous buildings and around Central. ⏲ *30 min. 1 Garden Rd. Mon–Fri 8am–8pm; Sat–Sun 8am–2pm. MTR: Central, exit J2.*

5 ★ L16 Cafe & Bar. The Thai and Western-style food served here is good, but the real reason to come is the view of lush Hong Kong Park and surrounding buildings. You can enjoy the spectacle either from the outdoor patio or from inside, where huge windows mean every seat has a view. The interior's combination of sleek wood and limestone give it an earthy feel, and the menu has dishes as varied as green curry and Boston lobster bisque. *Hong Kong Park.* ☎ *852/2522-6333. $$.*

6 Lippo Centre. Arguably the most eye-catching building in town, the Lippo consists of two hexagonal towers covered in reflective glass. Originally commissioned by the disgraced Australian tycoon Alan Bond, the patterning was designed to evoke climbing koala bears. There's not much to see inside, but the observation platforms in Hong Kong Park offer particularly good views. ⏲ *10 min. 89 Queensway. MTR: Admiralty, exit B.*

7 ★★★ Hongkong and Shanghai Banking Corporation (HSBC). Designed by Norman Foster and finished in 1985, HSBC's headquarters was built in such a way that it could be dismantled and shipped to Singapore in the event of the 1997 China takeover going badly. However, it's the interior view that really sparkles; cashiers work in an atrium that rises all the way to the top floors. In another ingenious step, Foster rejected a

One of the pair of lions that guard the entrance to the HSBC building.

A detail of the Lippo Centre's unique glass facade.

Nautical-style windows dot the exterior of Jardine House.

grand entrance hall and left the ground floor open to pedestrian traffic. 🕘 ***30 min. 1 Queen's Rd. Mon–Fri 10am–6pm; Sat 10am–1pm. MTR: Central, exit K.***

❽ **Jardine House.** Back in 1973, this brand-new 52-story building was a symbol of how innovative and fast-paced Hong Kong had become. It was the tallest building in Asia for nearly a decade and the porthole windows—evoking the Jardine Matheson company's maritime heritage—were considered cutting edge. Today it's slightly cowed amid the massive structures of Central, but its quirky design well reflects the fearless early days of Hong Kong's architectural boom. ***1 Connaught Place. MTR: Central, exit A.***

❾ ★ **Two International Finance Centre.** Completed in 2003, the previous holder of Hong Kong's height record is 415m (1,362 ft.), or 88 floors, tall. It's largely comprised of private office space, but the 55th floor, home of the Hong Kong Monetary Authority Information Centre, is open to the public. The center has interesting exhibits about Hong Kong's financial history, though the views of the skyline are limited to the Central district. 🕘 ***1 hr. 8 Finance St. Mon–Fri 10am–6pm; Sat 10am–1pm. MTR: Hong Kong, exit F.***

❿ ★ **Tsing Ma Bridge.** Nearly 100m (328 ft.) wider than the Golden Gate Bridge, the Tsing Ma Bridge is one part of the Lantau Link that joins outlying Lantau Island with mainland Hong Kong. Opened in 1997, it was the last major architectural contribution of the outgoing British government and remains the world's longest railway bridge. A viewing platform offers views of the Tsing Ma and nearby Ting Kau bridges, and is best visited around dusk. 🕘 ***1 hr. Tsing Yi Island. MTR: Tsing Yi, then taxi.***

The IFC tower is one of the newer additions to Hong Kong's ever-changing skyline.

British Hong Kong

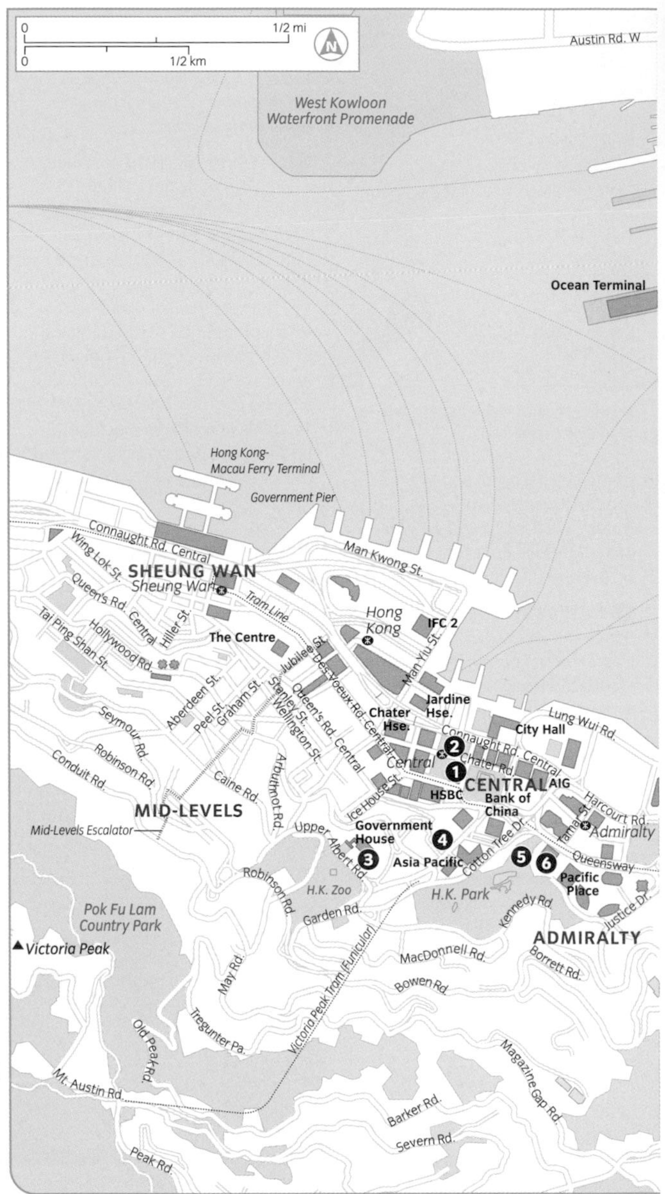

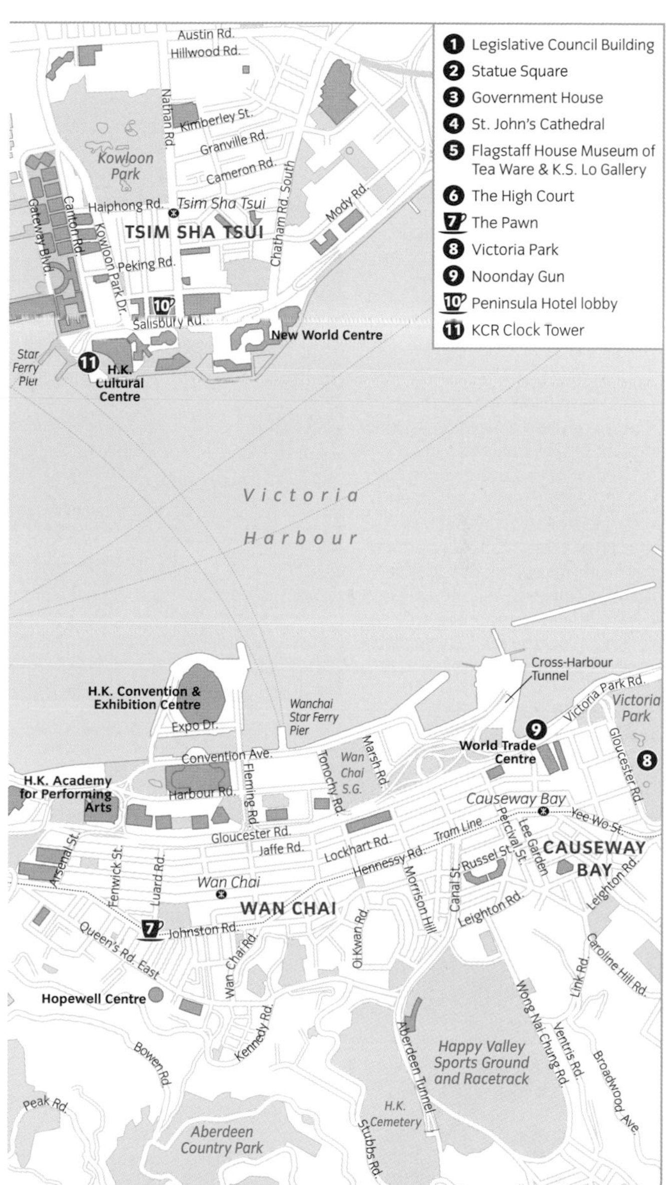
1 Legislative Council Building
2 Statue Square
3 Government House
4 St. John's Cathedral
5 Flagstaff House Museum of Tea Ware & K.S. Lo Gallery
6 The High Court
7 The Pawn
8 Victoria Park
9 Noonday Gun
10 Peninsula Hotel lobby
11 KCR Clock Tower
Austin Rd.
Hillwood Rd.
Nathan Rd.
Kimberley St.
Granville Rd.
Cameron Rd.
Kowloon Park
Haiphong Rd.
Tsim Sha Tsui
TSIM SHA TSUI
Chatham Rd. South
Mody Rd.
Gateway Blvd.
Canton Rd.
Kowloon Park Dr.
Peking Rd.
Salisbury Rd.
New World Centre
Star Ferry Pier
H.K. Cultural Centre
Victoria Harbour
Cross-Harbour Tunnel
Victoria Park Rd.
Victoria Park
H.K. Convention & Exhibition Centre
Expo Dr.
Wanchai Star Ferry Pier
Convention Ave.
Fleming Rd.
Tonochy Rd.
Wan Chai S.G.
Marsh Rd.
World Trade Centre
Gloucester Rd.
H.K. Academy for Performing Arts
Harbour Rd.
Causeway Bay
Yee Wo St.
Jaffe Rd.
Lockhart Rd.
Tram Line
Percival St.
Lee Garden
CAUSEWAY BAY
Arsenal St.
Fenwick St.
Luard Rd.
Hennessy Rd.
Morrison Hill
Canal St.
Russel St.
Leighton Rd.
Wan Chai
WAN CHAI
Johnston Rd.
Queen's Rd. East
Wan Chai Rd.
Oi Kwan Rd.
Caroline Hill Rd.
Link Rd.
Hopewell Centre
Kennedy Rd.
Wong Nai Chung Rd.
Ventris Rd.
Broadwood Ave.
Bowen Rd.
Aberdeen Tunnel
Happy Valley Sports Ground and Racetrack
Peak Rd.
H.K. Cemetery
Stubbs Rd.
Aberdeen Country Park

The British acquired Hong Kong Island as a spoil of the First Opium War in 1842 and seized Kowloon after the second installment in 1860. The New Territories were only ever leased so that in 1997, at the end of the 99-year term, the whole lot was handed back to China. Unsurprisingly given the length of the colonial stay, more than a hint of British influence remains. Don't be surprised if you sometimes feel you're closer to London than Beijing during this tour. **START: MTR to Central.**

1 ★★ Legislative Council Building. Just as she does at London's famous Old Bailey courthouse, Themis, the Greek god of justice, looks down from the top of this neoclassical building, opened in 1912 as the colonial-era Supreme Court. Now it's where the Hong Kong equivalent of Congress, Legco, meets. Half the delegates are elected while half are drawn from pro-China "functional constituencies," helping to ensure Beijing maintains a distant, but important, say in affairs. Line up outside the public entrance to see the action. Live translations are provided. *1 hr. 8 Jackson Rd. ☎ 852/2869-9399. MTR: Central, exit J1.*

What would the queen think? A replica of a Buckingham Palace guard's uniform for sale on Cat Street in Hong Kong.

The Greek god of justice stands atop the Legislative Council Building.

2 ★ Statue Square. This square was built toward the end of the 19th century and was so named because it originally contained a statue of Queen Victoria. The Japanese pulled the statue out when they invaded during World War II and it now stands in Victoria Park. The only remaining statue is of Sir Thomas Jackson, a manager of the Hongkong and Shanghai Banking Corporation (HSBC) in the 1870s. The latest incarnation of HSBC's head office is just across Des Voeux Road. *15 min. Chater Rd. and Des Voeux Rd. MTR: Central, exit K.*

❸ ★ **Government House.** Built in 1855, this white stucco house was home to most of Hong Kong's British governors. During World War II it was the headquarters for the Japanese commander, who added the Shinto shrine–style tower and the ceramic roof tiles. When the first Chinese leader, Tung Chee-hwa, came to power in 1997 he lived elsewhere because the building supposedly had bad feng shui (or perhaps just bad political history). The current chief executive, Donald Tsang, doesn't seem to mind. ⏱ *30 min. Upper Albert Rd. www.ceo.gov.hk. Bus: 3B, 12, 23, or 103.*

The Shinto shrine–style tower at the British-built Government House.

❹ ★★ **St. John's Cathedral.** Founded in 1849 by Christian missionaries, the oldest Anglican church in Hong Kong is shaped like a cross, with a large, airy interior and beautiful stained-glass windows. Look out for the ragged original flags beside the pulpit, and the royal insignia on the front pew; this is where visiting monarchs sat during services. With the city's skyscrapers looming in the background, the church makes for a stark contrast not only between the past and present, but also between the idealism of the missionaries and the realities of capitalism. ⏱ *30 min. 4–8 Garden Rd. www.stjohnscathedral.org.hk. Daily 6am–7pm. MTR: Central, exit J2.*

❺ ★★ **Flagstaff House Museum of Tea Ware and K. S. Lo Gallery.** This Greek revival–style home was built in 1846 and is the oldest colonial building in Hong Kong. It was originally the home of the commander of the British forces. Fittingly, it's now a tea museum showcasing teapots and tea ware from many Chinese dynasties. The attached K. S. Lo Gallery also has a variety of antique Chinese

St. John's Cathedral now sits in the shadow of skyscrapers.

ceramics along with Chinese seals. *1 hr. Hong Kong Park. 10 Cotton Tree Dr. Free admission. Wed–Mon 10am–5pm. MTR: Admiralty, exit C1.*

6 ★★ **The High Court.** This rather bland-looking high-rise was made the home of Hong Kong's Supreme Court after the 1997 handover to China. But in typical British fashion, the barristers here wear white wigs while arguing cases (which can be heard in Chinese or English). Stop by for a very visual reminder of Britain's rule. *30 min. 38 Queensway. Time varies depending on cases. MTR: Central, exit J2.*

At the High Court, lawyers and judges still wear wigs, in typical British style.

7 **The Pawn.** The British gastropub craze has arrived in Hong Kong, and its finest example is at this hip, three-storey eatery which previously housed a pawn shop. A full range of ales, ciders, and single-malt whiskeys are on offer, along with modern British fare. It has a rooftop garden, and traditional Sunday roasts are held each week. *62 Johnston Rd. ☎ 852/2866-3444. www.thepawn.com.hk. MTR: Wan Chai., exit B2.*

8 **Victoria Park.** Hop on the tram, itself a fascinating reminder of colonial days, and head for Causeway Bay. After being removed from Statue Square during Japanese occupation, the statue of Queen Victoria was restored and placed in this shady park in 1952. The park also has tennis courts, soccer fields, and many quiet spots to take a break. *30 min. MTR: Causeway Bay, exit E; Tin Hau, exit A2.*

9 ★ **Noonday Gun.** The original cannon was installed here in the 1860s by the powerful trading house Jardine's. Intended to be

You can fill up on cask ales and hearty British fare at gastropub The Pawn.

used against pirates, the cannon was ceremonially fired one day to mark a homecoming for Jardine's boss. Thinking such a welcome should be reserved exclusively for officers of Her Majesty, the Royal Navy punished Jardine's by forcing them to fire the cannon daily at noon as a time signal. The tradition continues today. Access is via a quirky subway from the Excelsior Hotel. ⌚ *20 min. 221 Gloucester Rd. MTR: Causeway Bay, exit D1.*

10 ★★★ **Peninsula Hotel Lobby.** Head to the nearby Wan Chai Ferry Pier and cross the harbor to reach this famous old hotel. Built in 1928, the Peninsula quickly became a popular stopover for the traveling elite. The squat building in front is original while the tower behind was added in 1994. The Peninsula's ornate lobby has long been a popular place to come for afternoon tea. Those wishing to enjoy butter scones and cucumber sandwiches should, in true British style, observe the dress code: strictly no sandals. *Salisbury Rd.* ☎ *852/2920-2888. Daily 2–7pm. $$$.*

⓫ ★★ **KCR Clock Tower.** The KCR Clock Tower is a British icon that today seems sadly out of place. Flanked by a Starbucks and a bus stop, the tower, completed in 1910, once marked the terminus of the Kowloon-Canton Railway (KCR), the main route into Hong Kong from China. City leaders decided such prime waterfront real estate could be better developed, and the train station was moved to make way for a promenade, shops, and museums, leaving only this tower behind as a reminder. ⌚ *10 min. Star Ferry terminal. MTR: Tsim Sha Tsui, exit E.*

Afternoon tea at the Peninsula Hotel is an elegant Hong Kong tradition.

Hip Hong Kong

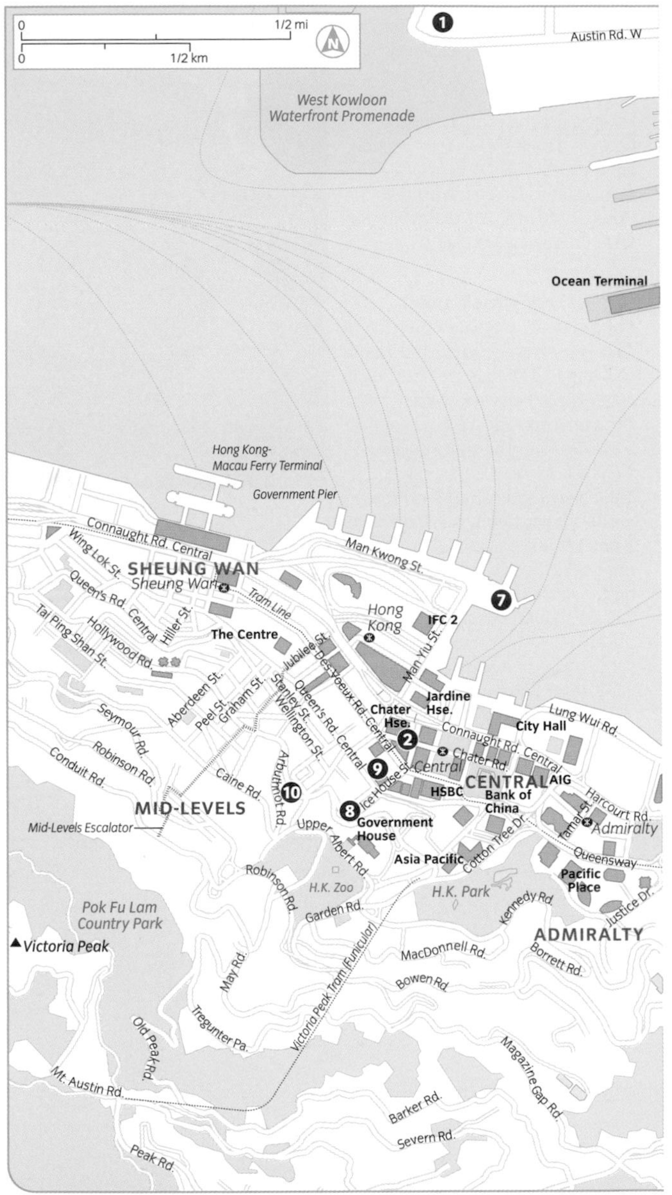

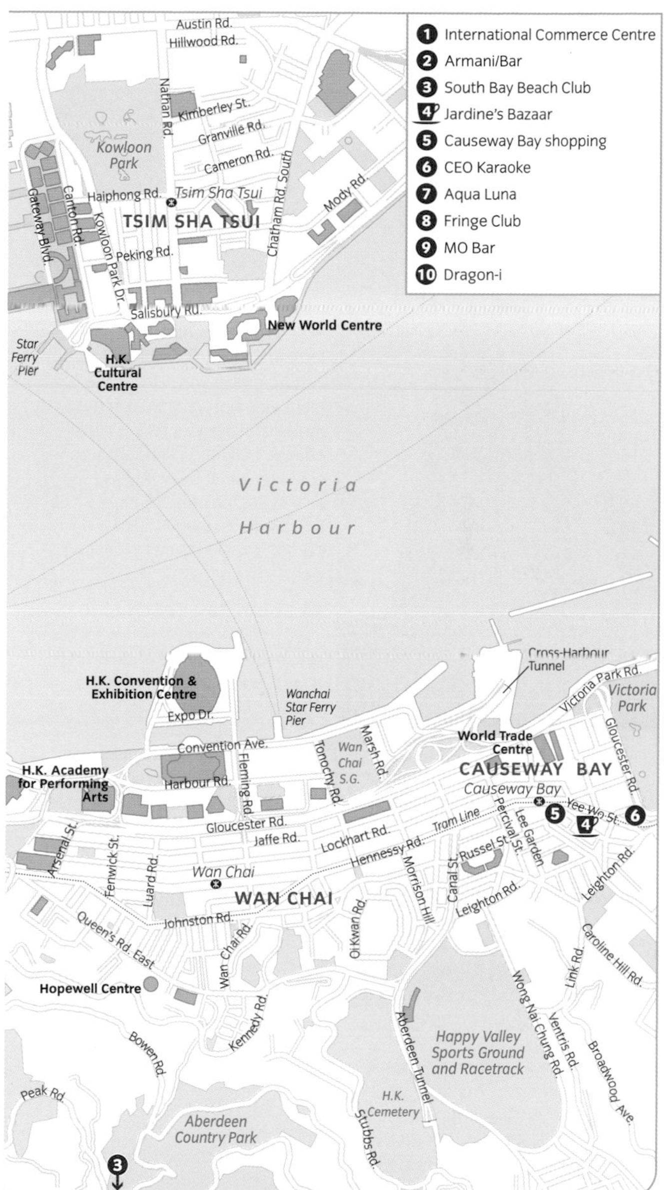
1 International Commerce Centre
2 Armani/Bar
3 South Bay Beach Club
4 Jardine's Bazaar
5 Causeway Bay shopping
6 CEO Karaoke
7 Aqua Luna
8 Fringe Club
9 MO Bar
10 Dragon-i
Austin Rd.
Hillwood Rd.
Nathan Rd.
Kimberley St.
Granville Rd.
Cameron Rd.
Kowloon Park
Haiphong Rd.
Tsim Sha Tsui
Chatham Rd. South
Mody Rd.
TSIM SHA TSUI
Gateway Blvd.
Canton Rd.
Kowloon Park Dr.
Peking Rd.
Salisbury Rd.
New World Centre
Star Ferry Pier
H.K. Cultural Centre
Victoria Harbour
Cross-Harbour Tunnel
Victoria Park Rd.
Victoria Park
H.K. Convention & Exhibition Centre
Expo Dr.
Wanchai Star Ferry Pier
Marsh Rd.
Tonochy Rd.
Wan Chai S.G.
World Trade Centre
Gloucester Rd.
Convention Ave.
Fleming Rd.
H.K. Academy for Performing Arts
Harbour Rd.
CAUSEWAY BAY
Causeway Bay
Percival St.
Lee Garden
Yee Wo St.
Tram Line
Jaffe Rd.
Lockhart Rd.
Hennessy Rd.
Russel St.
Arsenal St.
Fenwick St.
Luard Rd.
Wan Chai
Morrison Hill
Canal St.
Leighton Rd.
WAN CHAI
Oi Kwan Rd.
Johnston Rd.
Queen's Rd. East
Wan Chai Rd.
Caroline Hill Rd.
Link Rd.
Hopewell Centre
Wong Nai Chung Rd.
Kennedy Rd.
Aberdeen Tunnel
Happy Valley Sports Ground and Racetrack
Ventris Rd.
Broadwood Ave.
Bowen Rd.
Peak Rd.
H.K. Cemetery
Stubbs Rd.
Aberdeen Country Park

Hong Kong's famous East-West brew is no longer a straight two-parts China, one-part United Kingdom mix. Japan may have been a distinctly unwelcome interloper during WWII, but its recent invasion in the fields of fashion and design has brought a new hipness to Hong Kong. This tour introduces you to the city's landmarks of cool. Start late morning and plan to stay up well past midnight. **START: Kowloon MTR.**

International Commerce Centre.

1 ★★★ International Commerce Centre. Rising through 118 floors to a height of 484m (1,588 ft.), Hong Kong's tallest building is so of-the-moment it wasn't quite finished by the time this guide went to press. Pegged to open in December 2010, the ICC will offer sci-fi views of the city's gravity-defying sprawl from its 100th-floor observation outpost. High-tech telescopes and "MP5" audiovisual guided tours will point out local landmarks from the 360-degree viewing platform. *1 hr. 100/F, ICC, 1 Austin Rd. W., Daily 10am–10pm. MTR: Kowloon, exit D2.*

2 ★ Armani/Bar. Armani's largest retail space outside Milan is located in the heart of Central's gilded shopping district. Apart from the expected chic apparel and cosmetics, the complex contains a 40-seat restaurant with separate lounge and coffee bar, where you can sip espresso while enjoying a giant video projection of catwalk models on parade. With a clever change of lighting and furniture arrangements, the venue is reborn as a nightclub after 10pm. *1 hr. 2/F, Chater House, 11 Chater Rd. ☎ 852/2805-0028. MTR: Central, exit E.*

3 South Bay Beach Club. Just south of Repulse Bay lies a secluded sandy strip which develops elite appeal during warmer months. The South Bay Beach Club has the feel of a Mediterranean hipster hangout—all insistent club beats, skimpy bikinis, and wraparound shades. The champagne stocks are well drained most weekends. Come late afternoon and stick around for sunset. *3 hr. South Bay Rd., Repulse Bay. ☎ 852/2812-6015. Taxi.*

4 ★★★ Jardine's Bazaar. This grungy restaurant strip is popular with younger hipsters on account of its cheap hand-folded wanton and noodle shops. The Loon Wai diner (p 86) specializes in mixed-grill hot plates which include more meat than seems economically possible

Times Square at Causeway Bay.

for less than $HK40. After the beach posing, you'll appreciate the more down-to-earth scene. ***54–58 Jardine's Bazaar. ☎ 852/2576-6609. $.***

❺ ★★ **Causeway Bay shopping.** Formerly the commercial base of colonial traders the Jardines, Causeway Bay now has the feel of downtown Tokyo. Endless waves of consumers pulse down narrow roads and beneath the towering billboards and neon signs. Once the traffic stops, punk teens and platinum card–toters roam between famed department stores like Sogo, Times Square, and Island Beverley, while Kai Chiu Road is a rabbit's warren of smaller shops where youth culture breeds. Come after dark. 🕘 *2 hr. Causeway Bay. MTR: Causeway Bay.*

❻ ★★ **CEO Karaoke.** Karaoke may be a Japanese invention, but Hong Kongers have made it the bosom of local culture. My favorite spot to let loose is the **Causeway Bay CEO,** where you can choose from a huge selection of English songs. Shy types fear not: Hong Kong karaoke is conducted in private rooms rather than public arenas. Most have their own bathrooms, and to forestall the threat of microphone-hogs, some even come with PlayStations. ***Lok Sing Centre, 2–8 Sugar St., Causeway Bay. ☎ 852/2137-9777. www.ceokb.com. MTR: Causeway Bay, exit E.***

❼ ★★★ **Aqua Luna.** This wooden junk may look like the antithesis of hip, but trust the Aqua Group, one of Hong Kong's most successful purveyors of cool, to turn an old-fashioned tourist favorite into a "boutique" experience. The 45-minute cruise can be enjoyed from a top-deck lounge bed, with freshly made cocktail in hand. The glittering nighttime view of Central contrasts deliciously with the rough-hewn onboard furniture. The last sailing departs Central at 10:45pm. Book ahead. 🕘 *1 hr. Pier 9, Central. ☎ 852/2116-8821. Adults $HK180, kids 4–11 $HK150. MTR: Central, exit A.*

Aqua Luna *in Hong Kong Harbour.*

The Dragon-i is one of Hong Kong's most talked about clubs, thanks in part to its model clientele.

8 ★★★ **Fringe Club.** This is one of the best venues in Hong Kong for seeing contemporary theater, live music, and poetry readings. Some acts are international, but most are local performers and writers. There's also a rooftop bar. It's closed every Sunday. *2 Lower Albert Rd. ☎ 852/2521-7251. www.hkfringeclub.com. Tickets $HK100 and up. Bus: 13, 23A, or 26.*

The Fringe Club occupies a former dairy depot, and hosts many English-language acts.

9 ★★ **MO Bar.** This superchic hotel bar is all things to all people—coffee shop, cocktail lounge, performance venue, restaurant. It's played host to microgigs from the likes of Annie Lennox and Harry Connick, Jr., but the highlight for me is the slinky design, the centerpiece of which is a hypnotic red circle that glows mysteriously on the far wall. Be sure to sample a few of MO's expensive but delicious cocktails. *1 hr. MTR: Central, exit D2.*

10 ★ **Dragon-i.** No self-respecting see-and-be-seen card carrier can visit Hong Kong without making a late-night stop at Dragon-i, a club which has come to define the "it scene" thanks to the number of local and international celebs who intermittently parade through. Stop by after 11:30pm, and expect to have your fashion/beauty/wealth credentials examined by the bouncers. *UG/F The Centrium, 60 Wyndham St., Central. MTR: Central, exit D1.*

3 The Best Neighborhood Walks

Yau Ma Tei & Mong Kok

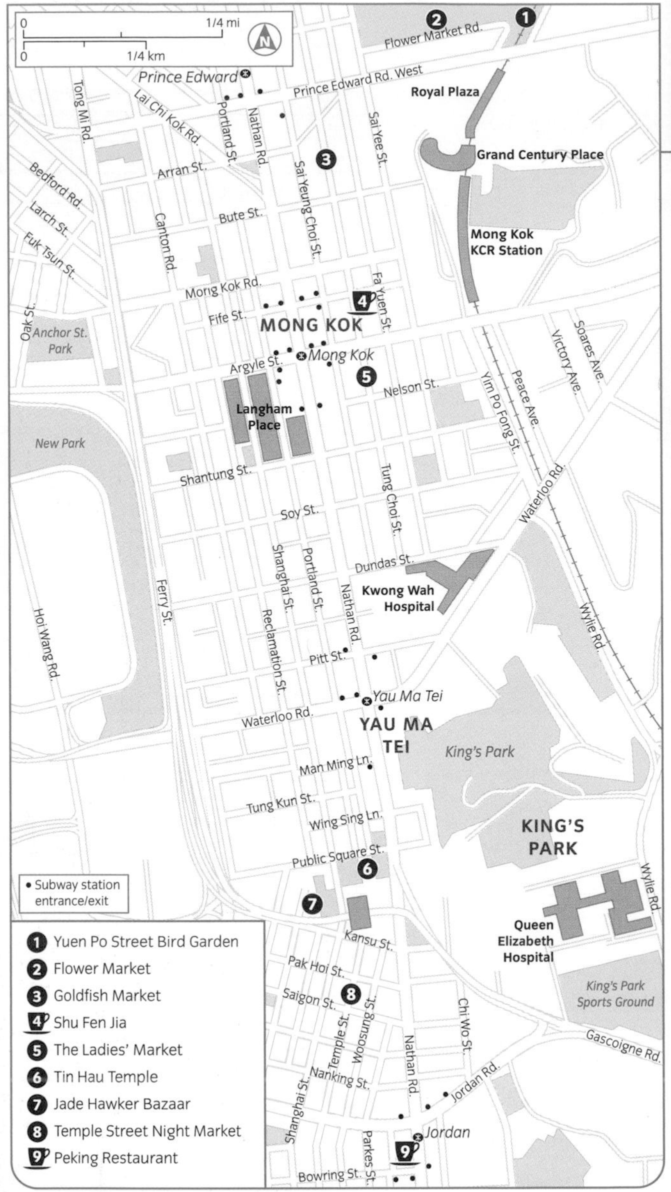

Previous page: Bamboo bird cages, complete with tiny porcelain water bowls, are for sale at the Bird Market.

This long walk will take you through some of the most crowded and vibrant parts of the city. The hustle is 24-7, but you'll be rewarded with a succession of insights into the remarkable vitality of Hong Kong's street life. Start the walk around 3 to 4pm to make the most of the attractions *en route* and to see the transition from day to night, when this part of the city really comes to life. **START: Mong Kok East or Prince Edward MTR.**

Birds, like this one for sale at the Bird Market, are prized pets here; prices are based on singing ability, not plumage.

1 ★★ Yuen Po Street Bird Garden. Enter this market through a traditional *pai lou* gateway to explore a series of courtyards containing a string of melodious songbird stalls. There are cockatoos and parakeets, along with exotic bird-keeping paraphernalia such as grasshoppers (a delicacy for some species). For enthusiasts, a day at Yuen Po Street is a social event, for both birds and keepers. At the northern end is Boundary Road, the dividing line between Hong Kong and mainland China up until the lease of the New Territories in 1898. Return to the main entrance to continue the walk. *30 min. MTR: Mong Kok East, exit D; Prince Edward, exit A.*

2 Flower Market. Turn right onto Flower Market Road, one of the most aromatic spots in Hong Kong where flora is traded with something approaching stock-market mania. *15 min. Flower Market Rd. MTR: Prince Edward, exit A.*

3 Goldfish Market. The Chinese believe fish bring good luck and that aquariums add great feng shui to any room. Tung Choi Street, south of Prince Edward Road, is packed to the gills with shops carrying everything from goldfish to rare tropical varieties. They're on display in tanks and in water-filled baggies that hang from doorways. Sensitive souls be warned: Most of the fish are kept in overcrowded tanks, and you'll also see puppies, kittens, and turtles waiting for homes. *30 min. Tung Choi St. MTR: Prince Edward, exit B2.*

4 ★ Shu Fen Jia. You're unlikely to spend long looking for food in Mong Kok—the options are many and varied. Down an alley on the south side of Fife Street, between Tung Choi Street and Fa Yuen Street, is my personal favorite snack joint, an open-air food counter which always reminds me of *Blade*

You can buy orchids, and other blooms, at the Flower Market.

A Taste of the Past

Dai pai dong (literally "big rows of food stalls") are a dying institution. These outdoor eateries, known for their cheap, wok-fried dishes, were all over the city less than 50 years ago but hygiene concerns and a fear of city clutter have led the government to shoo most of these stalls into covered areas. There are only 28 legal *dai pai dong* remaining, most of which are in Central and Sham Shui Po. The Temple Street outlets are, in fact, unlicensed but tolerated by the authorities on account of their tourist popularity. Unlike other *dai pai dong,* the Temple Street food stalls generally have English menus.

Runner. It specializes in potato-based snacks: Choose from chunky fries, Western filled baked potatoes, or Asian potato noodles, all fantastically cheap and available till 2am. The fresh fruit juices are a great remedy on steamy city nights. ***A2, 33–35 Fife St. ☎ 852/3481-6961. Daily 11am–2am. $.***

5 ★★ The Ladies' Market. South of Argyle Street, on Tung Choi Street, is Hong Kong's primary street market. Unlike other "markets" on this walk, the Ladies' Market comes complete with old-fashioned canopied stalls and the cries of competing vendors. After dark the street is almost permanently choked and movement is at shuffle pace. Once famous for women's gear, the market now offers pretty much everything, from brand-name rip-offs to apple peelers. Just keep in mind that even if you get a good price, the quality is likely to be as dubious as the label. ***1 hr. Tung Choi St. MTR: Mong Kok, exit D3.***

Bags of goldfish hang in a doorway at the Goldfish Market.

6 ★ Tin Hau Temple. Ready yourself for a few twists and turns: At the southern end of Tung Choi Street turn right onto Dundas Street, cross Nathan Road, and then do a left into Portland Street. It's then a right onto Man Ming Lane, followed by a quick left into Temple Street. This is a relatively quiet part of one of Kowloon's most famous streets but there'll still likely be a few *dai pai dong* and outdoor stalls. Keep going south until you hit Tin Hau Temple. It may seem hard to believe now, but this Buddhist shrine, dedicated to seafarers, was once on the waterfront. Arrive before 5pm to peer inside. There's still plenty to see for latecomers; the entire temple area becomes festive after dark, with soothsayers and amateur opera singers plying their trade on the south side of the temple. ***30 min. Daily 8am–5pm. MTR: Yau Ma Tei, exit C.***

The Tin Hau Temple is one of the oldest Buddhist temples in Hong Kong.

7 Jade Hawker Bazaar. Around 400 dealers are cooped together in this claustrophobic, tungsten-lit, caged compound. You can get everything from small pendants to large sculptures. A word of warning: Judging the quality of jade can be tricky. Think twice before spending large sums here, as foreigners are sometimes taken for a ride. If you like a piece but aren't sure the price is fair, ask if they'll allow you to have it tested for authenticity at the nearby Jade Plaza (about 150m/492 ft.) south on Canton Rd.). *30 min. Junction of Kansu and Battery sts. Daily 9am–6pm. MTR: Yau Ma Tei, exit C.*

Inexpensive jade jewelry is for sale at the Jade Market.

8 ★★★ Temple Street Night Market. Yes, you've already hit several markets, but this one, which stays open until midnight, has a very big draw—the *dai pai dong* stands selling delicious fried noodles and seafood. You can browse the DVDs, clothing, and other items, but I recommend you make a beeline to the Nanking Road junction, grab a stool at one of the outdoor tables, order a beer, and enjoy the scene. *1 hr. Daily 4pm–midnight. MTR: Yau Ma Tei, exit C.*

9 Peking Restaurant. Accessible through a narrow doorway and up a carpeted flight of stairs off busy Nathan Road, my favorite Peking duck restaurant hardly makes a fuss of advertising itself. The decor is faded and the service fusty, but the food makes up for it all. The duck is served in the traditional manner, with the crispy skin and tender flesh separated and served with scallion and a thick, sweet sauce to be made into DIY pancakes. There are a number of foreigner-friendly Sichuan dishes on offer too, including kung pao chicken and mapo doufu (spicy tofu with ground pork). *1/F, 227 Nathan Rd. ☎ 852/2730-1315. $$.*

Tsim Sha Tsui

1. Tsim Sha Tsui Promenade
2. KCR Clock Tower
3. 1881 Heritage
4. Harbour City
5. Haiphong Road Temporary Market
6. Kowloon Park
7. St. Andrew's Church
8. Tai Woo Restaurant
9. Knutsford Terrace

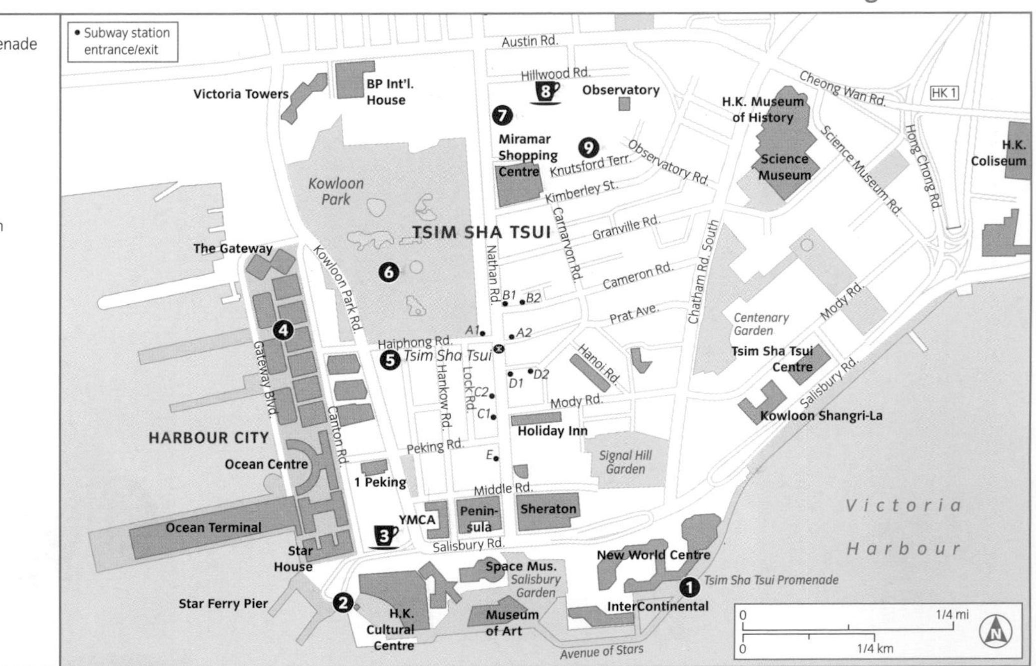

This walk skirts the touristy tip of the Kowloon peninsula before pitching you into the heart of Tsim Sha Tsui. As you'll discover on this fairly short walk, there are pockets of serenity amid the claustrophobic intensity of one of Hong Kong's most lively neighborhoods. Aim to end the walk around dinner time. **START: Tsim Sha Tsui East MTR.**

1 ★★★ Tsim Sha Tsui Promenade. You'll get the definitive view of the Hong Kong skyline from this long waterfront promenade. The river traffic, made up of commuter ferries, tourist junks, cruise liners, and cargo ships, is a reminder that for all its urban intensity, Hong Kong is a maritime city at heart. Your walk should begin east of the Hollywood-inspired Avenue of Stars and move westward towards the busy cultural zone with its mammoth galleries, museums, and auditoriums. *30 min. MTR: Tsim Sha Tsui East, exit J.*

2 ★ KCR Clock Tower. This used to be the terminus of the Kowloon-Canton Railway—the end point for those who crossed Europe and much of Asia by train to get here. All that's left today is the red-brick and concrete clock tower, built by the British government in 1915. The railway terminus was moved to Hung Hom in 1974, and the clock became an isolated symbol of Hong Kong's British past. *5 min. Star Ferry terminal. MTR: Tsim Sha Tsui, exit L6.*

The Kowloon-Canton Railway Clock Tower is a symbol of Hong Kong's fading colonial past.

Enjoy a quiet stroll along the Tsim Sha Tsui Promenade.

3 ★★★ 1881 Heritage. With classic Hong Kong panache, the colonial headquarters of the Marine Police was reopened in 2010 as an amphitheater of posh shopping and dining. It's an impressive development, crowned by Hullett House, a boutique hotel where you can enjoy a drink in a former pirate cell (see Mariner's Rest, p 98), or a meal in the Stables Grill. *1 hr. 2A Canton Rd. ☎ 852/2926-8000. www.1881heritage.com. Daily 10am–9pm.*

The British Are Coming

In the early part of the 19th century, the United Kingdom was desperate for Chinese tea and silks, but China wasn't interested in trade—that is until the British began importing large quantities of opium from India. Addiction ran rampant at every level of Chinese society and in the 1830s the emperor eventually banned opium imports. British traders ignored the ban, leading to the start of the First Opium War in 1839. Defeated by Britain's vastly superior naval strength, China was forced to hand over Hong Kong Island "in perpetuity." The Second Opium War (1856–58) resulted in the loss of Kowloon, and the UK expanded their colony with the lease of the New Territories in 1898. They remained in control until 1997.

❹ kids **Harbour City.** Housing over 600 high-end and midrange shops, four hotels, over 50 restaurants, and two cinemas, this mall is one of the largest in Asia. It also has stunning views of the harbor, in addition to its designer goods (including Louis Vuitton, Ferragamo, and Prada) and jewelry boutiques. If you're traveling with children, don't miss the KidX section, which includes the largest Toys "R" Us in Asia. ⌚ ***1 hr.*** *3–27 Canton Rd.* ☎ *852/2118-8601. www.harbourcity.com.hk. Daily 10am–9pm.*

❺ ★★ **Haiphong Road Temporary Market.** The word "temporary" is a misnomer in this fantastically grimy wet market; it's been located here, under the Kowloon Park Drive flyover, for many years now. There are great local *dai pai dong,* as well as flowers, meat, and fish galore. Interestingly, there's a flourishing trade in halal meat thanks to the large Muslim communities from the Indian subcontinent who live and work nearby. ⌚ ***30 min.*** *Entrance near gate to Kowloon Park. MTR: Tsim Sha Tsui, exit A1.*

❻ ★ **Kowloon Park.** Kowloon Park is one of the city's most diverse public spaces, with a variety of specialist gardens, an aviary, a walking trail enveloped by trees, public swimming pools, and, in the southeastern corner, Kowloon Mosque. There are outdoor martial arts in the Sculpture Garden between 2:30 and 4:30pm on Sundays. The park is also home to the Hong Kong Heritage Discovery Centre, which has an exhibition gallery and library. It's perhaps one for the connoisseur but the air-conditioning and free Wi-Fi can be appreciated by anybody. ⌚ ***30 min.*** *MTR: Tsim Sha Tsui, exit A1.*

The sculpture garden is just one of Kowloon Park's many charms.

7 ★ St. Andrew's Church. Built between 1904 and 1906 in what was then a remote corner of Kowloon, the distinctive Gothic, red-brick form of St. Andrew's represents an oasis of calm amid the incessant bustle and blaring neon of Nathan Road. Hong Kong's seafaring traditions, somewhat lost in Kowloon's concrete jungle, are referenced in the delightful stained-glass windows. Bible stories take place on the Hong Kong seashore, and a starfish stands in for the star of Bethlehem. *30 min. 138 Nathan Rd. MTR: Tsim Sha Tsui, exit B1.*

Massive neon signs dominate Hong Kong's high-end shopping street Nathan Road.

8 ★ Tai Woo Restaurant. This is a great place to try Hong Kong's hybrid cuisine. It's mostly Cantonese but there are invariably a few Western techniques that you don't find in Guangdong (Canton) proper. Take the scrambled egg whites with crab meat, served with breaded prawns and deep-fried oysters. As important as the food is the raucous, banquet-style atmosphere that's typical of local dining. Though part of a chain, this branch is by far the best. *14–16 Hillwood Rd. 852/2368-5420. $$.*

9 ★★ Knutsford Terrace. The most popular bar strip in Tsim Sha Tsui is a more refined take on Lan Kwai Fong and a great place to reward yourself at the end of the walk. The scene tends to be young, lively, and overwhelmingly foreign, with diners and drinkers mingling at tables lining the terrace. There are darts, TV sports, and other games in some of the bars. Try Merhaba (p 98), where the refreshments can be enjoyed alongside a hookah pipe. *1 hr.*

Celluloid City

Thanks to its political, economic, and artistic freedoms, Hong Kong was the center of Chinese-language filmmaking from the 1950s to the 1990s. Perhaps Hong Kong's biggest influence is felt in the kung fu genre; the city's most famous son, Jackie Chan, has a star on both the Avenue of Stars and Hollywood's Walk of Fame. Though Hong Kong's dominance has been undercut by rampant piracy and increased competition from Taiwan, South Korea, and mainland China, local filmmakers such as Wong Kar-wai and Stephen Chow continue to make international hits. Two of my favorite Hong Kong movies are Wong's vibrant and quirky *Chungking Express* and Chow's hilarious *Kung Fu Hustle*—great accompaniments on your long flight.

Central & Western

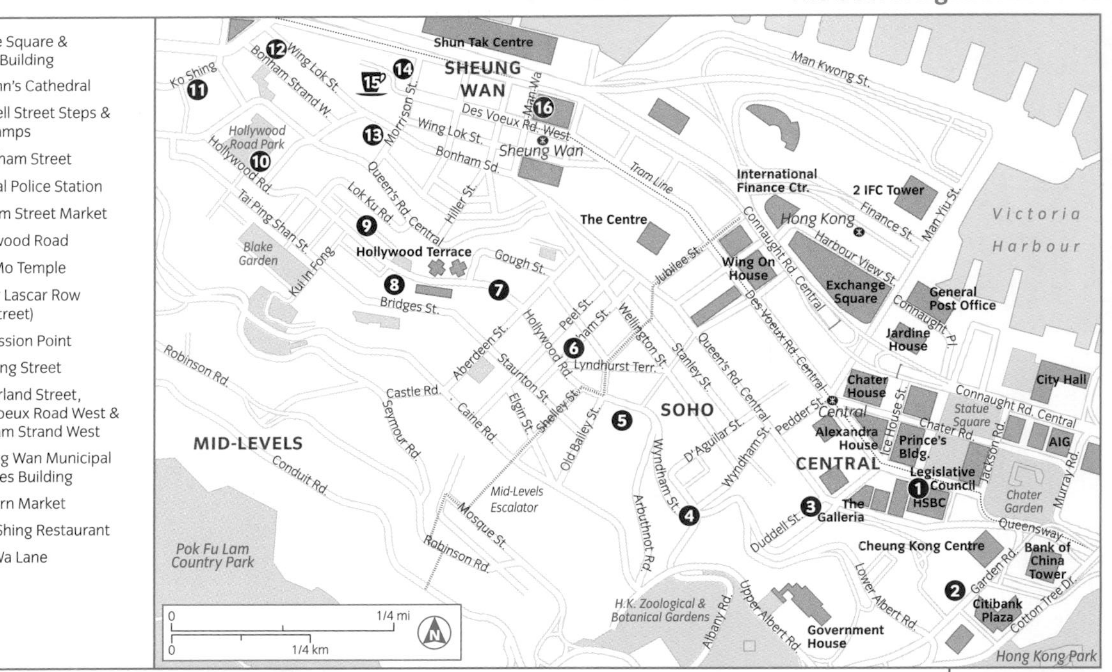

1. Statue Square & HSBC Building
2. St. John's Cathedral
3. Duddell Street Steps & Gas Lamps
4. Wyndham Street
5. Central Police Station
6. Graham Street Market
7. Hollywood Road
8. Man Mo Temple
9. Upper Lascar Row (Cat Street)
10. Possession Point
11. Ko Shing Street
12. Sutherland Street, Des Voeux Road West & Bonham Strand West
13. Sheung Wan Municipal Services Building
14. Western Market
15. Fung Shing Restaurant
16. Man Wa Lane

This long walk moves from Central, the center of colonial influence, to Sheung Wan, the home of Chinese commerce. You'll pass beneath bombastic skyscrapers and past handsome Victorian edifices before ending in one of the most palpably Chinese corners of Hong Kong. This route is best started early, since Sheung Wan tends to grind to a halt after sundown. If you are starting late, I recommend doing this walk in reverse. **START: Central MTR.**

1 ★ Statue Square & HSBC Building. Start in the heart of colonial Hong Kong. Named for a statue of Queen Victoria, the square's only permanent resident is now Sir Thomas Jackson, a 19th-century chief of the Hongkong and Shanghai Banking Corporation (HSBC) who faces the Legislative Council Building. HSBC's head office is across Des Voeux Road (p 51). Head inside to view the stunning banking hall. From here, you can walk directly into the adjacent, all-marble Standard Charter Bank and cross busy Queen's Road via an elevated walkway. ⌚ *20 min. MTR: Central, exit K.*

2 ★★ St. John's Cathedral. Climb Battery Path, once a seafront fortification, and pass the distinctive Edwardian exterior of the Court of Final Appeal to reach St. John's, the only building in all of Hong Kong which technically owns the land it stands on. Return down Battery Path and head for Duddell Street. ⌚ *30 min. 4–8 Garden Rd. Daily 7am–6pm.*

The Duddell Street Gas Lamps are a charming reminder of Hong Kong's colonialist past.

Stained glass at St. John's Cathedral.

3 Duddell Street Steps & Gas Lamps. The wide stone steps at the end of Duddell Street are a reminder of a time before the Mid-Levels escalator. In this city of neon, the old gas lamps—the last remaining in the city—that stand at the top of the steps are particularly evocative of days past. Turn right onto Ice House Street. ⌚ *10 min. Duddell St.*

❹ ★ **Wyndham Street.** Just where Ice House Street melts into Wyndham Street sits the grand old Dairy Farm Depot, formerly an ice storage depot dating back to 1892. Look south to see the distinctive but derelict former police barracks and magistracy building. Off to the right, as you continue up the hill, is Lan Kwai Fong, a riot of hedonism by night but fairly sleepy by day. Pop in for a happy-hour drink. 🕒 *10 min. Lan Kwai Fong.*

❺ **Central Police Station.** Past the Pottinger Street steps, Wyndham Street becomes Hollywood Road. To the left is the hulking gray form of the Central Police Station, the largest cluster of Victorian architecture left in the city. It's a relic of the past with an uncertain future. A fantastical development proposal by the designer of Beijing's Bird's Nest Stadium was rejected for being too outlandish. As Hong Kong gets increasingly serious about heritage preservation, it looks likely the original form will be preserved. 🕒 *10 min. 10 Hollywood Rd.*

❻ ★★ **Graham Street Market.** At Hollywood Road's five-way junction with Lyndurst Terrace and Graham Street, head downhill a few paces to experience one of Central's best-loved outdoor markets.

The Central Police Station is one of the best remaining examples of colonial architecture in Hong Kong.

Records show there was a small food bazaar here serving passing ships before the British arrived. This pedestrian-only lane is still crammed with fruit and vegetable stalls, with a wet market farther down the hill. Return to Hollywood Road. 🕒 *15 min. Graham St.*

❼ ★ **Hollywood Road.** See p 8, ❻. 🕒 *30 min.*

❽ ★★ **Man Mo Temple.** See p 9, ❽. 🕒 *30 min. Hollywood Rd. and Ladder St. ☎ 852/2803-2916. Free admission. Daily 8am–6pm.*

What's a SAR?

You may hear Hong Kong referred to as a SAR, which stands for Special Administrative Region. When the British handed the city back to Communist China in 1997, they negotiated an arrangement that allowed citizens of Hong Kong to retain certain rights for 50 years. The end result is that Hong Kong has far more economic and cultural freedoms than most of China, though not quite full democracy. Half of Hong Kong's lawmakers are freely elected but Beijing has a hand in selecting the other half, as well as appointing the Chief Executive.

Chinese Medicine

Though Hong Kong is a 21st-century city, many Chinese dispute the philosophy and assumptions of modern Western medicine, placing their faith instead in traditional remedies that go back thousands of years. You'll see shops selling exotic ingredients for these concoctions. Deer's horn is said to be effective against fever. Bones, teeth, and seashells are used as tranquilizers and cures for insomnia. Taking a holistic approach, Chinese herbalists prescribe medicine according to the state of a person's overall system; an eye complaint could just as easily be dealt with by treating the stomach, for example. If you have indigestion, a stuffed-up nose, a backache, or any other nagging pain (and you're not afraid to drink a mixture of crushed animal teeth), an herbalist can give you a remedy. You can always mime your symptoms—he'll probably figure out what you mean.

9 ★ Upper Lascar Row (Cat Street). See p 9, 9. 30 min. *Upper Lascar Row.*

10 ★ Possession Point. On January 26, 1841, a British naval party disembarked at a small fishing jetty and clambered up a steep hillock before planting the British union flag, nothing was ever the same. The hillock they climbed is now Possession Street, though land reclamation and development have wrecked the sea views. The flag-raising site is Hollywood Road Park, now a Chinese-style garden. *10 min. Possession St.*

11 ★★ Ko Shing Street. Hollywood Road heads downhill before meeting Queen's Road West. Turn left and take the first right into narrow Wo Fung Street. This leads down to a ramshackle old lane, fronted by traditional two-story Chinese houses selling an exotic array of ingredients used in Chinese herbal medicine (see "Chinese Medicine," above). Turn left here. *10 min.*

Hollywood Road is one of the best places to shop for antiques and for uniquely Chinese souvenirs like this wooden Buddha mask.

Bird's nest, for sale along Bonham Strand West, is a delicacy in Hong Kong. The nests are those of certain types of swifts.

12 ★ Sutherland Street, Des Voeux Road West and Bonham Strand West. Turn right into Sutherland Street, a pungent parade of shops and stalls selling dried seafood. Turn right onto Des Voeux

Exploring the dried seafood shops is a fascinating, albeit aromatic, experience.

Road West and follow the trams until you reach Bonham Strand West, which has the architectural feel of New York City but an aroma and ambience that's pure China. The shops here sell ginseng and bird's nest, ingredients used for both cooking and medicine. 🕘 *20 min.*

⑬ ★ **Sheung Wan Municipal Services Building.** Turn left onto Bonham Strand. Ahead on your right is this concrete monstrosity which houses a wet market on its ground floor and a traditional food court on level three, open until 1am. The Chinese value fresh food—and I do mean fresh. The squeamish may want to look away, but this remains a fascinating look at Chinese food culture. 🕘 *20 min. 345 Queen's Rd. C.*

⑭ **Western Market.** Head down Morrison Street to reach the red-brick Western Market, a handsome example of Edwardian architecture. The shops inside aren't terribly special, but they do sell clothing, tea, and souvenirs like Chinese seals and jade jewelry. The Grand Stage restaurant on the top floor is worth checking out, even if you don't stop for dinner. 🕘 *15 min. 323 Des Voeux Rd. C.*

15 ★ **Fung Shing Restaurant.** Located right beside the Western Market, this Chinese restaurant has a large menu (with plenty of pictures to help you choose), and offers classics such as shark's fin with shredded chicken or fried sliced pigeon. The staff is efficient and friendly, and the portions are huge. *7 On Tai St.* ☎ *852/2815-8689. $$.*

⑯ **Man Wa Lane.** Walk 3 blocks east down Des Voeux Road Central to reach this narrow street, home to one of China's oldest trades—carved seal making—since the 1920s. Vendors use materials like jade, clay, and marble to carve seals, or "chops." They can be custom-made at several of the booths here and you can choose to have your name written in English (difficult given the lack of space) or Chinese. It takes about an hour, so you may want to order before heading off for some well-earned food. 🕘 *30 min. Daily 10am–6pm. MTR: Sheung Wan, exit A1.* ●

An herbal medicine dealer measures out some of his wares.

4 The Best Shopping

Shopping Best Bets

Best **Chinese-Themed Gifts**
★★ Chinese Arts and Crafts Ltd., *3 Salisbury Rd. (p 60)*

Best **Contemporary Art**
★★★ Hanart T Z Gallery, *202 Henley Building, 2/F, 5 Queen's Rd. (p 59)*

Best **Designer Clothing**
★★ Joyce Boutique, *18 Queen's Rd. (p 62)*

Best **Jade Jewelry**
★★ Jade Market, *Junction of Kansu and Battery sts. (p 65)*

Best **Cheap Electronics**
★★★ Wan Chai Computer Centre, *130 Hennessy Rd. (p 61)*

Best **English-Language Books & Magazines**
★★★ Swindon Book Co. Ltd., *13–15 Lock Rd. (p 60)*

Best **Cheap Souvenirs**
★ Cat Street, *Upper Lascar Row (p 65)*

Best **Pottery**
★★ Dragon Culture, *231 Hollywood Rd. (p 58)*

Best **Designer Souvenirs**
★★★ Chocolate Rain, *Shop A, G/F, 67 Peel St. (p 63)*

Best **Chinese Furniture**
★★ Honeychurch Antiques, *29 Hollywood Rd. (p 58)*

Best **Hand-Woven Carpets**
★★ Chinese Carpet Centre, *Shop 5, G/F, Houston Centre, 63 Mody Rd. (p 60)*

Best **Night Shopping**
★★★ Temple Street Night Market, *34 Temple St. (p 65)*

Best **Local Fashion**
★★★ G.O.D., *Leighton Centre, Sharp St. E. (p 63)*

Best **Chinese Medicine**
★★★ Eu Yan Sang, *152–156 Queen's Rd. (p 66)*

Best **Mall**
★★★ Festival Walk, *80–88 Tat Chee Ave. (p 64)*

Best **Antiques for All Budgets**
★★★ Arch Angel Antiques, *53–55 Hollywood Rd. (p 58)*

The tailors at Sam's are world-famous for their custom suits and shirts.

Kowloon Shopping

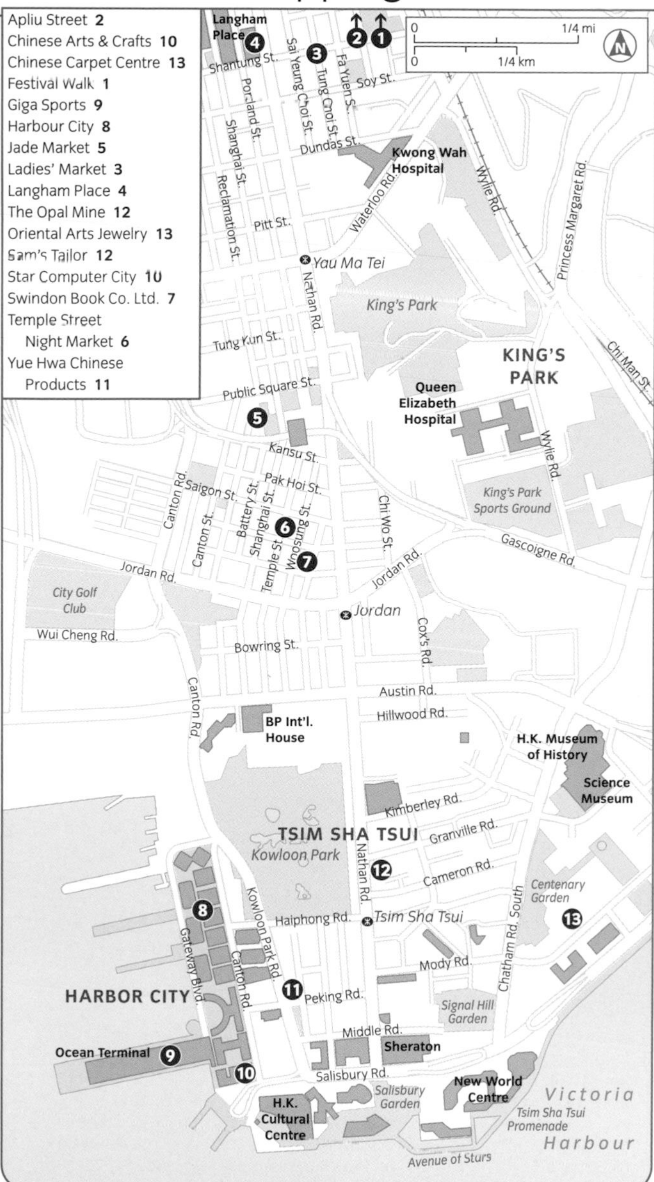

Photo p 53: Inexpensive Chinese silk dresses at the Temple Street Night Market.

Central Shopping

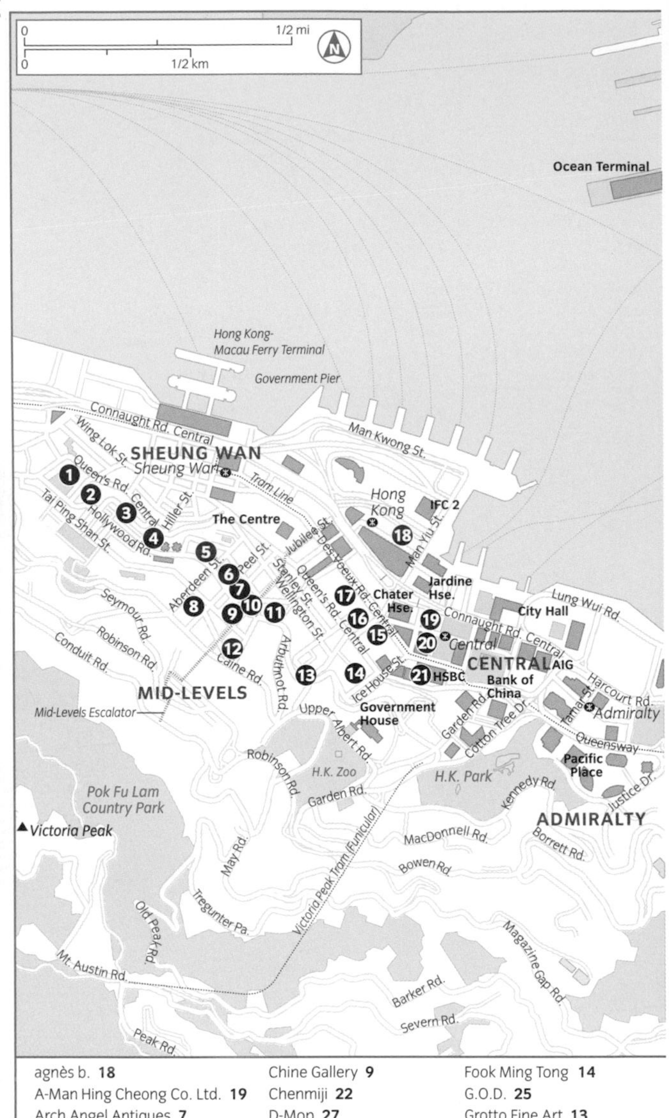

agnès b. **18**
A-Man Hing Cheong Co. Ltd. **19**
Arch Angel Antiques **7**
Blanc de Chine **16**
Cat Street **3**
Chocolate Rain **8**
Chine Gallery **9**
Chenmiji **22**
D-Mop **27**
Dragon Culture **2**
Dymocks Booksellers **18**
Eu Yan Sang **5**
Fook Ming Tong **14**
G.O.D. **25**
Grotto Fine Art **13**
Hanart T Z Gallery **21**
Homeless **5**
Honeychurch Antiques **10**

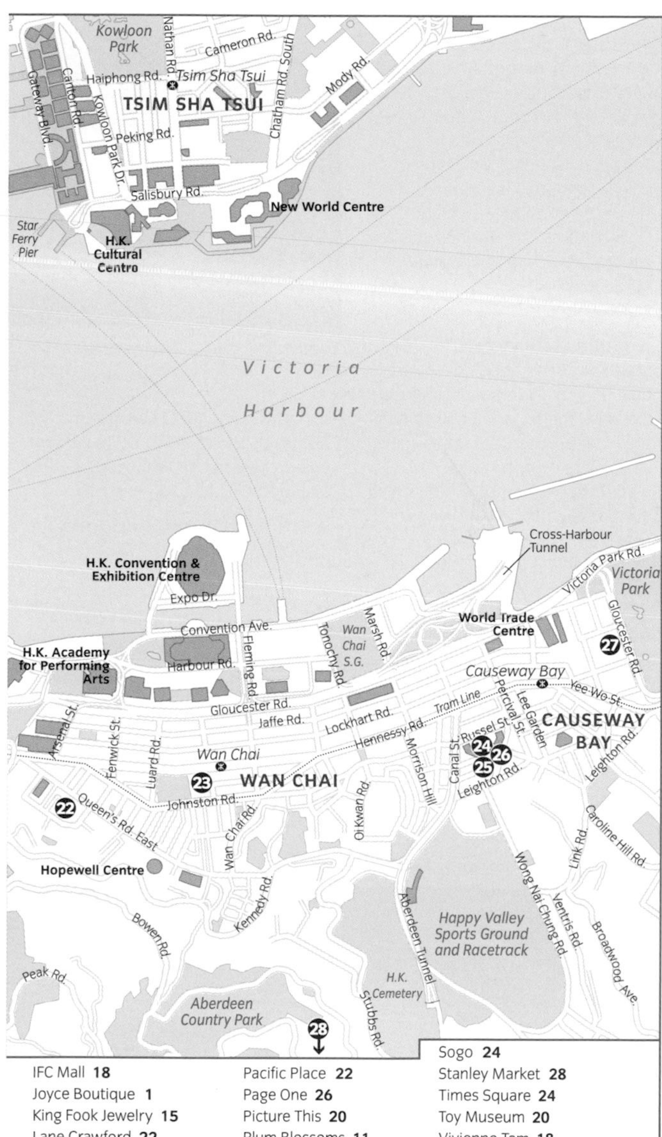

IFC Mall **18**
Joyce Boutique **1**
King Fook Jewelry **15**
Lane Crawford **22**
The Lanes **17**
Lock Cha Tea Shop **4**
Pacific Place **22**
Page One **26**
Picture This **20**
Plum Blossoms **11**
Schoeni Art Gallery **12**
Shanghai Tang **16**
Sogo **24**
Stanley Market **28**
Times Square **24**
Toy Museum **20**
Vivienne Tam **18**
Wah Tung China Company **6**
Wan Chai Computer Centre **23**

Shopping A to Z

Serious collectors of Asian antiques head to Honeychurch Antiques.

Antiques & Collectibles

★★★ Arch Angel Antiques CENTRAL There are pieces here for the serious collector—Chinese porcelain and terra cotta from the Tang (A.D. 618–907) and Ming (1368–1644) dynasties. But the shop's three floors also feature smaller items like mahjong sets and chopsticks. ***53–55 Hollywood Rd. ☎ 852/2851-6848. AE, MC, V. MTR: Sheung Wan. Bus: 26. Map p 56.***

★ Chine Gallery CENTRAL It's worth stopping at Chine to see the beautiful collection of chairs from Sichuan, Shanxi, and other regions of China. Brothers Zafar and Anwer Islam, who own the place, are experts in restoration. There's also a wide selection of hand-woven rugs from Tibet, Inner Mongolia, and Xinjiang. ***42A Hollywood Rd. ☎ 852/2543-0023. www.chinegallery.com. AE, MC, V. MTR: Central. Bus: 26. Map p 56.***

★★ Dragon Culture CENTRAL Owner Victor Choi, who also has a gallery in New York and has written books on Chinese antiques, has a huge stock of Tang dynasty pottery, Ming porcelain, snuff bottles, and other curios. The staff here is especially helpful. ***231 Hollywood Rd. ☎ 852/2545-8098. www.dragonculture.com.hk. AE, MC, V. MTR: Sheung Wan. Bus: 26. Map p 56.***

★★ Honeychurch Antiques CENTRAL Americans Glenn and Lucille Vessa, the art dealers who run this shop, can help guide you in buying furniture and collectibles from both China and other parts of Asia. They sell furniture, paintings, pottery, and porcelain ranging from 5th millennium B.C. to the early half of the 20th century. ***29 Hollywood Rd. ☎ 852/2543-2433. www.honeychurch.com/hongkong. AE, DC, MC, V. MTR: Central. Bus: 26. Map p 56.***

Terra-cotta horses are among the many unique items for sale at Dragon Culture.

Some of Hong Kong's hottest young artists show their work at Plum Blossoms.

Art Galleries

★★ Grotto Fine Art CENTRAL Founded in 2001, this small, avant-garde gallery shows Chinese artists, including major Hong Kong art stars like Lu Shou Kun and newcomers like painter Chow Chun-fai. The gallery's director and curator, Henry Au-yeung, is a specialist in 20th-century Chinese art history. *2/F. 31C–D Wyndham St. ☎ 852/2121-2270. www.grottofineart.com. AE, MC, V. MTR: Central. Map p 56.*

★★★ Hanart T Z Gallery CENTRAL Since 1983, this gallery has been influential in helping promote local artists (primarily painters and photographers) and has earned a reputation for showing some of the best new work out of mainland China. Closed Sundays. *202 Henley Building, 5 Queen's Rd. ☎ 852/2526-9019. www.hanart.com. AE, MC, V. MTR: Central. Map p 56.*

★★ Plum Blossoms CENTRAL Plum Blossoms stands out for showing Chinese textiles and antique Tibetan furniture alongside contemporary paintings and sculpture. Closed Sundays. *Shop 6, 1 Hollywood Rd. ☎ 852/2521-2189. www.plumblossoms.com. AE, MC, V. MTR: Central. Bus: 26. Map p 56.*

★ Schoeni Art Gallery CENTRAL This is the best place to see cutting-edge Chinese art. Schoeni represents artists like the surrealist painter Zhang Lin Hai, whose paintings incorporate Chinese landmarks and history. A second branch is at 27 Hollywood Rd. *21–31 Old Bailey St. ☎ 852/2869-8802. www.schoeniartgallery.com. AE, MC, V. MTR: Central. Map p 56.*

Books

★ Dymocks CENTRAL This Australian chain has a thorough selection of new releases and books about Hong Kong and China. It's not as sleek as Page One or as cool as Swindon, but the 11 branches, scattered around the city, have good magazine selections and plenty of airplane reading. *Shop 2007–2011, IFC Mall, 8 Finance St. ☎ 852/2117-0360. www.dymocks.com. AE, DC, MC, V. MTR: Central. Map p 56.*

★★ Page One CAUSEWAY BAY Page One stocks both Hong Kong books for the coffee table and Western titles for the plane trip, as well as greeting cards, notebooks, and journals. There are two more branches at Festival Walk and Harbour City. *Shop 922, 9/F, Times*

For Chinese-made rugs that look great on the floor or as wall hangings, head to the Chinese Carpet Centre.

Square, 1 Matheson St. ☎ *852/2536-0111. www.pageonegroup.com. AE, DC, MC, V. MTR: Central. Map p 56.*

★★★ **Swindon Books** TSIM SHA TSUI You'll find everything from pocket Cantonese phrase books to magazines from the U.S. and UK at this sprawling bookstore. Founded in 1918, it has the feel of an old library, with large stacks and a huge selection of new and used books. *13–15 Lock Rd.* ☎ *852/2366-8001. www.swindonbooks.com. AE, DC, MC, V. MTR: Tsim Sha Tsui. Map p 55.*

Carpets

★★ **Chinese Carpet Centre** TSIM SHA TSUI In business 30 years, this large showroom has a huge selection of both hand- and machine-woven Chinese carpets and stands out from the rest for its reasonable prices. *Shop 5, G/F, Houston Centre, 63 Mody Rd.* ☎ *852/2730-7230. www.cccrugs.com.hk. AE, MC, V. MTR: Tsim Sha Tsui. Map p 55.*

Wah Tung China Company sells ceramics ranging from small statues to oversize floor vases.

Ceramics & Glass

★ **Wah Tung China Company** CENTRAL Wah Tung offers a wide selection of Chinese hand-painted ceramics and pieces from various dynastic periods. It also sells European makes and designs. *7/F, Lee Roy Commercial Building, 57–59 Hollywood Rd.* ☎ *852/2543-2823. www.wahtungchina.com. AE, DC, MC, V. MTR: Central. Bus: 26. Map p 56.*

Chinese Emporiums

★★ **Chinese Arts and Crafts** TSIM SHA TSUI The prices here are high, but so is the quality of the goods. You'll find Chinese silk dresses, jade jewelry, and Chinese herbs and tea. Items are clearly labeled, the staff is knowledgeable, and the store is large and easy to navigate. *Star House, 3 Salisbury Rd.* ☎ *852/2735-4061. www.crcretail.com. AE, DC, MC, V. MTR: Tsim Sha Tsui. Map p 55.*

★ **Yue Hwa Chinese Emporium** TSIM SHA TSUI This chain is as close to mainland Chinese shopping as you can get in Hong Kong—it's packed with uniquely Chinese goods such as snake wine, which comes with an actual snake in the bottle. The items here are of lesser quality than Chinese Arts and Crafts but they're cheaper. *301–309 Nathan Rd.* ☎ *852/3511-2222. www.yuehwa.com. AE, MC, V. MTR: Tsim Sha Tsui. Map p 55.*

If you're looking for uniquely Chinese items, Yue Hwa will have just what you're looking for.

Electronics & Photography Equipment

★ **Apliu Street** SHAM SHUI PO A street market packed with secondhand electronics, ranging from cellphones to video game consoles, worked back into shape by Hong Kong's electronics aficionados. Best to stick to small-ticket items, as some goods may not have a long lifespan and there are no warranties. *MTR: Sham Shui Po. Map p 55.*

★★ **Star Computer City** TSIM SHA TSUI Hong Kong is a techie lover's town, and this is a good place to dive into the offerings, with hundreds of shops selling laptops, PCs, computer screens, and a host of new gadgets. It can be a little tricky to find what you want, so give yourself time to explore. *3 Salisbury Rd.* ☎ *852/2736-2608. Many shops take AE, MC, V. MTR: Tsim Sha Tsui. Map p 55.*

★★★ **Wan Chai Computer Centre** WAN CHAI I'm writing this book on a laptop I bought at this crowded, messy, and very cheap electronics center. It can be claustrophobic, but it's worth it if you're looking for great deals. *130 Hennessy Rd. Many shops take AE, MC, V. MTR: Wan Chai. Map p 56.*

Apliu Street is a tech geek's dream come true.

The founder of Joyce Boutique helped introduce European fashions to Hong Kong.

Fashion

★★ **agnès b.** CENTRAL This outlet of the French fashion house is a plush minimall within the IFC, with individual shops for women's and men's gear, plus travel, sports, and bags. *Shop 3089–3097, 3/F, IFC Mall. ☎ 852/2805-0611. www.agnesb.com. AE, MC, V. MTR: Central. Map p 56.*

★★★ **Blanc de Chine** CENTRAL This stylish, Chinese-influenced clothing line features elegant silk dresses, jackets with Chinese characters, and jewelry. *Shop 201–203A, 12 Pedder St. ☎ 852/2524-7875. www.blancdechine.com. AE, MC, V. MTR: Central. Map p 56.*

★★ **D-Mop** CAUSEWAY BAY A popular local label specializing in urban street wear from Japan, the U.S., and Europe. Hong Kong's hip kids love it. *Shop A–C, 8 Kingston St., Fashion Walk. ☎ 852/2203-4130. AE, MC, V. MTR: Causeway Bay. Map p 56.*

★★ **Joyce Boutique** CENTRAL Joyce Boutique is a well-known chain selling designer brands like Yves Saint Laurent and Issey Miyake. Joyce Ma started the store in the 1970s to bring European fashion to Hong Kong women, but now she also showcases Asian and local designers. *G/F, New World Tower, 18 Queen's Rd. ☎ 852/2810-1120. AE, MC, V. MTR: Central. Map p 56.*

★★★ **Shanghai Tang** CENTRAL When founder David Tang launched his clothing line in 1994, his goal was to make traditional Chinese clothing—collarless shirts, loose-fitting pants—stylish and modern. He now has stores in New York, Paris, and London selling his chic designs for men and women. Buy off the rack or get custom tailoring. *12 Pedder St. ☎ 852/2525-7333. www.shanghaitang.com. AE, DC, MC, V. MTR: Central. Map p 56.*

★ **Vivienne Tam** CENTRAL One of China's best-known designers, Vivienne Tam now sells her elegant fashions worldwide, but she got her start here in Hong Kong. This cool boutique, in Central's superexclusive Landmark mall, is one of five in

Designer David Tang made traditional Chinese styles hip, and fashionistas flock to Shanghai Tang for his gear.

Hong Kong. *Shop 309, The Landmark, Des Voeux Rd.* ☎ *852/2868-9268. www.viviennetam.com. AE, DC, MC, V. MTR: Central. Map p 56.*

Homeware

★★ **Chenmiji** ADMIRALTY Fans of Wong Kar-wai's nostalgic films will love this retro furniture store. It stocks a host of one-offs and attic-finds with everything from disco-era turntables to flip clocks to rotary dial telephones, all arranged in a wonderfully bohemian jumble. *4 Sun St.* ☎ *852/2549-8800. www.chenmiji.com. Cash only. MTR: Admiralty. Map p 56.*

★★★ **G.O.D.** CAUSEWAY BAY The initials stand for "Goods of Desire," and even when I stop in with the intention of just window-shopping, I usually can't resist. There's a lot to choose from: clothes, CDs, funky furniture, small gifts, and cards. *Leighton Centre, Sharp St. E.* ☎ *852/2524-5555. www.god.com.hk. AE, MC, V. MTR: Causeway Bay. Map p 56.*

★★ **Homeless** CENTRAL The frontage alone—a Gothic tangle of flexi-exhaust pipes—is indicative of the imagination behind Homeless's range of trendy lifestyle products. Look out for the sci-fi surrealist motifs of local designer Carrie Chau, founder of the Wun Ying label. *29 Gough St.* ☎ *852/2581-1880. www.homeless.hk. AE, MC, V. MTR: Central, then Mid-Levels escalator. Map p 56.*

Jewelry

★★★ **Chocolate Rain** SOHO Founded by two young Hong Kong fine-arts graduates, Chocolate Rain specializes in handmade patchwork bags, dolls, and jewelry. With a distinct hybrid Hong Kong–Japan chic, they make great souvenirs for fashionably minded friends. *Shop A, G/F,*

Stock up on mahjong sets while you hunt for fashion finds at G.O.D.

67 Peel St. ☎ *852/2975-8318. www.chocolaterain.com. MC, V. MTR: Central. Map p 56.*

★ **King Fook Jewelry** CENTRAL King Fook has been selling consumer-brand women's and men's jewelry, watches, and pens by makers like Christine Dior, Tag Heuer, and Gucci since 1949. There's a lot to choose from here, and the staff is especially friendly. *Shop 21, G/F, Central Building, 1–3 Pedder St.* ☎ *852/2822-8524. www.kingfook.com. AE, MC, V. MTR: Central. Map p 56.*

★★ **The Opal Mine** TSIM SHA TSUI Billed as Hong Kong's "only opal cave shop," the duly cavernous Opal Mine specializes in both refined opal jewelry and raw mineraloids. *Shop G–H, Burlington House, 92 Nathan Rd.* ☎ *852/2721-9933. www.opalnet.com. AE, MC, V. MTR: Tsim Sha Tsui. Map p 55.*

★ **Oriental Arts** TSIM SHA TSUI There's an excellent selection of jade and other jewelry at this elegant shop in the Peninsula Hotel. It's also the perfect stop for those who like to make their own jewelry, as there are a number of loose items (like beads and stones) to choose from. *The Peninsula Hotel, Salisbury Rd.* ☎ *852/2369-0820. AE, DC, MC, V. MTR: Tsim Sha Tsui. Map p 55.*

Oriental Arts shows off some of its finest wares.

Malls & Department Stores

★★★ **Festival Walk** KOWLOON TONG One of Hong Kong's newest and most attractive malls, Festival Walk is located immediately beside the Kowloon Tong metro interchange. It has the largest bookshop and cinema in town and a huge ice rink to boot. *80–88 Tat Chee Ave.* ☎ *852/2844-2222. www.festivalwalk.com.hk. Most shops take AE, DC, MC, V. MTR: Kowloon Tong. Map p 55.*

★ **Harbour City** TSIM SHA TSUI Before mainland China started opening megamalls, this one was billed as the biggest in Asia. With more than 700 stores, it's a huge draw for both mainland and Western visitors, making it one of Hong Kong's best people-watching spots. *3–27 Canton Rd.* ☎ *852/2118-8601. www.harbourcity.com.hk. Most shops take AE, DC, MC, V. MTR: Tsim Sha Tsui. Map p 55.*

★★ **IFC Mall** CENTRAL This sleek mall in the center of the city has high-end shops, a movie theater, restaurants, and bars. It also connects to the Mid-Levels escalator so it's within easy reach of Lan Kwai Fong and Soho. *8 Finance St.* ☎ *852/2295-3308. www.ifc.com.hk. Most shops take AE, DC, MC, V. MTR: Central. Map p 56.*

★★ **Langham Place** MONG KOK With around 300 stores spread over 15 stories, this building is part of an attempt to rejuvenate historically down-at-the heels Mong Kok. There is a branch of posh Japanese department store Seibu, as well as a huge Muji store. *8 Argyle St.* ☎ *852/3520-2800. www.langhamplace.com.hk. Most shops take AE, DC, MC, V. MTR: Mong Kok. Map p 55.*

★★★ **Pacific Place** ADMIRALTY The best thing about this mall is its sweeping, curved interior. The high-end goods (think Prada, Dior, Louis Vuitton) are an added bonus. With a plethora of shops, grocery stores, and restaurants, it's easy to spend an afternoon here. *88 Queensway.* ☎ *852/2844-8988. www.pacific-place.com.hk. Most shops take AE, DC, MC, V. MTR: Admiralty. Map p 56.*

★ **Sogo** CAUSEWAY BAY This tight, often-crowded Japanese department store is popular with locals. It carries clothing, toys, household goods, and electronics at

The cool, calm Pacific Place mall offers a refreshing break from market shopping.

The quality may not always be top-notch, but the jewelry on sale at the Jade Market is still very pretty.

competitive prices. *555 Hennessy Rd. ☎ 852/3556-1212. www.sogo.com.hk. AE, DC, MC, V. MTR: Causeway Bay. Map p 56.*

★★ **Times Square** CAUSEWAY BAY Located at the center of bustling Times Square, this mall is a good place if you're looking for reasonably priced Western-style duds. Stores include Timberland, Nike, and the UK's Marks & Spencer. *1 Matheson St. ☎ 852/2118-8900. www.timessquare.com.hk. Most shops take AE, DC, MC, V. MTR: Causeway Bay. Map p 56.*

Markets

★ **Cat Street** SHEUNG WAN I love browsing this quaint street for cheap Communist kitsch. Mao's image adorns everything from buttons to watches and clocks, and there are heaps of socialist-realist posters and prints. You can also pick up cool souvenirs like Chinese compasses and calligraphy brushes. *Upper Lascar Row. No credit cards. MTR: Sheung Wan. Map p 56.*

★★ **Jade Market** YAU MA TEI You can find small jade items at low prices in this quirky caged compound which houses more than 400 stalls. You'll need to bargain for the best deals but big-ticket items at this market sometimes turn out to be rip-offs. *Kansu and Battery sts. Some sellers take AE, MC, V. MTR: Yau Ma Tei. Map p 55.*

★★ **Ladies' Market** MONG KOK A bustling market where you can buy your fill of rip-off designer handbags, sunglasses, and watches. It can be very crowded, so plan to spend at least an hour. *Tung Choi St. btw. Argyle and Dundas sts. No credit cards. MTR: Mong Kok. Map p 55.*

★★ **The Lanes** CENTRAL Collectively known as "The Lanes," Li Yuen Street West and Li Yuen Street East are crowded parallel alleys full of stalls selling knickknacks and cheap clothing. You might well have to elbow your way to the front in order to properly rummage. If you're not planning a trip to mainland China, this is about the next best thing. *Li Yuen St. W. and Li Yuen St. E. Cash only. MTR: Central. Map p 56.*

★ **Stanley Market** STANLEY VILLAGE Although this was once a great place for bargains, it's a bit of a tourist trap now. It's still worth a visit if you're in the market for silk clothing. *Main St. Some shops take AE, MC, V. Bus: 6, 6A, 6X, or 260 from Exchange Square in Central; 973 from Mody Rd. in Tsim Sha Tsui E. Map p 56.*

★★★ **Temple Street Night Market** YAU MA TEI With hundreds of vendors selling everything from cheap CDs to handbags, this is one of Hong Kong's liveliest markets. It's also famous for its popular

Shop for accessories at the Ladies' Market.

dai pai dong food stalls. Come anytime after 5pm. ***Temple St. MTR: Jordan. Map p 55.***

Medicine

★★★ **Eu Yan Sang** CENTRAL This chain is a foreigner-friendly place to buy Chinese medicine (see "Chinese Medicine," p 51). Some, but not all, staff speak English. ***152–156 Queen's Rd. ☎ 852/2544-3870. www.euyansang.com. AE, MC, V. MTR: Central. Map p 56.***

Posters

★★ **Picture This** CENTRAL Specializing in antique maps, prints, and vintage travel posters from the colonial era (including many from Hong Kong), this easy-to-browse shop offers a taste of the Age of Empire. ***Shop 212, 2/F, Prince's Building, 10 Chater Rd. ☎ 852/2525-2803. www.picturethiscollection.com. AE, MC, V. MTR: Central, exit K. Map p 56.***

Sporting Goods

★ **Giga Sports** TSIM SHA TSUI Giga is one of the few places in Hong Kong where you can find a large selection of gear for outdoor sports activities such as hiking, running, or swimming. ***Shop 244–247, 2/F, Ocean Terminal, Harbour City, 3–27 Canton Rd. ☎ 852/2115-9930. AE, MC, V. MTR: Tsim Sha Tsui. Map p 55.***

Tailors

★★ **A-Man Hing Cheong** CENTRAL This Hong Kong tailor makes shirts and suits with a European cut, making it popular among expatriates from the UK. ***Mandarin Oriental Hotel, 5 Connaught Rd. ☎ 852/2522-3336. AE, DC, MC, V. MTR: Central. Map p 56.***

★★★ **Sam's Tailor** TSIM SHA TSUI The most famous tailor in Hong Kong, Sam's has made clothing for everyone from former British Prime Minister Tony Blair to tennis star Serena Williams. You can find cheaper tailors in Hong Kong but you won't get that Sam's quality. ***Shop K, Burlington Arcade, 92–94 Nathan Rd. ☎ 852/2367-9423. www.samstailor.com. AE, MC, V. MTR: Tsim Sha Tsui. Map p 55.***

Tea & Tea Sets

★★ **Fook Ming Tong** CENTRAL This shop blends its own tea and lets you take a taste to help you decide what to buy. Teapots, teacups, and tea caddies are all available. ***1 Duddell St. ☎ 852/2521-8626. AE, MC, V. MTR: Central. Map p 56.***

★★★ **Lock Cha Tea Shop** SHEUNG WAN With its traditional Chinese furniture and comprehensive stock of over 100 types of tea, this is the place to buy your tea in Hong Kong. You can pick up flavors like jasmine green and peony white, and the staff will even show you the proper way to pour. ***UG/F, 290A, Queen's Rd. ☎ 852/2805-1360. www.lockcha.com. AE, MC, V. MTR: Sheung Wan. Map p 56.***

Toys

★★ kids **Toy Museum** CENTRAL If your child needs a new toy for the plane home, this store has loads of options, including dolls, action figures, and Pokémon. ***Shop 320, Prince's Building, 10 Chater Rd. ☎ 852/2869-9138. AE, MC, V. MTR: Central. Map p 56.*** ●

Stop in to Fook Ming Tong to try their specially blended teas.

5 The Best of the **Outdoors**

Hong Kong **Hiking**

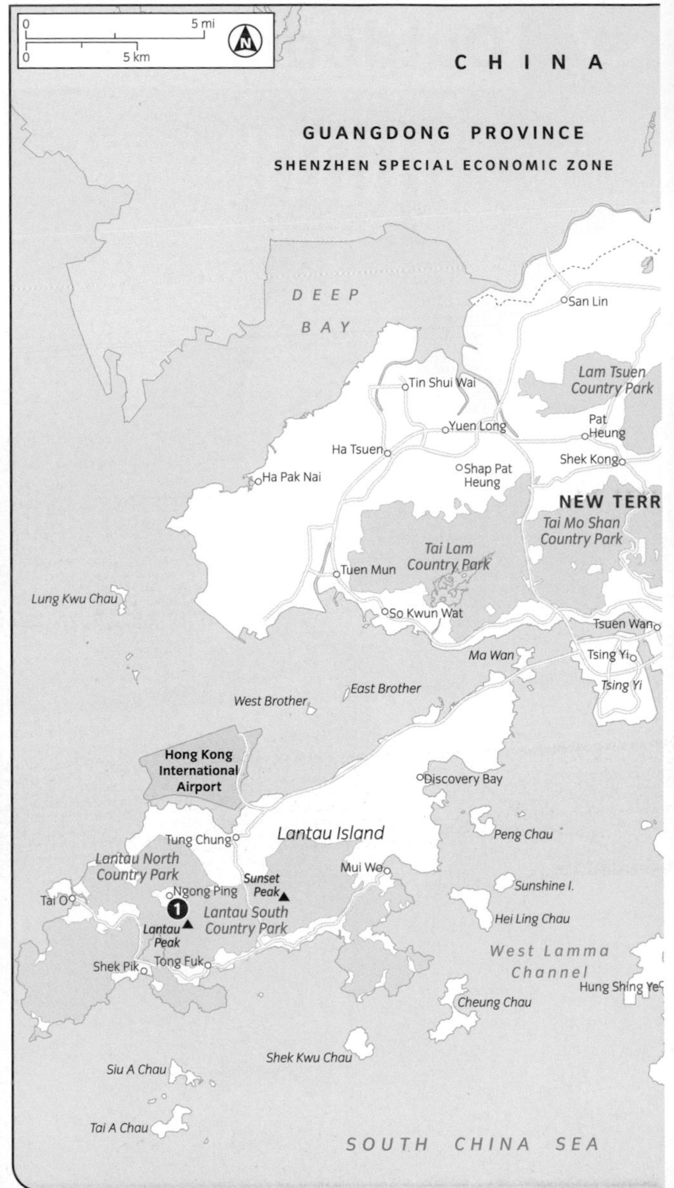

Previous page: Huge statues of Chinese gods stand at an outdoor temple along the southern edge of Repulse Bay beach.

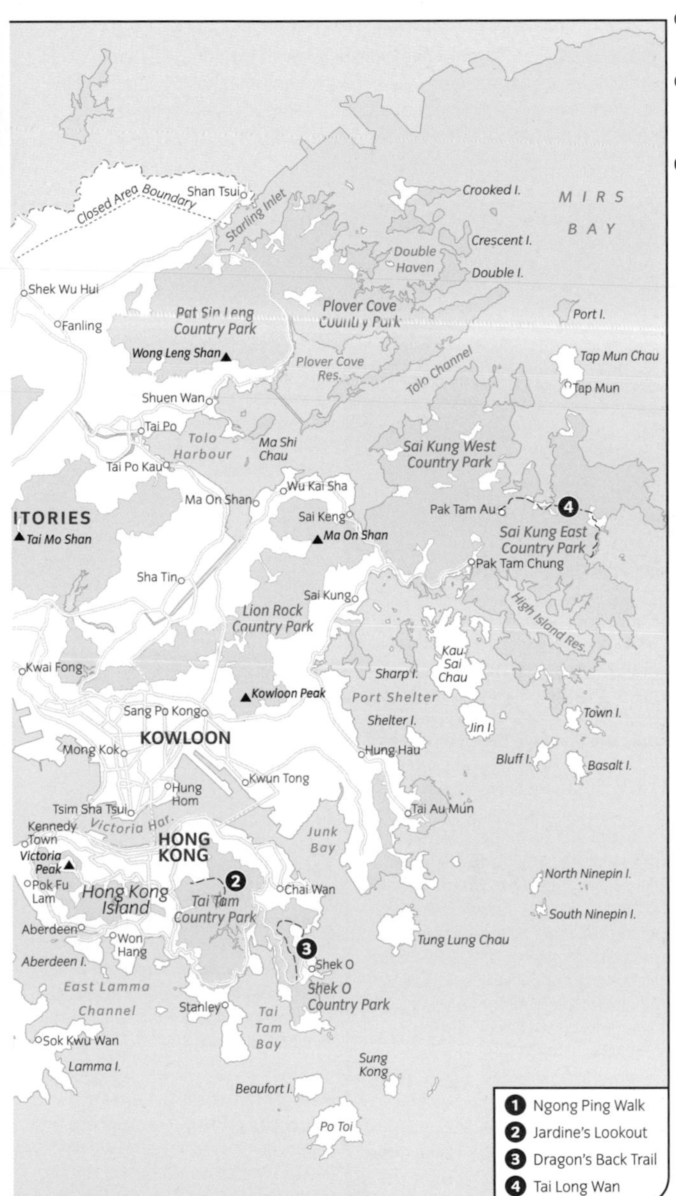
Closed Area Boundary
Shan Tsui
Starling Inlet
Crooked I.
MIRS BAY
Crescent I.
Double Haven
Double I.
Shek Wu Hui
Fanling
Pat Sin Leng Country Park
Plover Cove Country Park
Port I.
Wong Leng Shan
Plover Cove Res.
Tolo Channel
Tap Mun Chau
Tap Mun
Shuen Wan
Tai Po
Tolo Harbour
Ma Shi Chau
Sai Kung West Country Park
Tai Po Kau
Wu Kai Sha
Ma On Shan
Pak Tam Au
Sai Keng
ITORIES
Tai Mo Shan
Ma On Shan
Sai Kung East Country Park
Pak Tam Chung
Sha Tin
Sai Kung
High Island Res.
Lion Rock Country Park
Kwai Fong
Sharp I.
Kau Sai Chau
Kowloon Peak
Port Shelter
Sang Po Kong
Shelter I.
Jin I.
Town I.
KOWLOON
Mong Kok
Hung Hau
Bluff I.
Basalt I.
Kwun Tong
Hung Hom
Tsim Sha Tsui
Tai Au Mun
Kennedy Town
Victoria Har.
HONG KONG
Junk Bay
Victoria Peak
North Ninepin I.
Pok Fu Lam
Hong Kong Island
Tai Tam Country Park
Chai Wan
South Ninepin I.
Aberdeen
Won Hang
Tung Lung Chau
Aberdeen I.
Shek O
East Lamma Channel
Shek O Country Park
Stanley
Tai Tam Bay
Sok Kwu Wan
Lamma I.
Sung Kong
Beaufort I.
Po Toi
1 Ngong Ping Walk
2 Jardine's Lookout
3 Dragon's Back Trail
4 Tai Long Wan

Hong Kong's natural beauty often comes as a surprise to visitors who know only its famous skyline. More than three-quarters of Hong Kong remains totally undeveloped, and well-crafted trails crisscross the wilderness. Walking can be as easy or as difficult as you want, from weeklong mountain hikes to spectacular strolls that can be squeezed into an afternoon. What follows is a selection of the best; times reflect the duration of the walk itself. Don't forget to bring water and sunblock.

The stunning views from Dragon's Back include this look down at Shek O beach.

Hong Kong Island

★★★ Dragon's Back. Once voted the best walk in Asia by *Time* magazine, the Dragon's Back is a Hong Kong classic and I highly recommend it if you're only in town for a few days. After climbing steeply from the bus stop, the 4.5km-long (2¾-mile) trail begins with a long, flat section through a shady forest dotted with small streams. You'll eventually emerge to walk on the undulating spine of D'Aguilar Peninsula, Hong Kong Island's most easterly headland, which has spectacular views of Big Wave Bay, the islands, and Stanley Peninsula. The walk can be done in 90 minutes, but consider stopping for lunch in nearby Shek O (p 74). ⏱ *90 min. MTR: Shau Kei Wan, then bus 9. Get off at the Cape Collison bus stop.*

Before heading out to Dragon's Back, stop in at ★★ **Cafe Too** in the Island Shangri-La Hotel. There's a lot to choose from at this casual food hall: Options are laid out buffet style at seven separate stations and include sushi, Peking duck, dim sum, and pizza. *Island Shangri-La Hong Kong, Pacific Place.* ☎ *852/ 2820-8571. $$.*

★★ Jardine's Lookout. Named after the highest point of the walk—a spot once used by Jardine's to descry the firm's clippers coming from London or India—this midlength hike is easily accessible from Central and is unique in its blend of glimpses of the high-rise-studded corridor on the north of Hong Kong Island and wild, verdant southern fringes. The first 90 minutes involve two hard climbs. After passing Mount Butler it's mainly downhill before you skirt the Tai Tam Tuk Reservoir. From Tai Tam Road there are buses to Shau Kei Wan MTR or south to Stanley. ⏱ *3–4 hr. Bus: 6 or 66 from Exchange Square. Get off at Wong Nai Chung Gap, next to a petrol station on your left. Climb stairs marked* TAI TAM RESERVOIR RD.*, turn left and walk uphill for 10 min. before joining the track.*

New Territories & Lantau

★★ Ngong Ping. I recommend enhancing your visit to the Big Buddha (p 17) with a walk to two of the surrounding peaks. From the Buddha,

Trek Smart

The Hong Kong Tourism Board publishes ***Discover Hong Kong Nature: A DIY Guide*** which can be picked up for free in any of its offices (p 157). Hong Kong is incredibly hiker-friendly, but if you're nervous about heading out alone, there are organizations to help. Hong Kong Trampers (☎ 852/8209-0517; www.hktrampers.com) is an informal group that organizes Sunday hikes around the island. Trips depend on volunteer availability so inquire ahead. Outdoor Adventure Tours (☎ 852/9300-5197; www.kayak-and-hike.com) specializes in hikes and kayak trips around the Sai Kung Peninsula and is led by an expat local. Prices vary depending on the trip.

follow signs to the Lantau Tea Garden from where you can join section three of the 70km-long (43-mile) Lantau Trail. It's steep, so expect the climb up to the 934m (3,064-ft.) Lantau Peak to take up to an hour. The Wisdom Path is close to the start of the trail, while the Ngong Ping Tree Walk will lead all the way to 751m (2,464-ft.) Nei Lak Shan peak. The path curves around the mountainside and has great views back down to the Po Lin Monastery and Big Buddha, before a junction points the way back to the cable car. 🕘 ***2–3 hr. MTR: Tung Chung, then Ngong Ping Skyrail.***

★★★ **Tai Long Wan (Big Wave Bay).** More than 100km (62 miles) long, the MacLehose Trail connects the coasts of the New Territories and can take experienced hikers up to a week to complete. This walk, along one of the least hilly of the 10 sections, takes you along the gorgeous coastline of Sai Kung, past two hamlets, Tao Long and Ham Tin, to Tai Long Wan with its cluster of beaches. You can walk south all the way to Sai Wan Beach (see Sai Wan, p 74). 🕘 ***5–6 hr. MTR: Diamond Hill, exit C2, then bus 96R to Pak Tam Au. From Pak Tam Au, bus 94 takes you to Sai Kung Village.***

Mist enshrouds part of the Lantau Trail, which winds its way along Lantau Island's rolling green hills.

Hong Kong **Beaches & Parks**

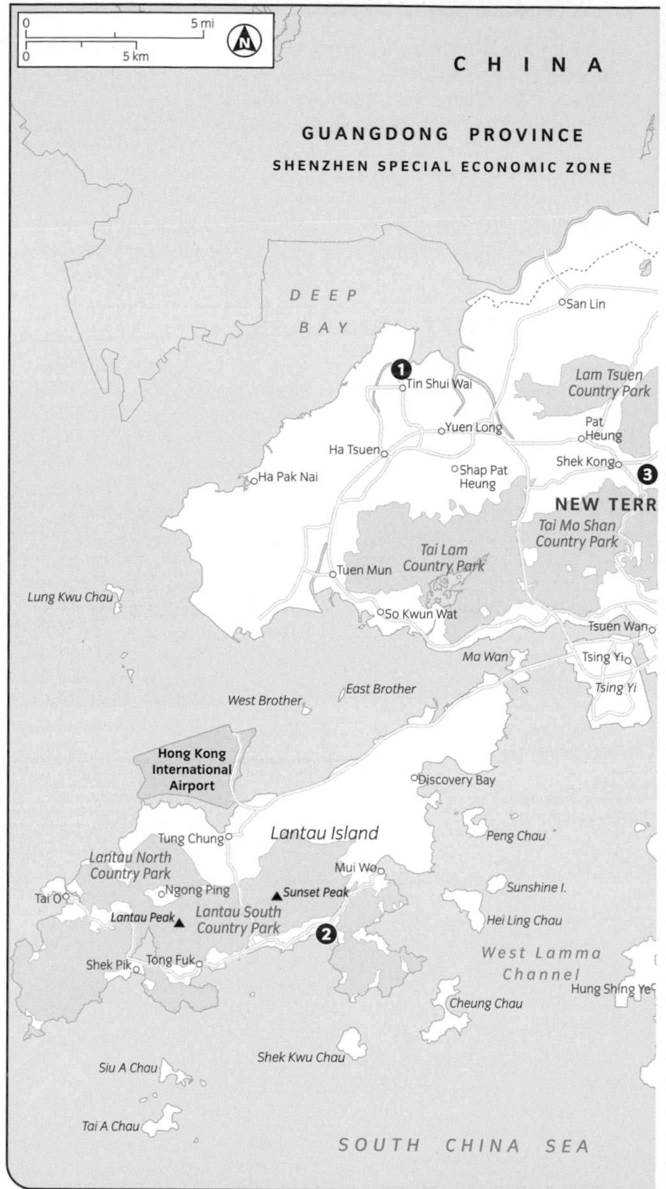

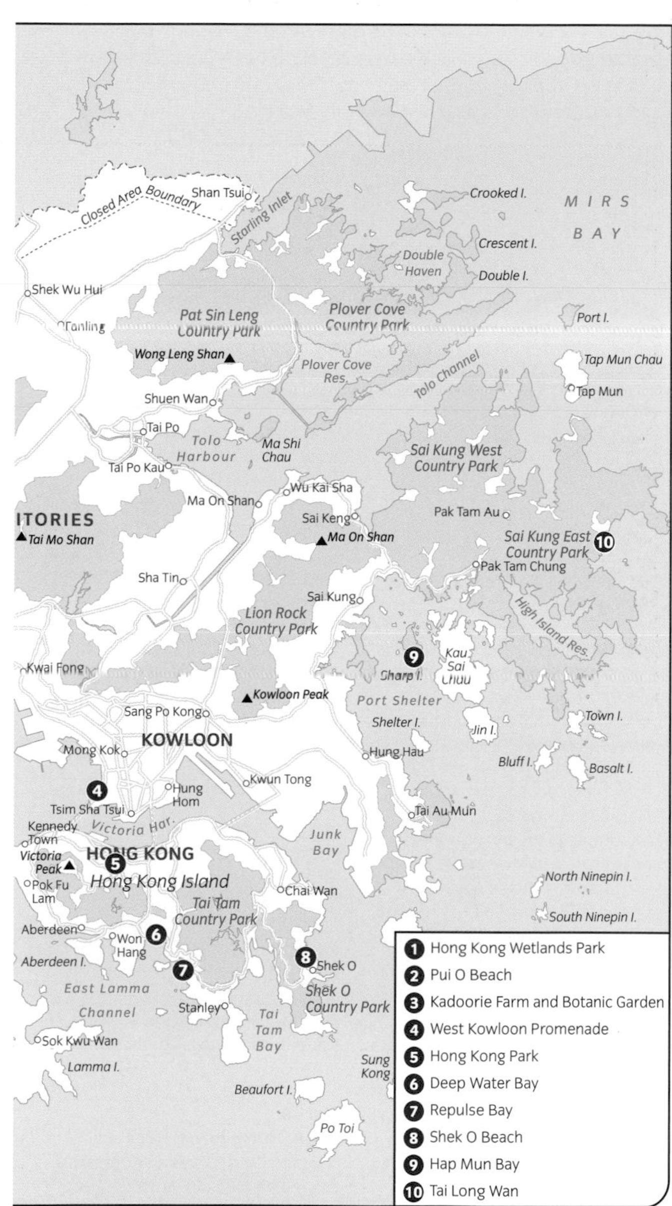
Closed Area Boundary
Shan Tsui
Starling Inlet
Crooked I.
MIRS BAY
Crescent I.
Double Haven
Double I.
Shek Wu Hui
Pat Sin Leng Country Park
Plover Cove Country Park
Port I.
Tanling
Wong Leng Shan
Plover Cove Res.
Tolo Channel
Tap Mun Chau
Tap Mun
Shuen Wan
Tai Po
Tolo Harbour
Ma Shi Chau
Sai Kung West Country Park
Tai Po Kau
Wu Kai Sha
Ma On Shan
Pak Tam Au
ITORIES
Sai Keng
Tai Mo Shan
Ma On Shan
Sai Kung East Country Park
Pak Tam Chung
Sha Tin
Sai Kung
High Island Res.
Lion Rock Country Park
Kau Sai Chau
Kwai Fong
Sharp I.
Kowloon Peak
Port Shelter
Sang Po Kong
Shelter I.
Town I.
KOWLOON
Jin I.
Mong Kok
Hung Hau
Bluff I.
Basalt I.
Kwun Tong
Hung Hom
Tsim Sha Tsui
Tai Au Mun
Kennedy Town
Victoria Har.
Junk Bay
Victoria Peak
HONG KONG
Hong Kong Island
North Ninepin I.
Pok Fu Lam
Chai Wan
Tai Tam Country Park
South Ninepin I.
Aberdeen
Won Hang
Aberdeen I.
Shek O
East Lamma Channel
Shek O Country Park
Stanley
Tai Tam Bay
Sok Kwu Wan
Lamma I.
Sung Kong
Beaufort I.
Po Toi
1 Hong Kong Wetlands Park
2 Pui O Beach
3 Kadoorie Farm and Botanic Garden
4 West Kowloon Promenade
5 Hong Kong Park
6 Deep Water Bay
7 Repulse Bay
8 Shek O Beach
9 Hap Mun Bay
10 Tai Long Wan

There are about 40 free public beaches in and around Hong Kong. They tend to be busy on the island itself but there are acres of empty strands to be discovered elsewhere, most with changing rooms and snack stands. If you're not a fan of tanning under the tropical sun, you may opt to visit one of Hong Kong's leafy parks or eco-resorts as a respite from the city.

High-rise apartments line the hills around Repulse Bay.

Beaches

★ Repulse Bay and Deep Water Bay. A short drive from Central, these adjacent bays may be open to public visitors but to live here you need more than a fistful of (Hong Kong) dollars. Artificially enlarged Repulse Bay is lined with restaurants, high-end apartment complexes, and the historic Repulse Bay Hotel. The beach's name is quite literal, as it refers to the way the British "repulsed" pirates from the shore in the mid-1800s. Deep Water Bay, a pleasant 30-minute walk away around a headland, has a smaller, quieter beach. *Beach Rd. Bus: 6, 6A, 6X, or 260.*

★★★ Sai Wan. Arguably the prettiest of the secluded beaches along Tai Long Wan (Big Wave Bay), Sai Wan has a wide swathe of sand backed by rolling green hills and rocky ridges, with a small cafe at the far end of the beach. If you're in the mood, you can join the MacLehose Trail, stretching north, which leads on to several more beaches, before meandering off into the hills (see Tai Long Wan walk, p 71). *MTR: Choi Hung, then any minibus with* SAI KUNG *written on the front. From Sai Kung, take a 20-min. taxi ride to "Tai Long Sai Wan." Follow the path to the beach.*

★★ Shek O. Shek O is on Hong Kong Island but feels a world away from the urban center. Shek O, which means "rocky cove," has a craggy headland on which you can walk. There's a shaded promenade next to the beach and plenty of simple village restaurants. A mile or so up the road is (another) Big Wave Bay, a quieter spot popular with surfers. If you're heading out to Shek O, I heartily recommend doing the Dragon's Back walk (p 70). *MTR: Shau Kei Wan, then bus 9.*

If you make it out to Shek O, stop in at the **Paradiso Beach Club.** It has artificial seashells for tables, floors comprised totally of sand, and tropical aquariums, but there's a touch of class about the place. The cocktails go down particularly well on the open beachfront deck, and the pizzas are excellent. *G/F, Government Building, Shek O beach. ☎ 852/2809-2080. $$.*

Parks

★★★ Hong Kong Park. Undulating paths and stairways ripple across this green oasis, located just behind some of Central's most famous

Skim boarding is a popular pastime on Hong Kong's beaches.

skyscrapers. There are fountains, lily ponds, kids' playgrounds, observation towers, and a restaurant, but the highlight is the spectacular walk-through aviary, home to more than 150 species of birds. Hong Kong's oldest building, the Flagstaff House Museum of Tea Ware (p 31) is also on-site. *MTR: Admiralty, exit C1. Bus: 12A.*

★ **Hong Kong Wetlands Park.** Located beside the huge Tin Shui Wai new town, this excellent nature park acts as a buffer between urban Hong Kong and the extensive Mao Po Marshes. The reserve's most famous resident is Pui Pui, a celebrity crocodile who caused a scare when he was spotted roaming around the city in 2003. There's also a wide variety of bird, insect, and butterfly species. Four boardwalks trace a path through the mangroves. *Wetland Park Road, Tin Shui Wai. ☎ 852/2708-8885. www.wetlandpark.com. Adults $HK30, kids $HK15. Mon, Wed–Fri 10am–5pm.*

★ kids **Hong Kong Zoological & Botanical Gardens.** Founded in 1864 in the foothills of the Peak, this garden maintains much of its Victorian charm despite the skyscrapers in the distance. There's a wrought-iron greenhouse, a terrace garden, and a playground with slides and swings. The animals are the real stars: 400 bird species, 70 mammals, and 50 reptiles, including the rare Yangtze alligator. *Albany Rd. ☎ 852/2530-0154. Daily 6am–7pm. Bus: 3B, 12, or 13.*

★★ **Kadoorie Farm and Botanic Garden.** Built into the side of the Lam Tsuen Valley, the Kadoorie Farm showcases the best of Hong Kong's natural flora and fauna in a spectacular setting. There are organic vegetable terraces, orchid gardens, butterfly sanctuaries, flamingos, birds of prey, even pigpens. The garden was built to both assist and honor local farmers, and a museum pays testament to

Sun lovers enjoy clear skies and warm waters at Shek O Beach.

Best of the Rest

If you're planning on doing some walking or dining on the Sai Kung Peninsula, consider spending the afternoon at **Hap Mun Bay.** The beach is beautiful and the sampan ride from Sai Kung is part of the fun. With its faraway feel, **Pui O,** on Lantau, is a popular destination for campers and has quite a wild, dark-sand beach. There is a restaurant right on the beach that serves drinks and snacks. You'll need to take a minibus from Mui Wo. **Mui Wo** itself has a pleasant beach that's walkable from the ferry port and the town center. Downtown Kowloon has two parks that are not quite destinations in their own right, but well worth visiting if you're nearby. Lush **Kowloon Park** is a few steps off manic Nathan Road (p 12). The **Kowloon Walled City Park,** built on the site of a notoriously grim housing project, was designed to re-create the style of a classical Southern Chinese garden, with winding paths past bonsai, bamboo, ponds, and streams. **Hong Kong National Geopark** is a 50-sq.-km (19-sq.-mile) area across parts of the northeastern New Territories which serves to conserve Hong Kong's unique landforms and landscapes. For more, see www.discoverhongkong.com.

The Flagstaff House Museum of Tea Ware at Hong Kong Park.

their techniques and skills. ***Adults $HK10, free for kids & seniors. Daily 9.30am–5pm. MTR: Tai Wo, then bus 64K and get off at Kadoorie Farm.***

★★ West Kowloon Promenade. This large swathe of reclaimed land will likely remain in limbo until at least 2015, while the government resolves a long-running dispute over how it should be used. This offers tourists a window to enjoy Hong Kong Island's stunning high-rise panorama in a quiet, natural setting. There's currently a boardwalk but not much else. It's fantastic if you're looking for peace and quiet. ***MTR: Kowloon, then cross bridge over the cross-harbor toll booths.*** ●

6 The Best Dining

Dining Best Bets

Best **Roast Goose**
★ Yung Kee Restaurant $$ *32–40 Wellington St. (p 90)*

Best **Fusion**
★★★ Spoon $$$ *InterContinental Hong Kong, 18 Salisbury Rd. (p 88)*

Best **Japanese**
★★ Wasabisabi $$$ *1 Matheson St. (p 89)*

Best **Frog**
★ Fook Lam Moon $$ *35–45 Johnston Rd. (p 84)*

Best **Italian**
★★★ Isola $$$ *3/F, IFC Mall (p 85)*

Best **Village Restaurant**
★★ Anthony's Catch $$$ *Po Tung Rd. (p 83)*

Best **Floating Restaurant**
★ Jumbo Kingdom $$$ *Aberdeen Harbour (p 85)*

Best **View of Hong Kong Island**
★★★ Hutong $$$ *1 Peking Rd. (p 85)*

Best **Elegant Dim Sum Dining**
★★★ Lung King Heen $$$ *8 Finance St. (p 86)*

Best **Vegetarian Chinese**
★★★ Kung Tak Lam $$ *Shop 1001, World Trade Centre, 280 Gloucester Rd. (p 85)*

Best **Local Diner**
★★★ Loon Wai $ *54–58 Jardine's Bazaar (p 86)*

Best **Mexican**
★ Agave $$ *93–107 Lockhart Rd. (p 83)*

Best **Dumplings**
★★ Din Tai Fung $ *Shop 130, 3/F, Silvercord Centre,30 Canton Rd. (p 84)*

Best **French**
★★ Chez Patrick $$$ *G/F, 26 Peel St. (p 83)*

Best **Western-Food Fix**
★ California Pizza Kitchen $ *1 Matheson St. (p 83)*

Best **Beach Dining**
★ The Stoep $$ *32 Lower Cheung Sha Village (p 89)*

Previous page: Dim sum from trolleys at Maxim's Palace. Below: Dining alfresco at Isola.

Kowloon Dining

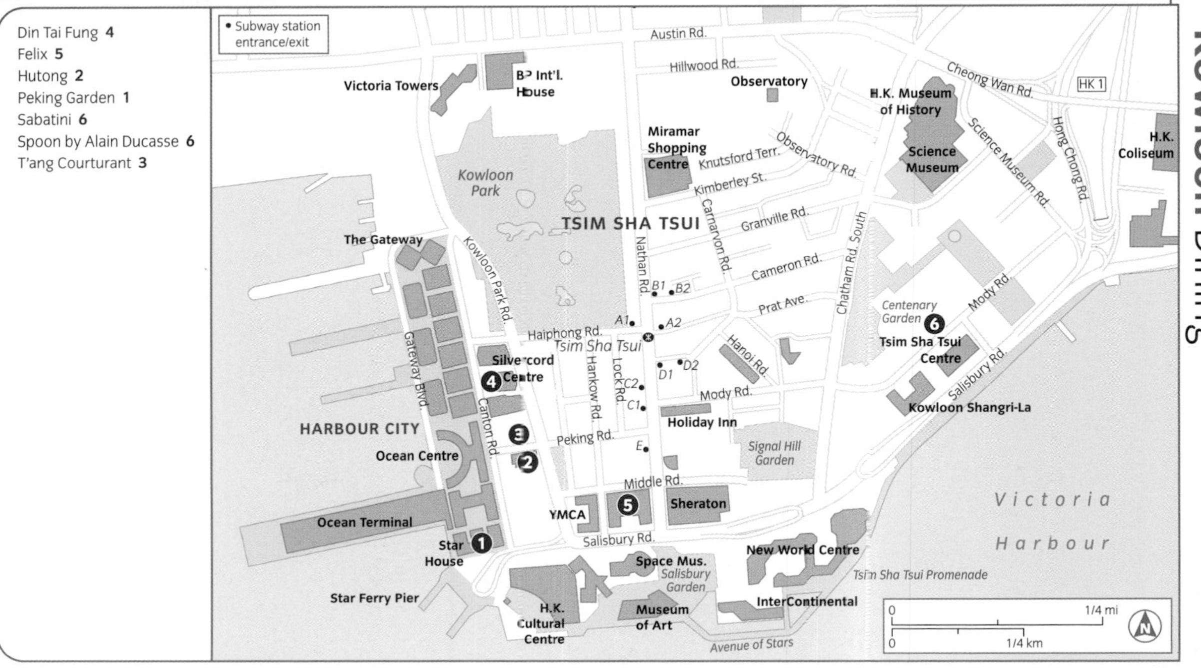

Central Dining

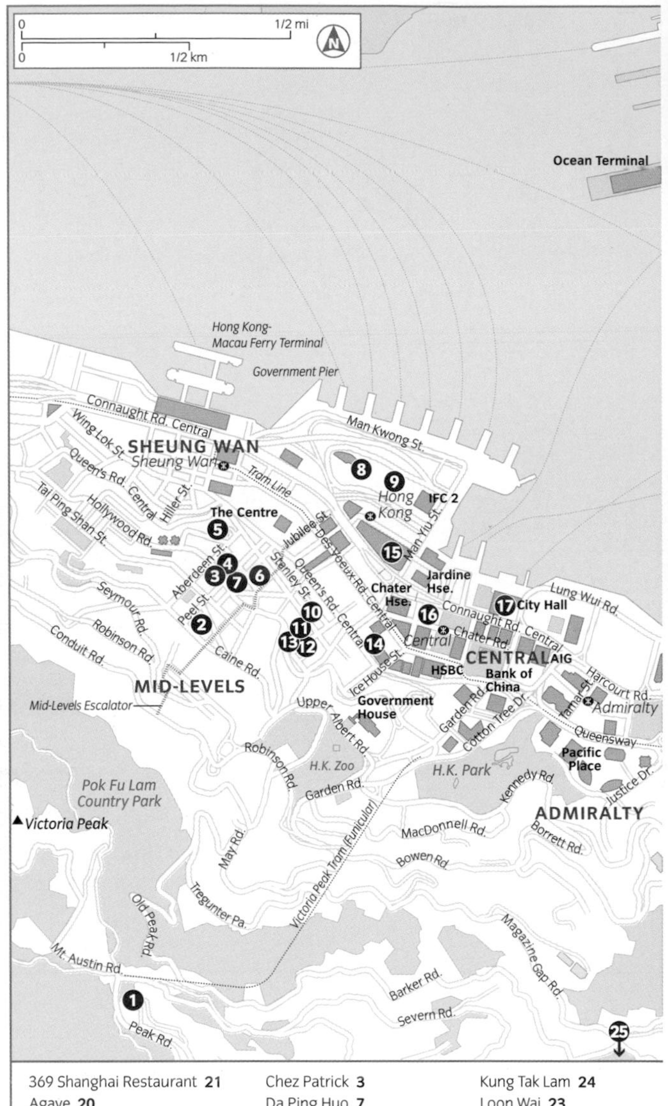

369 Shanghai Restaurant **21**
Agave **20**
Amber **14**
Café Deco **1**
California Pizza Kitchen **22**
Chez Patrick **3**
Da Ping Huo **7**
Fook Lam Moon **19**
Isola Bar and Grill **9**
Jumbo Kingdom **25**
Kung Tak Lam **24**
Loon Wai **23**
Luk Yu Teahouse **10**
Lung King Heen **8**
Mandarin Grill **16**

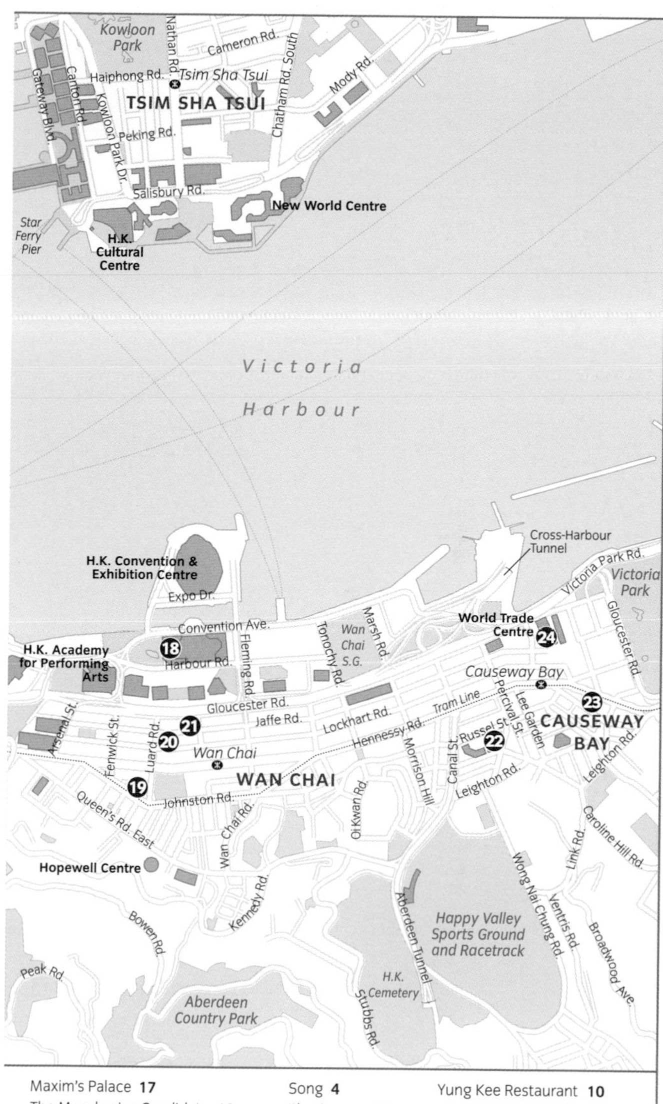

Maxim's Palace **17**
The Manchurian Candidate **12**
One Harbour Road **18**
Shanghai Lane **5**
Shui Huju **2**
Song **4**
The Square **15**
Wasabisabi **22**
Yellow Door Kitchen **6**
Yun Fu **13**
Yung Kee Restaurant **10**

Sai Kung/Lamma/Lantau Dining

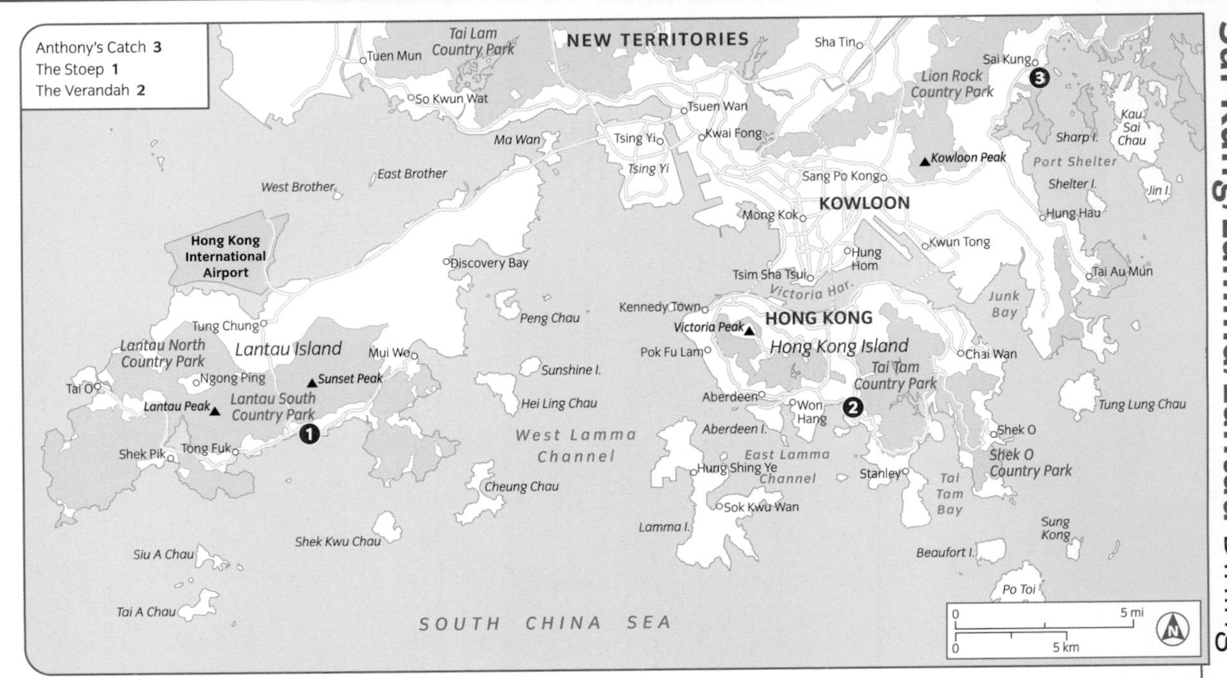

Restaurants A to Z

★ **Agave** WAN CHAI *MEXICAN* Decent Mexican is hard to find in Asia, so Agave's sizzling fajitas and chunky guacamole are a treat. The clientele is lively, thanks in part to the 150 tequilas on offer, and the street-side views are perfect for people-watching. A second branch is in Lan Kwai Fong. *93–107 Lockhart Rd. ☎ 852/2866-3228. Entrees $HK120–$HK188. AE, MC, V. Lunch & dinner daily. MTR: Wanchai, exit A1. Map p 80.*

★★★ **Amber** CENTRAL *EUROPEAN* The Landmark Mandarin Oriental's double-Michelin-star fine-diner is a stunner. The food is as creative as the Adam Tihany decor: Try the pistachio and apricot samosas, olive-oil-poached trout with shrimp and duck confit, and for dessert, caramel, sea salt, and milk fondant with caramelized peanuts. *15 Queen's Rd. ☎ 852/2132-0188. Entrees $HK300–$HK500. AE, DC, MC, V. Breakfast, lunch & dinner daily. MTR: Central, exit G. Map p 80.*

At Amber, the ceiling art is as impressive as the menu.

★★ **Anthony's Catch** SAI KUNG *ITALIAN/SEAFOOD* This small spot in the beach village of Sai Kung offers up dishes with fish imported from Australia and New Zealand and ingredients brought in from Italy by chef Anthony Blair Sweet. *G/F 1826B Po Tung Rd. ☎ 852/2792-8474. Entrees $HK165–$HK355. AE, MC, V. Lunch & dinner daily. MTR: Diamond Hill, exit C, then bus 92. Map p 82.*

★ **Café Deco** VICTORIA PEAK *INTERNATIONAL* Oddly, many of the Peak's restaurants don't have great views. Café Deco is the exception—it's an airy space with windows overlooking the city. The food, while okay, won't blow you away but the view certainly will. *Level 1–2, Peak Galleria, 118 Peak Rd. ☎ 852/2849-5111. Entrees $HK136–$HK248. AE, DC, MC, V. Lunch & dinner Mon–Sat; breakfast, lunch & dinner Sun. Peak tram. Map p 80.*

★ **kids** **California Pizza Kitchen** CAUSEWAY BAY *PIZZA* If you have a hankering for Western food, but still want a taste of Asia, this chain offers up Peking duck pizza alongside its cheese and tomato pie. The atmosphere, though, is decidedly Western, with large tables and fast service. *13/F, Times Square, 1 Matheson St. ☎ 852/3102-9132. Entrees $HK72–$HK112. AE, DC, MC, V. Lunch & dinner daily. MTR: Causeway Bay, exit A. Map p 80.*

★★ **Chez Patrick** WAN CHAI *FRENCH* "Patrick" is globetrotting former hotel chef Patrick Goubier and this is his attempt to re-create the feel of a Parisian dinner party in downtown Hong Kong. It's a favorite haunt of well-heeled French expats in search of a taste of home. The pan-fried duck served with sweet-and-sour cherry sauce is divine.

Private Dining

Private-dining restaurants, where families open their homes and lay out set menus for patrons, are some of Hong Kong's best dining options. They first sprang up in the 1990s during the Asian financial crisis. While many of these places are humble in atmosphere, they often surpass four-star spots in terms of freshness, originality, and flavor; Yellow Door Kitchen and Manchurian Candidate are two fine examples in this chapter. Call a few days in advance for bookings.

G/F, 26 Peel St. ☎ 852/2541-1401. Set dinners from $HK499. AE, MC, V. Lunch & dinner Mon–Sat. MTR: Central, then Mid-Levels escalator. Map p 80.

★★★ **Da Ping Huo** CENTRAL *SICHUAN* One of Hong Kong's most popular private-dining options, Da Ping Huo is run by a husband-and-wife team specializing in spicy Sichuan food. Be prepared to eat, as meals consist of up to 14 courses, including Sichuan dumplings in garlic chili oil, spicy shrimp, and melon soup. The chef sings Chinese opera to guests at the end of the meal. ***L/G, 49 Hollywood Rd. ☎ 852/2559-1317. Set menu $HK250 per person. AE, DC, MC, V. Dinner Mon–Sat. Bus: 26. Map p 80.***

★★ **Din Tai Fung** TSIM SHA TSUI *SHANGHAINESE* This ever-popular Taiwanese chain is the best place in town to try *xiao long bao,* Shanghai's nationally adored hot broth dumpling snack. Staples like wonton soup and braised bamboo shoots also feature prominently. There's a bit of a food-court feel to the place, but the quality is superb. Expect to wait in line on weekends. ***Shop 130, 3/F, Silvercord Centre, 30 Canton Rd. ☎ 852/2730-6928. Entrees $HK70–$HK128. AE, MC, V. Lunch & dinner daily. MTR: Tsim Sha Tsui, exit A1. Map p 79.***

★★★ **Felix** TSIM SHA TSUI *FUSION* The all-white interior of this Philippe Starck–designed restaurant competes with the spectacular view of Hong Kong Island (call ahead for a seat by the windows). The fusion food matches the funky setting, with dishes such as honeyed tempura prawns and Atlantic cod marinated with Japanese *misoyaki* sauce, which are complemented by a large selection of French wines. ***Peninsula Hotel, Salisbury Rd. ☎ 852/2315-3188. Entrees $HK225–$HK350. AE, DC, MC, V. Dinner daily. MTR: Tsim Sha Tsui, exit E. Map p 79.***

★ **Fook Lam Moon** WAN CHAI *CANTONESE* Pay homage to Hong Kong fare in all its glory at this four-story restaurant with large tables to

The view of the Hong Kong skyline is stunning from Hutong's chic dining room.

Jumbo is like a theme-park version of a Chinese restaurant, complete with huge gold dragons lurking in the massive dining rooms.

accommodate large portions of braised shark's fin soup, deep-fried crispy chicken, and sweetened double-boiled bird's nest in fresh coconut. ***35–45 Johnston Rd.* ☎ *852/ 2866-0663. Entrees $HK100–$HK190. AE, DC, MC, V. Breakfast, lunch & dinner daily. MTR: Wan Chai, exit B2. Map p 80.***

★★★ **Hutong** TSIM SHA TSUI *NORTHERN CHINESE* This is an enticing spot, with rustic Chinese furniture and floor-to-ceiling windows revealing the harbor and skyline. The clientele is a bit stuffy, but the menu makes up for it, with excellent drunken raw crabs in rice wine, braised veal shank in osmanthus flower sauce, and an extensive wine list. ***28/F, 1 Peking Rd.* ☎ *852/ 3428-8342. Entrees $HK118–$HK288; $HK300 minimum. AE, DC, MC, V. Lunch & dinner daily. MTR: Tsim Sha Tsui, exit H. Map p 79.***

★★★ **Isola Bar and Grill** CENTRAL *ITALIAN* A firm favorite for lunch dates among the expat *taitais* (local slang for ladies who lunch), Isola claims one of Hong Kong's finest harbor views and best Italian kitchens. The classic Mediterranean menu has everything from hand-spun pizzas upward, while the dreamy white interior and long outdoor balcony combine to make this my favorite of Hong Kong's upmarket independent restaurants. Book ahead. ***3/F, IFC Mall.* ☎ *852/2383-8765. Entrees $HK138–$HK368. AE, DC, MC, V. Lunch & dinner daily. MTR: Central, exit A. Map p 80.***

★ kids **Jumbo Kingdom** ABERDEEN *SEAFOOD* You take a free shuttle past fishing junks to arrive at this campy family eatery, billed as the world's largest floating restaurant. The menu features seafood like fresh lobster salad and Chinese dishes like Peking duck. ***Aberdeen Harbour.* ☎ *852/2553-9111. Entrees $HK80–$HK400. AE, DC, MC, V. Breakfast, lunch & dinner daily. Bus: 7 or 70 from Central, then Jumbo's boat from pier. Map p 80.***

★★★ **Kung Tak Lam** CAUSEWAY BAY *SHANGHAINESE VEGETARIAN* Popular among vegetarians, this place is a win-win for those looking to take a break from meat and still get a taste of Shanghai cuisine.

Meat substitutes are used for dishes such as *mapo doufu,* a spicy tofu dish usually made with minced pork. ***Shop 1001, World Trade Centre, 280 Gloucester Rd.*** ☎ ***853/2890-3127. Entrees $HK100–$HK250. AE, MC, V. Lunch & dinner daily. MTR: Causeway Bay, exit D1. Map p 80.***

★★★ **Loon Wai** CAUSEWAY BAY *CANTONESE* My favorite casual diner in Hong Kong is a must if you find yourself in Causeway Bay after dark. Popular with young groups of friends, Loon Wai does simple Cantonese dishes, but the menu highlight is the ridiculously generous mixed-grill hot plate that costs just $HK40 (only available after 6pm). There's no English on the sign but English menus are available inside. ***54–58 Jardine's Bazaar.*** ☎ ***853/2890-6909. Entrees $HK26–$HK30. No credit cards. Lunch & dinner daily. MTR: Causeway Bay, exit F. Map p 80.***

★★★ **Luk Yu Teahouse** CENTRAL *DIM SUM* This teahouse has been serving dim sum since 1933, and the atmosphere, with its golden colors and Chinese landscape paintings, is a blast from Hong Kong's past. The food is some of the tastiest and freshest in town (try the steamed rice wrapped in lotus leaves). Come before 10:30am, when the dim sum is served from trays carried by the waitstaff, but be prepared to wait. ***24–26 Stanley St.*** ☎ ***852/2523-5464. Entrees $HK100–$HK220. MC, V. Breakfast, lunch & dinner daily. MTR: Central, exit D2. Map p 80.***

Noodle soups are a Hong Kong staple and can be found at many restaurants.

You'll find old-fashioned Chinese favorites like spring rolls at Luk Yu Teahouse.

★★★ **Lung King Heen** CENTRAL *CANTONESE* The only restaurant to be awarded three stars during Michelin's first survey of Hong Kong in 2008, this hotel restaurant combines a supremely elegant dining room with fabulous views. The Cantonese cuisine is creatively done, with dishes such as crispy glutinous rice dumplings stuffed with beef satay, and steamed shrimp dumplings with bamboo. ***4/F, Four Seasons, 8 Finance St.*** ☎ ***852/3196-8888. Entrees $HK68–$HK158. AE, DC, MC, V. Lunch & dinner daily. MTR: Central, exit A. Map p 80.***

★★★ **Mandarin Grill** CENTRAL *CONTINENTAL* The gleaming white interior of this popular hotel restaurant is flanked by an oyster bar with a long, wooden serving table. Once you've had a taste of the grilled tuna or the succulent Australian *wagyu* beef, you can take in the view of downtown Hong Kong. ***5 Connaught***

Rd. ☎ ***852/2825-4004. Entrees $HK358–$HK528. AE, DC, MC, V. Breakfast, lunch & dinner daily. MTR: Central, exit F. Map p 80.***

★★ **Maxim's Palace** CENTRAL *DIM SUM* Sprawling, cheap, and packed on Sundays, this is a can't-miss Hong Kong experience. Hong Kong families gather here to choose dim sum from rolling trolley carts (today, such service is increasingly rare). I recommend the fried squid tentacles and steamed pork buns. ***Low Block, City Hall, Connaught Rd. Central and Edinburgh Place.*** ☎ ***852/2526-9931. Dim sum $HK17–$HK29. AE, DC, MC, V. Lunch Mon–Sat; breakfast & lunch Sun. MTR: Central, exit K. Map p 80.***

★★ **The Manchurian Candidate** CENTRAL *SICHUAN* Deep inside a nondescript apartment building off Lan Kwai Fong, this down-home Chinese restaurant is a refreshing contrast to the trendiness below. The family team who runs it serves wonderfully spicy Sichuan dishes that include hand thrown noodles, homemade dumplings, and chicken flavored with star anise. ***Room 7B, 5/F, Winners Building, 37 D'Aguilar St.*** ☎ ***852/2522-0338. Evening set menu only $HK200. No credit cards. Lunch & dinner daily. MTR: Central, exit D2. Map p 80.***

Stir-frying at a Chinese outdoor restaurant.

Dim sum is like tapas—lots of different dishes served in small portions.

★★★ **One Harbour Road** WAN CHAI *CANTONESE* There's a seemingly inexhaustible number of five-star hotel restaurants in this city of wealthy business travelers. This one stands out not only for its view of the harbor, but also for its spacious dining room, complete with a lotus pond. The food is classed-up traditional Cantonese. ***7–8/F, Grand Hyatt, 1 Harbour Rd.*** ☎ ***852/2584-7722. Entrees $HK145–$HK250. AE, DC, MC, V. Lunch & dinner daily. MTR: Wan Chai, exit A5. Map p 80.***

★ **Peking Garden** TSIM SHA TSUI *PEKINGESE* The house specialty at this northern Chinese restaurant is stir-fried noodles. You can watch the staff making hand-pulled "la mian" noodles at 8pm every day. ***Star House, 3 Salisbury Rd.*** ☎ ***852/2735-8211. Entrees $HK86–$HK188. AE, DC, MC, V. Lunch & dinner daily. MTR: Tsim Sha Tsui, exit E. Map p 79.***

★★ **Sabatini** TSIM SHA TSUI *ITALIAN* Sabatini serves Italian fare in a rustic, relaxed setting within the Royal Garden Hotel. The menu includes handmade pastas, delicious veal with morel sauce, and a huge selection of Italian wines that all go well with the evening guitar serenades. ***69 Mody Rd.*** ☎ ***852/2733-2000. Entrees $HK250–$HK385. AE, DC, MC, V. Lunch & dinner daily.***

MTR: Tsim Sha Tsui East, exit P2. Map p 79.

★ **Shanghai Lane** CENTRAL *SHANGHAINESE* Located on trendy Gough Street, this ye olde diner is filled with pictures of old Shanghai and faux wooden fittings. With a variety of Huaiyang dishes from eastern China, the menu will satisfy those seeking exoticism (pig trotters and sea cucumbers) as well as those in need of the comforting staples of "Western" Chinese food. Given the surrounds, it's really quite cheap. ***G/F, 35–37 Gough St. ☎ 852/ 2850-7788. Entrees $HK38–$HK88. No credit cards. Lunch & dinner daily. MTR: Sheung Wan, exit E2. Map p 80.***

★★ **Shui Huju** SOHO *NORTHERN CHINESE* The dark-wood interior makes this place feel more like a neighborhood spot in Beijing. The menu is superb, and the clams with Chinese wine and spicy sauce, deep-fried lamb shank, and lychee wine are all standouts. ***68 Peel St. ☎ 852/2869-6927. Entrees $HK100–$HK300. AE, MC, V. Dinner daily. MTR: Central, then Mid-Levels escalator. Map p 80.***

★★ **Song** CENTRAL *VIETNAMESE* Sheathed in white and tucked away down a tiny alley off Hollywood Road, this small restaurant serves quality Vietnamese food at reasonable prices. The lemon grass beef with rice vermicelli is excellent, as is the sautéed pumpkin with cashews. ***LG/F, 75 Hollywood Rd. ☎ 852/2559-0997. Entrees $HK75–$HK180. AE, MC, V. Lunch & dinner Mon–Sat. MTR: Central, then Mid-Levels escalator. Map p 80.***

★★★ **Spoon by Alain Ducasse** TSIM SHA TSUI *FRENCH* This famous spot offers a lovely view of the harbor, but you may be happily distracted by the collection of 550 handblown Murano glass spoons that hang from the ceiling. The French fusion menu includes steamed duck foie gras, pear and ginger chutney, and puff pastry with frogs' legs, tomato marmalade, mixed herbs, and pesto. ***InterContinental Hong Kong, 18 Salisbury Rd. ☎ 852/2313-2256. Entrees $HK330–$HK680. AE, DC, MC, V. Dinner Mon–Sat; lunch & dinner Sun. MTR: Tsim Sha Tsui, exit F. Map p 79.***

★★★ **The Square** CENTRAL *CANTONESE* The big draws here are the steamed lobster dumplings and the jumbo shrimp and asparagus rolls. The dim sum menu is rather

An expert noodle maker plies his trade at Peking Garden.

The lobster cocktail at Spoon is not to be missed.

small on the weekdays, but it expands on the weekends. Whenever you go, make sure you book ahead. *4/F, Exchange Square II. ☎ 852/2525-1163. Dim sum $HK40–$HK58. AE, DC, MC, V. Lunch daily. MTR: Central, exit A. Map p 80.*

★ **The Stoep** LANTAU *SOUTH AFRICAN* This is a favorite of mine, as there's nothing more wonderfully surreal than eating a plate of South African *braai,* or barbequed meat, on a laid-back beach in Hong Kong. Try a bottle of South African red wine and take a walk along the water when you're done. *32 Lower Cheung Sha Village. ☎ 852/2980-2699. Entrees $HK100–$HK200. AE, MC, V. Lunch & dinner daily. Central Pier, ferry 6 to Mui Wo. Take a cab from bus station. Map p 82.*

★★ **T'ang Court** TSIM SHA TSUI *CANTONESE* The Langham's best restaurant is known more for its food than its ambience (it's in a nearly windowless room). The quality of the Cantonese classics earned the restaurant two Michelin stars in 2008. There's an English menu that clearly explains what's in each dish. Good set-menu deals are available. *8 Peking Rd. ☎ 852/2375-1133. Entrees $HK150–$HK280. AE, DC, MC, V. Lunch & dinner daily. MTR: Tsim Sha Tsui, exit H. Map p 79.*

★ **369 Shanghai Restaurant** WAN CHAI *SHANGHAINESE* This relaxed, family-run eatery has worn booths and chipped plates, but delicious dishes like juicy sweet and sour fish and shredded pork with green pepper make up for the lack of atmosphere. *30–32 O'Brien Rd. ☎ 852/2527-2343. Entrees $HK40–$HK120. AE, MC, V. Lunch & dinner daily; open until 4am. MTR: Wan Chai, exit A1. Map p 80.*

★★ **The Verandah** REPULSE BAY *CONTINENTAL* This colonial throwback, perched above Repulse Bay's wide sand beach, has benefited from a recent renovation. High ceiling fans whirl softly while crisp white tablecloths flutter in the sea breeze. The menu offers grilled fish, meat, and seafood like lobster and crab, but it's also well known for its posh afternoon tea sets. *109 Repulse Bay Rd. ☎ 852/2292-2822. Entrees $HK280–$HK330. AE, DC, MC, V. Lunch & dinner Tues–Sun. Bus: 6, 260, or 973. Map p 82.*

Stir-fried flour rolls with chili are among the dim sum offerings at the Square.

★★ **Wasabisabi** CAUSEWAY BAY *JAPANESE* With its funky interior and plethora of sushi, sashimi, and tempura choices, this place feels straight out of Tokyo. Try the *temaki* (hand-rolled sushi) and grilled

Yung Kee is famous for its roast goose.

salmon, which is moist and tasty. ***13/F, Times Square, 1 Matheson St. ☎ 852/2506-0009. Entrees $HK118–$HK198. AE, DC, MC, V. Lunch & dinner daily. MTR: Causeway Bay, exit A. Map p 80.***

★★ **Yellow Door Kitchen** SOHO *SICHUAN* This private restaurant is a very small room reached by a rickety elevator, but the owners and staff are dedicated to offering the best Sichuan food around. The set menu changes—depending on the night, you may be treated to spicy bean curd, smoked lamb shank, or tasty Hangzhou-style duck. ***6/F, 37 Cochrane St. ☎ 852/2858-6555. Set menu $HK250. AE, MC, V. Lunch & dinner Mon–Fri; dinner Sat. MTR: Central, then Mid-Levels escalator. Map p 80.***

★★ **Yun Fu** CENTRAL *NORTHERN CHINESE* You'd be forgiven for thinking you had mistakenly wandered into a Himalayan spa as you enter this seductive subterranean restaurant. Themed around minority Chinese culture, the rustic designs and costumes suggest the charm of village life. Dishes from northern China are simply cooked; try the roast suckling pig, served with flaming sauce. ***B/F, 43–55 Wyndham St. ☎ 852/2116-8855. Entrees $HK138–$HK288. AE, DC, MC, V. Dinner daily. MTR: Central. Map p 80.***

★ **Yung Kee Restaurant** CENTRAL *CANTONESE* Yung Kee has been a Hong Kong institution for around 70 years thanks to its famous roast goose—which you can see hanging from the windows. The interior has grown a little worn, but it's clean and comfortable and you'll get complimentary dishes like preserved eggs and pickled ginger to go along with the goose. ***32–40 Wellington St. ☎ 852/2522-1624. Entrees $HK70–$HK120. AE, MC, V. Lunch & dinner daily. MTR: Central, exit D2. Map p 80.*** ●

7 The Best Nightlife

Nightlife Best Bets

Best Dance Club
★★★ Drop, *38–43 Hollywood Rd. (p 100)*

Best Wan Chai Bar
★★★ The Pawn, *62 Johnston Rd. (p 98)*

Best for Models and Celebs
★★ Dragon-i, *66 Wyndham St. (p 100)*

Best Place for Absinthe
★★★ Gecko Lounge, *15–19 Hollywood Rd. (p 101)*

Best Retro Bar
★★ Club Feather Boa, *38 Staunton St. (p 96)*

Best Unpretentious Bar
★★ Soho Corner, *43 Staunton St. (p 99)*

Best for Views
★★★ Aqua Spirit, *1 Peking Rd. (p 96)*

Best Outdoor Patio
★★ Inn Side Out, *Sunning Plaza, 10 Hysan Ave. (p 97)*

Best African Bar
★★ Makumba, *Garley Building, 48–52A Peel St. (p 98)*

Best Gay Venue
★★★ Propaganda, *1 Hollywood Rd. (p 101)*

Best Bohemian Vibe
★★★ Senses 99, *2–3/F, 99 Wellington St. (p 99)*

Best Space
★★★ 1/5, *Starcrest Building, 9 Star St. (p 100)*

Best Place to Drink on the Street
★ Stormies, *46–50 D'Aguilar St. (p 99)*

Best Laid-Back Dance Spot
★★ Yumla, *LB/F, 79 Wyndham St. (p 100)*

Many of Hong Kong's best bars have patios, where you get a ringside view of the city's nightlife.

Central Nightlife

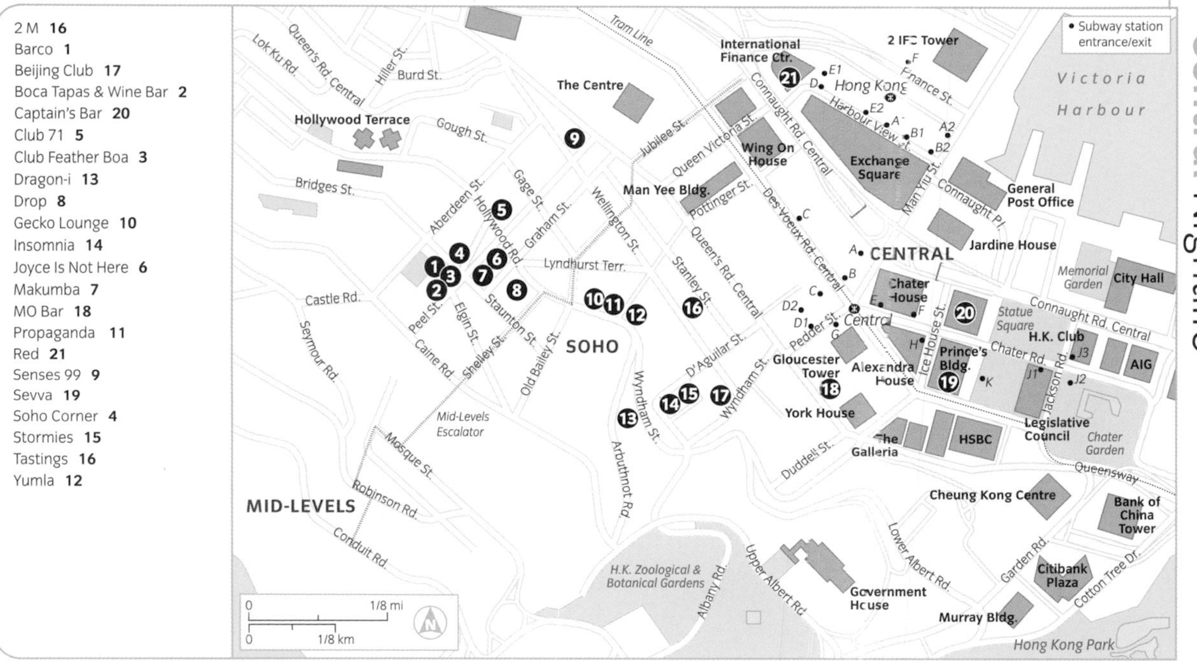

Page 91: Neon signs light up the night in Hong Kong.

Wan Chai Nightlife

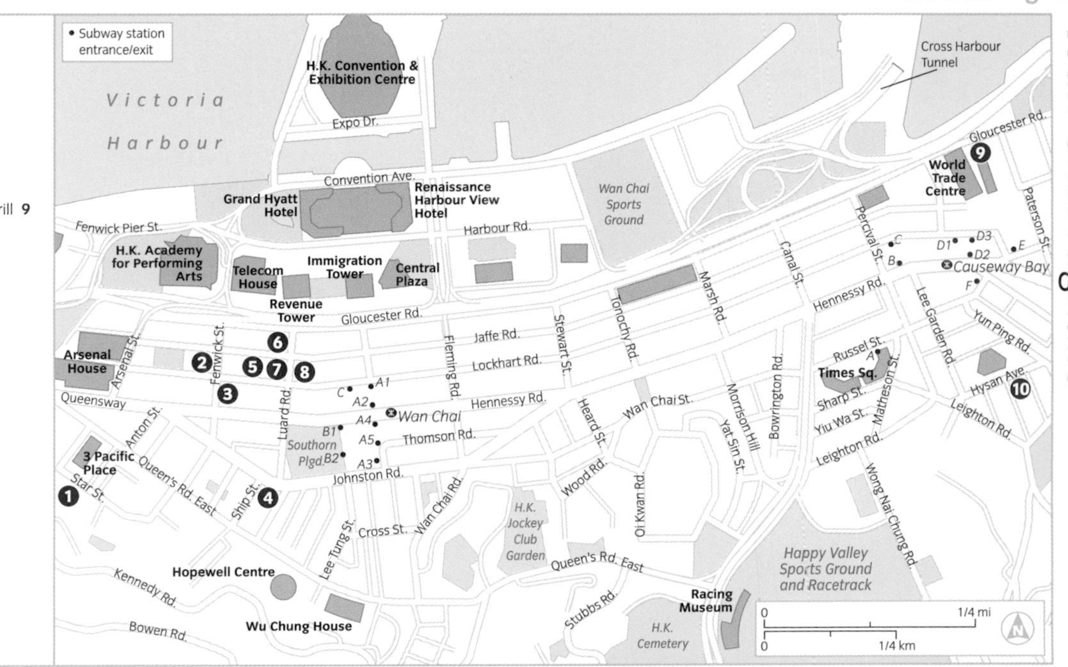

1/5 **1**
Delaney's **8**
Devil's Advocate **3**
Dicken's Bar **9**
Dusk Til Dawn **5**
Inn Side Out **10**
Joe Bananas **6**
Mes Amis **7**
ToTT's Asian Bar & Grill **9**
Typhoon **2**

Kowloon Nightlife

Aqua Spirit 1
Courtney's Bar 4
Lobby Lounge 3
Mariner's Rest 2
Merhaba 5

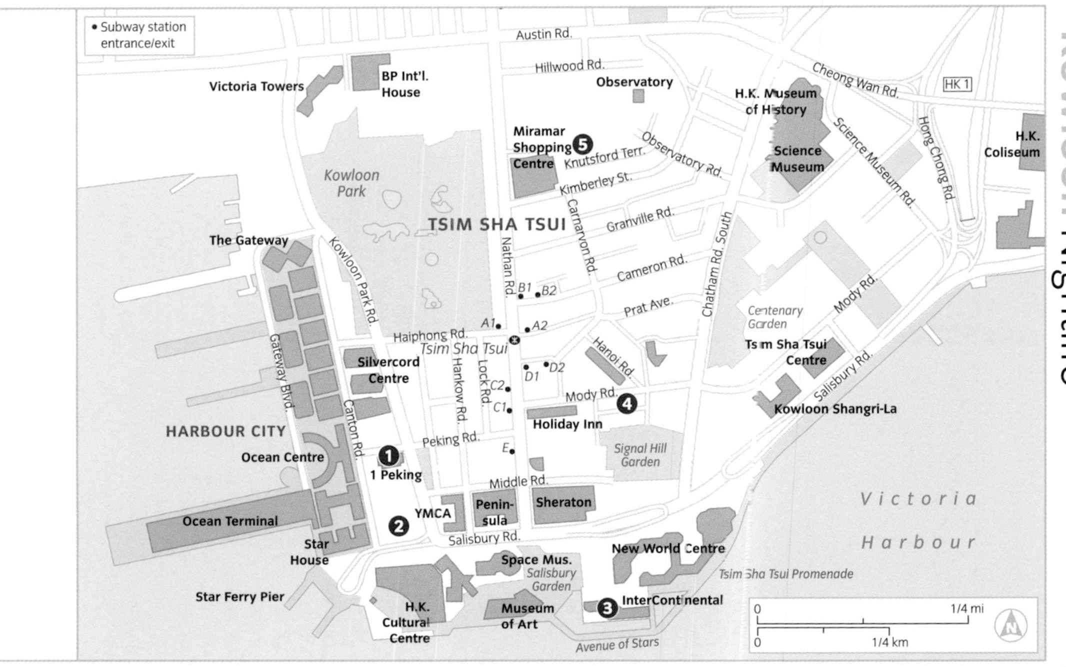

Nightlife A to Z

The nighttime view from the elegant Aqua Spirit bar is a big draw.

Bars

★★★ Aqua Spirit TSIM SHA TSUI Located on the 29th floor, this achingly hip lounge has floor-to-ceiling windows and what could well be the world's finest bar view. When seats are available (go early or be prepared to wait) you can choose from tall stools or couches, and a creative drink list that includes the Aquatini, made of Ketel One, lychee liqueur, Chambord, and gold leaves. *29/F, 1 Peking Rd.* ☎ *852/3427-2288. MTR: Tsim Sha Tsui, exit E. Map p 95.*

★ Barco SOHO This is a bar for the rest of us, with wooden stools and tables, couches in the back, and board games and magazines to pass the time. The beer and wine selection isn't vast, but it's got Carlsberg beer on tap and red wines from Australia. *42 Staunton St.* ☎ *852/2857-4478. Bus: 13, 26, or 40M. Map p 93.*

★ Captain's Bar CENTRAL This dark, clubby spot where the patrons wear their work duds (albeit with ties loosened and sleeves rolled up) and smoke cigars is as close to the feel of an old British Hong Kong pub as you're likely to get. The martinis are outstanding and beer is served in silver tankards. There's live music later in the night and a small dance floor. *Mandarin Oriental, 5 Connaught Rd.* ☎ *852/2522-0111. MTR: Central, exit F. Map p 93.*

★★ Club Feather Boa SOHO There's no sign outside the Feather Boa, but it's easy enough to find—just look for French windows covered with heavy curtains. Behind those curtains is a small, 1920s-style sitting room where the specialty is delicious frozen daiquiris. The only drawback is that the place gets packed beyond comfort after 10pm on weekends. *38 Staunton St.* ☎ *852/2857-2586. Bus: 13, 26, or 40M. Map p 93.*

★★ Club 71 CENTRAL Tucked away on a tree-lined alley just below Hollywood Road, this is an untouristy bar where the regulars play board games on outdoor tables. *B/F, 67 Hollywood Rd. (entrance off Man Hing Lane).* ☎ *852/2858-7071. Bus: 26. Map p 93.*

★ Courtney's Bar TSIM SHA TSUI This lounge, located in the hip boutique hotel the Minden, is named after local artist Pauline Courtney, whose Sri Lankan/Australian/Hong Kong–influenced paintings adorn the walls. There's an outdoor terrace that extends the space, and snacks are served in the early evening (as is breakfast in the morning). *7 Minden Ave.* ☎ *852/2729-7777. MTR: Tsim Sha Tsui, exit G. Map p 95.*

★★ Delaney's WAN CHAI It's been said more than once (especially after a few pints) that there is at least one good Irish pub in every major city in the world. Delaney's is Hong Kong's. The Guinness flows in abundance and the televised sports are never-ending. *18 Luard Rd.* ☎ *852/2804-2880. MTR: Wan Chai, exit C. Map p 94.*

★★ Devil's Advocate WAN CHAI This is a surprisingly unpretentious sports bar in the heart of Wan Chai. With huge booths, a long bar, and tables near the street, it's a good place to hit for happy hour, when drinks are two for one. ***48–50 Lockhart Rd. ☎ 852/2865-7271. MTR: Wan Chai, exit C. Map p 94.***

★ **Dicken's Bar** CAUSEWAY BAY The Excelsior Hotel's sprawling basement bar comes with loads of tables, multiple TVs, and great pub food, served until 11pm. Soccer fans often brave the high prices to watch games here. It's a relaxing stop after a day of shopping in Causeway Bay. ***B/F, 281 Gloucester Rd. ☎ 852/2837-6782. MTR: Causeway Bay, exit D1. Map p 94.***

★★ **Inn Side Out** CAUSEWAY BAY With big-screen sports and international beers that can be enjoyed under the stars on the huge outdoor patio, this is a pub for the man's man. There's something pleasingly slovenly about being able to throw the shells from the complimentary peanuts on the ground. Start the night here and see if you can pull yourself away. ***Sunning Plaza, 10 Hysan Ave. ☎ 852/2895-2900. MTR: Causeway Bay, exit F. Map p 94.***

★★ **Insomnia** LAN KWAI FONG Come early to this live-music venue

Patrons at Inn Side Out enjoy the outdoor seating.

in the center of Lan Kwai Fong and you may be lucky enough to nab a seat at the bar, which is open to the street. Bands (mostly covering Western hits) play in the back, and the dance floor can get very crowded as the night wears on. Open 24 hours. ***38–44 D'Aguilar St. 852/2525-0957. MTR: Central. Map p 93.***

Grab a spot on one of the comfortable couches and enjoy one of Captain's Bar's famous martinis.

★ **Joe Bananas** WAN CHAI Joe Bananas is one of Hong Kong's oldest bars, and over the years it has transformed from a place where men picked up women of ill repute to a place where both men and women get picked up in a totally nondiscriminatory manner. ***23 Luard Rd. ☎ 852/2529-1811. MTR: Wan Chai, exit C. Map p 94.***

★★ **Joyce Is Not Here** SOHO Joyce bills her bar as an artists' haven, and holds poetry readings and movie screenings throughout the week. The place is small and a bit cluttered with paintings, books, and even mannequins dressed in hats and boas. The crowd is bohemian and (largely) banker free. ***38–44 Peel St. ☎ 852/2851-2999. Bus: 13, 26, or 40M. Map p 93.***

★★ **Lobby Lounge** TSIM SHA TSUI This sea of tables and booths is located behind the check-in desk at the InterContinental, but that doesn't detract from its amazing view of Hong Kong Island, comfortable seating, and chilled-out live music in the evenings. *18 Salisbury Rd. ☎ 852/2721-1211. MTR: Tsim Sha Tsui, exit F. Map p 95.*

★★ **Makumba** CENTRAL A real bar-with-a-difference, the cavernous Makumba is decked out with furniture and art from Africa. African bands perform daily and even the cocktails come with a wild, safari spirit. *G/F, Garley Building, 48–52A Peel St. ☎ 852/2522-0544. MTR: Central. Bus: 13, 26, or 40M. Map p 93.*

★★ **Mariner's Rest** TSIM SHA TSUI Worth a stop for novelty alone, this British pub within the boutique 1881 Heritage development has three cold concrete cells out back. The building was formerly used by the Hong Kong Maritime Police but, unlike pirates of old, you'll be able to enjoy a pint of English ale during your voluntary incarceration. *Hullett House, 2A Canton Rd. ☎ 852/3988-0103. MTR: Tsim Sha Tsui, exit E. Map p 95.*

★★ **Merhaba** TSIM SHA TSUI One of the least generic of Knutsford Terrace's manifold drinking offerings, Merhaba comes with Middle Eastern flavor thanks to the mandatory hookahs. Grab an outdoor seat and get warmed up for the belly dancing with a *raki* (a Turkish anise-flavored spirit). *12 Knutsford Terrace. ☎ 852/2367-2263. MTR: Tsim Sha Tsui, exit B1. Map p 95.*

★★ **MO Bar** CENTRAL This chic hotel bar is the kind of place where afternoon business meetings tend to spill over into expensive evenings of cocktail indulgence. Voted "Best Bar in the World" by luxury travel mag *Virtuoso,* it's played host to low-key sets by visiting superstars, including Alicia Keys and Harry Connick, Jr. *G/F, Landmark Mandarin Oriental, 15 Queen's Rd. ☎ 852/2132-0077. MTR: Central, exit G. Map p 93.*

Enjoy the pub fare and the water views at the Pickled Pelican.

★★★ **The Pawn** WAN CHAI Retaining many of the original design features of the 19th-century pawn shop in which it's housed, the Pawn shows off the new spirit of heritage preservation in Wan Chai. It's classy without being stuffy, and there's a great balcony from where you can watch the trams go by below on busy Johnston Road. *62 Johnston Rd. ☎ 852/2866-3444. MTR: Wan Chai, exit A3. Map p 28.*

★ **Pickled Pelican** STANLEY This British-style pub has a large selection of whiskey and sports on the TVs around the bar. Although there's a crush of options on the waterfront in Stanley, this bar is notable for its excellent service and better-than-average pub food, like the potato fish cakes and garden salad. *90 Stanley Main St. ☎ 852/2868-6026. Bus: 6, 6X, 6A, 260, or 973.*

★★ **Red** CENTRAL This hip bar on the fourth floor of the IFC Mall offers an outdoor patio with panoramic views of Victoria Harbour and the skyline. You can order healthy California fare while watching the lights come on in Central. There is live jazz on Thursday nights starting at 10pm. *4/F, IFC Mall, 8 Finance St. ☎ 852/8129-8882. MTR: Central, exit A. Map p 93.*

★★★ **Senses 99** SOHO Open only on Friday and Saturdays, this bohemian bar takes up a couple of sparsely decorated upstairs rooms in a pre-war heritage building. Indie tracks play downstairs while upstairs a bunch of instruments dare the crowd to improvise. *2–3/F, 99 Wellington St. No phone. MTR: Central, exit D2. Map p 93.*

★★★ **Sevva** CENTRAL One of the hottest spots in the heart of Central, Sevva's crowning glory is the 360-degree terrace. It's perched amid some of Hong Kong's most famous buildings and festooned with low-slung sofas and luxuriant pillows, so customers can enjoy the combined city and harbor views in comfort. *25/F, Prince's Building, 10 Chater Rd. ☎ 852/2537-1388. MTR: Central, exit K. Map p 93.*

★★ **Soho Corner** SOHO Away from the glitz, glam, and high prices, the real essence of Soho is distilled in this humble corner joint. Take up a street-side stool and watch well-dressed partygoers scurry back and forth while you relax with a beer and a curry. There's no finer place for people-watching. *43 Staunton St. ☎ 852/2543-2632. Bus: 13, 26, or 40M. Map p 93.*

The patio at Red offers fantastic views of the city.

Revelers take to the streets during a typical night out in Lan Kwai Fong.

★ **Stormies** LAN KWAI FONG On a weekend night, it's easy to find Stormies: Just look for the hordes of people holding plastic cups on the street outside. The interior is huge, with two floors and plenty of seating, but the best way to enjoy this place is to take a drink out onto the street with the masses. *46–50 D'Aguilar St. ☎ 852/2845-5533. MTR: Central, exit D2. Map p 93.*

★ **Typhoon** WAN CHAI Typhoon is a chic newcomer to Wan Chai, with a stylish round bar and a huge TV screen for sporting events. Even when it's packed, it's less raucous than many other options in this part of the city, though the music can be very loud. *37–39 Lockhart Rd. ☎ 852/2527-2077. MTR: Wan Chai, exit C. Map p 94.*

Clubs

★ **Beijing Club** CENTRAL Spreading over three floors, the Beijing Club offers a superclub experience in cramped Hong Kong. Unlike some other venues in this neighborhood, Chinese make up the bulk of the

Night Touring

Not in the mood for barhopping? Take a tour of the harbor and see the glittering lights of Hong Kong in all their glory. The Aberdeen & Harbour Night Cruise takes you on a nearly 5-hour ride, which includes drinks and dinner. Go to www.watertours.com.hk for information, or call ☎ 852/2926-3868. Tour companies like **Gray Line** (☎ 852/2368-7111; www.grayline.com.hk), and **Splendid Tours & Travel** (☎ 852/2316-2151; www.splendidtours.com) also offer night tours of the city—you'll get a sense of what Hong Kong is really like after the sun goes down.

crowd. There's a fairly steep cover charge and don't expect to get in if you're not dressed up. *2–5/F, Wellington Plaza, 2–8 Wellington St. ☎ 852/2526-8298. MTR: Central, exit D2. Map p 93.*

★★ **Dragon-i** CENTRAL This restaurant, bar, and dance club has long been a hot spot in Hong Kong. The tables that surround the dance floor are often occupied by models, who are invited to eat here for free.

Many bars and nightclubs in Hong Kong have dance floors, and DJs get the crowds moving.

Getting past the doorman can be challenging, but dressing well and using a touch of silver-tongue charm may yield success. *The Centrium, 60 Wyndham St. ☎ 852/3110-1222. MTR: Central, exit D2. Bus: 26. Map p 93.*

★★★ **Drop** CENTRAL Located down a narrow alley, this club has a square bar flanking a dance floor, couches, and a high-rise stage for the DJ. The music is usually in-your-face deep house, and there are some cozy tables in the back, which are easier to commandeer if you arrive early. *38–43 Hollywood Rd. ☎ 852/2543-8856. Bus: 26. Map p 93.*

★★★ **1/5** WAN CHAI Though it's not an out-and-out dance club, this is one of my favorite late-night haunts in Hong Kong. It's both elegant and comfortable, with a dance floor near the entrance and tables and couches tucked in the back. Crowds often spill out onto quiet Star Street during warmer months. *Starcrest Building, 9 Star St. ☎ 852/2520-2515. MTR: Admiralty, exit F. Map p 94.*

★★ **Yumla** CENTRAL A small, somewhat gritty basement club, Yumla offers terrific music in a laid-back, welcoming atmosphere—it's one for the alternative clubber. The bar is sometimes hard to reach across the packed dance floor, so be patient. Access is off the Pottinger Street steps. ***LB/F, 79 Wyndham St. ☎ 852/2147-2383. MTR: Central. Bus: 26. Map p 93.***

Gay Clubs & Bars

★★★ **Propaganda** CENTRAL This is Hong Kong's best-known gay club, with a massive dance floor, a wide drink selection, and a balcony perfect for watching the crowd below. It's popular among tourists even though it's a bit hard to find (it's in the alley off Pottinger St.). ***B/F, 1 Hollywood Rd. ☎ 852/2868-1316. MTR: Central. Bus: 13, 26, or 40M. Map p 93.***

★ **2M** CENTRAL A relaxed and intimate neighborhood spot that functions as a good pre-clubbing stop, largely thanks to its long 6-to-10pm happy hours. The entrance is down a small alley off Wellington Street. ***B/F, 27–29 Wellington St. ☎ 852/2869-9990. MTR: Central, exit D2. Map p 93.***

Live Music

★★ **Dusk til Dawn** WAN CHAI This spot has seating along the edges of the room and at the bar, with a dance floor in the center with a stage for live acts. They book some very good cover bands, playing mostly American rock. The place stays open late, but the crowd can get a little less appealing as the night winds down, so plan to come on the early side. ***76–84 Jaffe Rd. ☎ 852/2528-4689. MTR: Wan Chai, exit A1. Map p 94.***

★★★ **Gecko Lounge** CENTRAL Gecko is a hugely popular midweek drinking stop on account of the live jazz which runs Tuesday to Thursday (DJ stuff takes over on weekends). It's a reclusive setting, accessible down an alley off Pottinger Street, with comfortable couches lining the walls. Fiery absinthe is a specialty at the bar. ***15–19 Hollywood Rd. ☎ 852/2537-4680. Bus: 26. Map p 93.***

★★ **ToTT's and Roof Terrace** CAUSEWAY BAY The Excelsior Hotel's recently renovated rooftop bar has a gorgeous slinky feel, but the real reason to come is the new roof terrace, which has spectacular views over Causeway Bay to Central. Try the sangria where the fruit is suspended midglass with some mixologist trickery. Live bands play later in the evening. ***281 Gloucester Rd. ☎ 852/2837-6786. MTR: Causeway Bay, exit D1. Map p 94.***

Happy hour at Dusk til Dawn runs from 5 to 11pm, and draws a mostly expat crowd.

Try the absinthe at Gecko Lounge.

Wine Bars

★★ Boca Tapas and Wine Bar SOHO This candlelit Spanish-themed bar is dark and moody in the best possible way. The wine selection is good, with the best offerings from Spain. It's a bit pricey, but the pours are generous and the tapas excellent. *65 Peel St. ☎ 852/2548-1717. Bus: 13, 26, or 40M. Map p 93.*

★★ Tastings CENTRAL The major drawcard of this stylish wine bar is the Italian-designed Enomatic wine-dispensing system which allows patrons to sample one of 40 featured wines, from a rolling stock of 160, in smaller-than-usual tasting glasses. *27–29 Wellington St. ☎ 852/2523-6282. MTR: Central, exit D2. Map p 93.*

From Cheesy to Sleazy

Bars and clubs in Hong Kong often come in dense clusters where a distinct atmosphere prevails. Here's a look at what to expect.

Lan Kwai Fong: Loud, expensive, and crowded, this area is aimed at 20-somethings looking for a party, though plenty of 40-somethings seem to enjoy it as well. Dress up and be prepared to spend.
Mong Kok: Dominated by small independent bars where the beer is served in buckets and the karaoke is deafening. It's charmingly local but not always suited to tourist tastes.
Soho: More artsy and bohemian than LKF, though it can be exponentially more pretentious as a result. Less glitz, more conversation.
Tsim Sha Tsui: Knutsford Terrace is the closest thing to LKF you'll find in Kowloon. It's popular with young expat residents and is a good spot to find an outdoor seat. The busy bar strip along Minden Avenue has more of a Chinese vibe.
Wan Chai: An area defined by the antics of U.S. servicemen during breaks from the Vietnam War. North of Hennessey Road is still a bit seedy, but Star Street is the epitome of refined cool.

8 The Best Arts & Entertainment

Arts & Entertainment Best Bets

Best **Movie Theater**
★★★ Broadway Cinematheque, *Prosperous Garden, 3 Public Square St. (p 109)*

Best **Horse Racing Track**
★★★ Sha Tin Racecourse, *Sha Tin (p 110)*

Best **Live Music**
★★★ Peel Fresco, *49 Peel St. (p 111)*

Best **Place to Learn a Karate Chop**
★★ Kung Fu Corner, *22 Austin Rd. (p 112)*

Best **Boat Ride**
★★★ Duk Ling Ride, *Kowloon Public Pier (p 108)*

Best **New Orleans Jazz**
★★ Ned Kelly's Last Stand, *11A Ashley Rd. (p 111)*

Best **Ballet Dancers**
★★★ Hong Kong Ballet, Hong Kong Cultural Centre, *10 Salisbury Rd. (p 109)*

Best **Nighttime Horse Races**
★★★ Happy Valley Racecourse, *2 Sports Rd. (p 110)*

Best **Place for Kung Fu Movies**
★★ Film Archive Cinema, *50 Lei King Rd. (p 109)*

Best **Cantonese Opera**
★ Ko Shan Theatre, *77 Ko Shan Rd. (p 109)*

Best **Theme Park**
★★ Ocean Park, *Aberdeen (p 107)*

Best **Massage**
★★★ Chuan Spa, *41/F, 555 Shanghai St. (p 111)*

Horses come out of the gate at Happy Valley Racecourse, where both locals and visitors put money on the races.

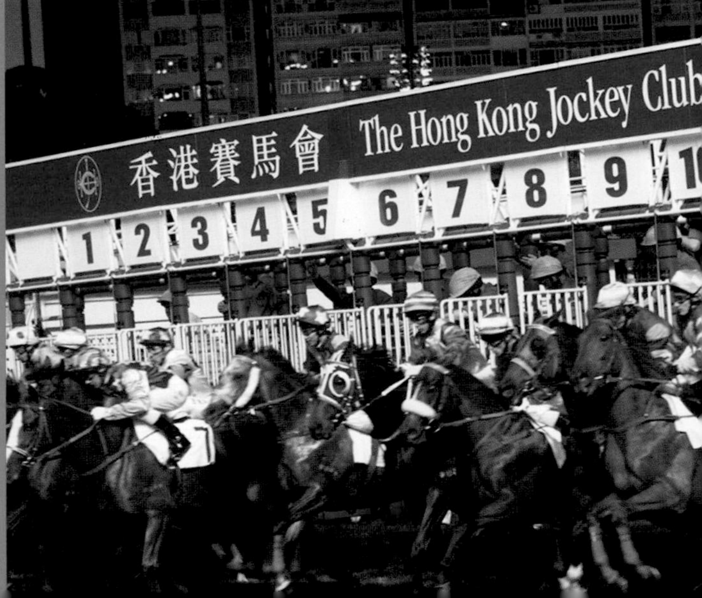

Kowloon Arts & Entertainment

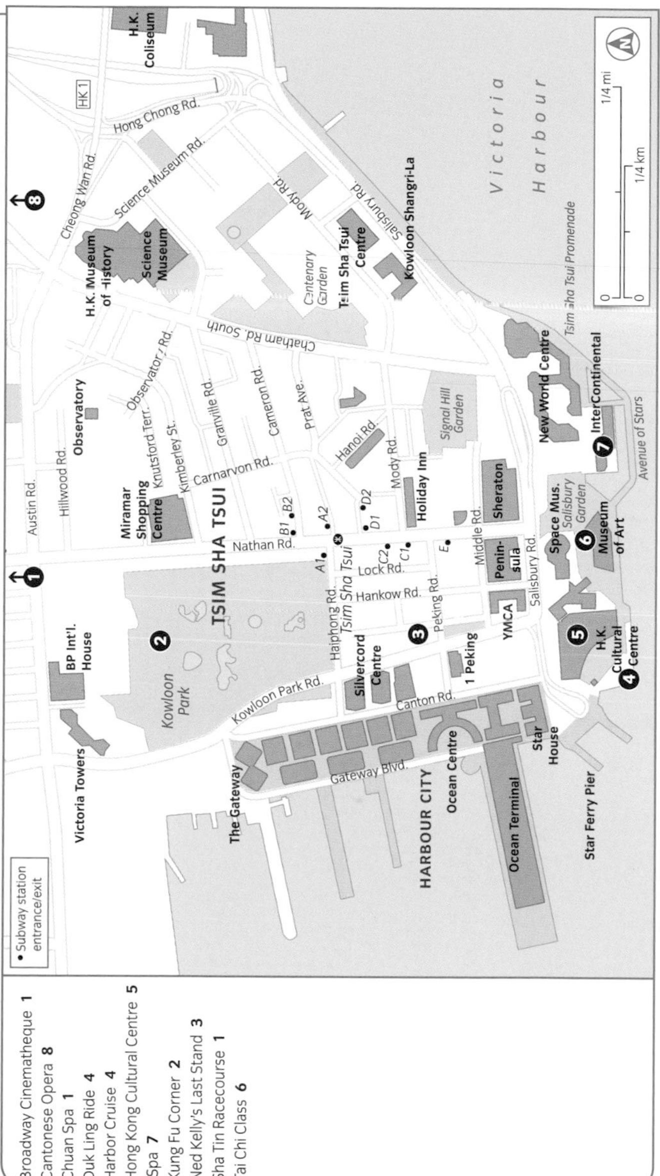

Page 103: A dancer with the Hong Kong Ballet rehearses at the Hong Kong Cultural Centre.

Central Arts & Entertainment

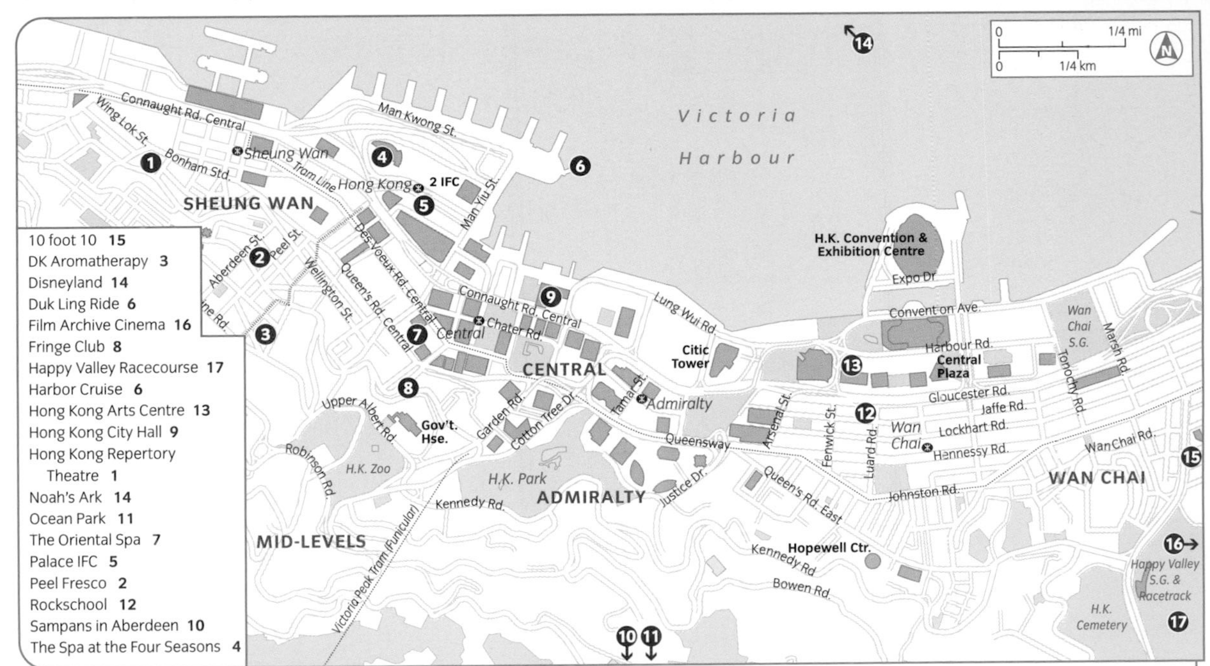

Arts & Entertainment A to Z

Amusement Parks

★ kids Hong Kong Disneyland

LANTAU The press skewered Disneyland when it opened here for being too small, but there's enough here to keep you busy for at least a day. Most of the attractions are Disney standards—the one unique standout is a garden where Mickey, Minnie, and the rest of the crew mingle with visitors. ☎ *852/1-830-830. www.park.hongkongdisneyland.com. Admission $HK350 adults, $HK250 kids 3–11. MTR: Disneyland. Map p 106.*

★ kids Noah's Ark MA WAN

Seemingly propping up Tsing Ma Bridge, a life-size replica of Noah's Ark is the centerpiece of this not-for-profit resort on Ma Wan island, a boat ride from Central. There are multimedia exhibits on the environment, a park with full-size animal sculptures, and an adventure playground. It's overtly educational and its Christian conception is obvious, though neither is so overdone that it's off-putting. ☎ *852/3411-8888. www.noahsark.com.hk. Admission $HK100 adults, $HK85 kids 3–11. Ferry: Pier 2, Central. Map p 106.*

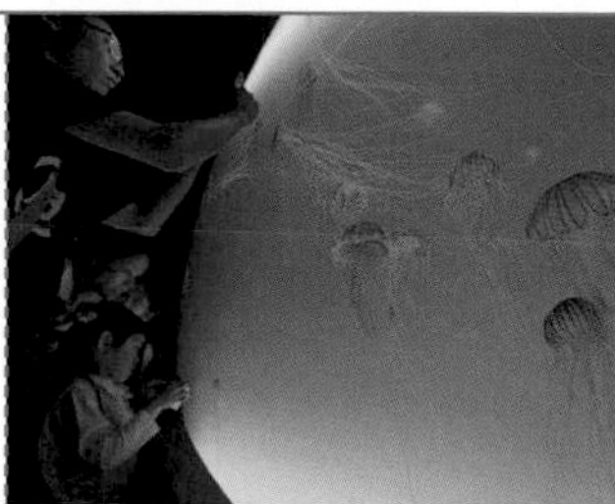

Visitors can get an up-close look at jellyfish and other marine creatures at Ocean Park.

★★ kids Ocean Park ABERDEEN

Ocean Park's rides include a "turbo drop," which sends thrill-seekers into free fall for 5 seconds; a roller coaster called the Dragon; and a large Ferris wheel. There are also marine and bird exhibits, a butterfly walk, and daily performances by the park's seals and dolphins. It's also the only place in Hong Kong to see the giant panda. ☎ *852/2552-0291. www.oceanpark.com.hk. Admission $HK250 adults, $HK125 kids 3–11. Bus: 6A, 6X, 70, 75, 90, 97, or 260. Map p 106.*

Mickey Mouse is dressed in a traditional Chinese outfit for a parade at Hong Kong Disneyland.

The Duk Ling, *a traditional Chinese junk, sails through Victoria Harbour.*

Boat Rides

★★ kids Dolphinwatch Cruise TSIM SHA TSUI Hong Kong's pink dolphins are local celebrities—not surprising, given their attractive flamingo hue and the fact that they're not found anywhere else in the world. Dolphinwatch runs eco-trips to see these creatures in the waters around Lantau. ☎ *852/2984-1414. www.hkdolphinwatch.com. Tickets $HK360 adults, $HK180 kids 11 and under. Pickup from various hotels.*

★★★ Duk Ling Ride TSIM SHA TSUI The creaky old *Duk Ling* stands out amid the high-speed ferries and container ships in Victoria Harbour. The last of the genuine junks which once dominated Hong Kong's waters has been saved for tourism by the Hong Kong Tourism Board. Be sure to book ahead for one of the hour-long trips. *Kowloon Public Pier (beside the Star Ferry Pier) and Central Pier 9.* ☎ *852/2508-1234. www.dukling.com.hk. Tickets $HK50. MTR: Tsim Sha Tsui/Central. Map p 106.*

★★ Harbor Cruise TSIM SHA TSUI There are a variety of morning, afternoon, and evening cruises offered on Victoria Harbour; some even include onboard dining. Boats generally pick up on both sides of the harbor. I recommend an evening trip to coincide with the harborside laser-and-light show, though wait for a clear night. Departure points can vary in the evening. *Kowloon Public Pier 3, Central Pier 9.* ☎ *852/2118-6201. www.discoverhongkong.com. Tickets $HK150 30-min. cruise; $HK330 night cruise with buffet. Map p 106.*

★★ Sampans in Aberdeen ABERDEEN On the pier just across the street from the bus station in Aberdeen, you can hire sampans, traditional Chinese fishing boats, for a short spin. The harbor here was once home to fishing families who were born, raised, and died living on their boats. Development has changed the life of this community, but you can still see a few of these boats out in the water. *Aberdeen Promenade, south of Aberdeen Praya Rd. Price is negotiable, around $HK50 for a short trip. Bus: 70, 73, or 973. Map p 106.*

Don't miss a chance to see Hong Kong's endangered pink dolphins.

A sign outside a Cantonese opera performance explains who is playing each character.

Cinema

★★★ **Broadway Cinematheque** YAU MA TEI Showing international mainstream hits and art-house films, this theater is my favorite spot for a night at the movies. There's a lobby shop selling posters and postcards and a bookshop/cafe that offers English-language books on film and other topics. *Prosperous Garden, 3 Public Square St.* ☎ *852/2388-3188. www.cinema.com.hk. Tickets $HK80. MTR: Yau Ma Tei, exit C. Map p 105.*

★★ **Film Archive Cinema** SAI WAN HO This is a great resource for those who want to delve into Hong Kong filmmaking, past and present. On any given night, you'll see films like the 1959 Cantonese opera movie *The Purple Hairpin*, or kung fu epics like *Sacred Fire, Heroic Wind* from 1966. *50 Lei King Rd.* ☎ *852/2734-9011. www.filmarchive.gov.hk. MTR: Sai Wan Ho, exit A. Map p 106.*

★ **Palace IFC** CENTRAL The Palace is my favorite place to catch mainstream, Western films. If you get popcorn, ask for a mix of sweet and salty. *1/F, IFC Mall, 8 Finance St.* ☎ *852/2388-6268. www.ifc.com.hk/english/cinema.aspx. Tickets $HK50–$HK75. MTR: Central. Map p 106.*

Dance, Opera & Classical Music

★ **Cantonese Opera** HUNG HOM Given Cantonese opera's prized place at the heart of popular culture, it's possible you'll stumble upon a performance by chance. You can also buy tickets to more formal shows at venues like the **Ko Shan Theatre** in Hung Hom. Though the operas are, of course, in Cantonese, you'll usually be handed a summary of the plot so you can follow along. *Ko Shan Park, Ko Shan Rd.* ☎ *852/2750-9222. www.lcsd.gov.hk/kst. Tickets $HK70–$HK150. Bus: 5,11, 14, 26, or 28. Map p 105.*

★ **Hong Kong Academy for Performing Arts** WAN CHAI This funky glass building in the heart of Hong Kong is both a school and a hot spot for art, theater, and music. Though not everything here is polished or professional, you'll see emerging local and international artists at work. *1 Gloucester Rd.* ☎ *852/2584-8500. www.hkapa.edu. Tickets $HK80 and up. MTR: Wan Chai, exit A1. Bus: 18.*

★ **Hong Kong City Hall** CENTRAL There is a constant stream of shows at this harborside venue, from theater to dance and jazz. Check the website for listings or just drop by to see what's on. *5 Edinburgh Place.* ☎ *852/2921-2840. www.cityhall.gov.hk. Tickets $HK100 and up. MTR: Central, exit K. Map p 106.*

★★★ **Hong Kong Cultural Centre** TSIM SHA TSUI Opened in 1989 on the site of the former Kowloon-Canton Railway station, this saddle-shaped monstrosity (a waterfront building with no windows?) is Hong Kong's largest center for performing arts. There are free family

I've Got a Horse Right Here

Although there are only two horse-racing tracks in Hong Kong, you can see the sport's presence all over the city in the form of Hong Kong Jockey Club betting shops. On Wednesdays and on weekends you'll notice locals (mostly older men) going about their business while carrying a radio and a marked-up newspaper—a sure sign they've got money on. Both courses are run by the Hong Kong Jockey Club which uses some of its mammoth profits in ensuring high-quality facilities and cheap admission and food costs, as well as giving lots to local charities. Horse-racing is the only form of legal gambling in Hong Kong, though people often make bets on mahjong, card games, and liar's dice.

performances every Saturday between 2:30 and 4:30pm, ranging from traditional Chinese dance to magic shows. The Hong Kong Philharmonic, the Hong Kong Chinese Orchestra, and Hong Kong Ballet all perform here. *10 Salisbury Rd.* ☎ *852/2734-2009. www.hkculturalcentre.gov.hk. Tickets $HK100 and up. MTR: Tsim Sha Tsui, exit F. Map p 105.*

Horse Racing

★★★ Happy Valley Racecourse HAPPY VALLEY Dating to 1846, Happy Valley is one of the few urban racecourses left in the world. Encircled by glittering apartment blocks and popular with both expats and locals, the course is well worth a visit even if you're not into gambling. Dining options range from hamburgers to dim sum, and cheap beer is available on tap. Races are generally held every Wednesday (and occasionally weekends) though the track shuts down for most of July and all of August. *2 Sports Rd.* ☎ *852/2895-1523. www.happyvalleyracecourse.com. Admission $HK10. Tram: Happy Valley. Bus: 75, 90, or 97. Map p 106.*

★★★ Sha Tin Racecourse SHA TIN I'll confess: I actually prefer this place to Happy Valley. It's far newer, less claustrophobic, and draws a mostly local crowd to

The Hong Kong Cultural Centre is the home of many of the city's best known performing arts groups.

Organ trio performs at Peel Fresco.

watch the horses run on either Saturday or Sunday. More attention is paid to the races and less to socializing. There are also abundant Cantonese and Western fast-food options. *Sha Tin Racecourse.* ☎ *852/2695-6223. www.sha-tin.com. Tickets $HK10. MTR: Racecourse. Map p 105.*

Live Music

★★ Ned Kelly's Last Stand TSIM SHA TSUI The bands at this dark-wood bar mostly play New Orleans jazz—it's great stuff but not so conducive to conversation. The beer selection is excellent and the service fast and friendly. *11A Ashley Rd.* ☎ *852/2376-0562. MTR: Tsim Sha Tsui, exit H. Map p 105.*

★★★ Peel Fresco SOHO A rotation of local jazz stars plays to packed houses in this intimate Soho venue. The specific jazz genre varies on a nightly basis, from rockabilly blues to organ trios, and the musicians play literally inches from their audience. *49 Peel St.* ☎ *852/2540-2046. www.peelfresco.com. MTR: Central, then Mid-Levels escalator to Stanton St. Map p 106.*

★★ Rockschool WAN CHAI This rock club is one of the most active music venues in town and, unusually for Hong Kong, both stage and dance floor are generously proportioned. It's loud and brash, and focuses on local indie and metal bands. *2/F, The Phoenix, 21–25 Luard Rd.* ☎ *852/2510-7339. MTR: Wan Chai, exit C. Map p 106.*

Spas & Foot Massages

★★★ Chuan Spa MONG KOK Located in the beautiful Langham Place Hotel, this spa is an oasis of calm, with private, pre-treatment tea rooms and decor that evokes the elements of feng shui. They offer everything from massages and facials to a combination package called the Tao of Detox ($HK1,645). *41/F, Langham Place Hotel, 555 Shanghai St.* ☎ *852/3552-3388. www.chuanspa.com. Prices start at $HK550 for facials; $HK795 for 1-hr massage. MTR: Mong Kok. Map p 105.*

DK Aromatherapy SOHO This bright, modern spa specializes in aromatherapy, but you can also get a massage or other treatments while you're here. There's even an "Animal Communications Workshop" where you'll learn to commune with your pets. *16A Staunton St.* ☎ *852/2771-2847. www.aroma.com.hk. Treatments $HK380 and up. Bus: 12, 13, or 26. Map p 106.*

★★ I Spa TSIM SHA TSUI What sets I Spa apart from the myriad five-star hotel spa options in Hong Kong are the harbor views available from within the treatment rooms. The Beauty Tox treatment (prices start at $HK1,100) is reputed to have a "Botox effect" without the use of needles. *3/F, InterContinental Hong Kong, 18 Salisbury Rd.* ☎ *852/2721-1211. www.hongkong-ic.intercontinental.com. Prices vary based on treatment. MTR: Tsim Sha Tsui. Map p 105.*

★★ The Oriental Spa CENTRAL This five-star spa has got it all, from traditional Chinese medicine to Swedish massages. They even offer a Chinese Herbal Steam Room. The facilities are elegant, with Chinese art and marble interiors throughout. There's also an old-fashioned barbershop where men can get a shave and a haircut. *5–6/F, Landmark Mandarin Oriental, 15 Queen's Rd.* ☎ *852/2132-0011. www.mandarinoriental.com/landmark/spa. Prices vary based on treatment. MTR: Central. Map p 106.*

★★ **The Spa at the Four Seasons** CENTRAL This five-star spa offers two spa suites where you can spend the night, and 18 spa rooms with earth-tone designs that use stone and glass materials to make for a relaxed atmosphere. Many rooms have excellent views of the harbor, which can be enjoyed while you have your massage. *The Four Seasons Hotel, 8 Finance St.* ☎ *852/3196-8900. www.fourseasons.com/hongkong/spa. Prices vary based on treatment. MTR: Central. Map p 106.*

★★ **10 foot 10** CAUSEWAY BAY This small acupuncture and foot reflexology shop stands out for its high-quality treatments and helpful staff. Whether or not it's effective, their technique certainly feels good. Stop in and give your toes a real Hong Kong treat. *5/F, Bartlock Centre, 3 Yiu Wa St.,* ☎ *852/2591-9188. www.10-foot-10.com. Prices start at $HK128 for 30-min. foot reflexology treatment. MTR: Causeway Bay. Map p 106.*

The spa at the Four Seasons offers serious luxury and excellent skyline views.

Sports & Activities

★★ **Kung Fu Corner** TSIM SHA TSUI Every Sunday between 2:30 *and* 4:30pm in Kowloon Park's Sculpture Walk, the Hong Kong Tourism Board organizes a demonstration of traditional kung fu, drumming, and dragon dancing. After the show, those brave enough can learn a few moves themselves. *22 Austin Rd.* ☎ *852/2724-3344. www.discoverhongkong.com. MTR: Tsim Sha Tsui, exit A1. Map p 105.*

★★ **Tai Chi Class** TSIM SHA TSUI Technically a form of martial arts, tai chi is really a slow, deliberate exercise suitable for all ages and fitness levels. Master William Ng gives free beginner's classes between 8 and 9am, Monday, Wednesday, and Friday. Call in advance to book a spot. *Sculpture Court, Museum of Art.* ☎ *852/2508-1234. www.discoverhongkong.com. MTR: Tsim Sha Tsui, exit F. Map p 105.*

Theater

★★ **Hong Kong Arts Centre** WAN CHAI You can catch plays and other performances, mostly by local groups, at this arts center, which also houses galleries and the **agnès b. cinema,** which screens independent films, classics, and revivals. *2 Harbour Rd.* ☎ *852/2582-0200. www.hkac.org.hk. Tickets $HK80 and up. MTR: Wan Chai, exit A1. Bus: 18. Map p 106.*

★★ **Hong Kong Repertory Theatre** CENTRAL The troupe here puts on both original works and established classics from China and elsewhere. The venue feels slightly industrial, with its seats crammed together. *4/F, Sheung Wan Municipal Services Building, 345 Queen's Rd.* ☎ *852/3103-5930. www.hkrep.com. MTR: Sheung Wan, exit A2. Map p 106.*

9 The Best **Lodging**

Lodging Best Bets

Best **Historic Hotel**
★★★ Peninsula Hotel $$$$$ *Salisbury Rd. (p 124)*

Best **Luxury Hotel**
★★★ Four Seasons $$$$ *8 Finance St. (p 119)*

Best **Outdoor Pool**
★★★ Grand Hyatt $$$ *1 Harbour Rd. (p 119)*

Best **Spa Rooms**
★★★ Langham Place Hotel $$$$ *555 Shanghai St. (p 122)*

Best **Elevation**
★★★ Ritz-Carlton $$$$$ *102–118/F, International Commerce Centre, 1 Austin Rd. (p 125)*

Best **Airport Hotel**
★★ Novotel Hong Kong Citygate $$ *50 Man Tung Rd. (p 124)*

Best **for Hiking**
★ Hong Kong Bank Foundation SG Davis Hostel $ *Ngong Ping (p 120)*

Best **Rooftop Tennis Court**
★★ The Excelsior $$ *281 Gloucester Rd. (p 119)*

Best **Boutique Hotel**
★★★ Hullett House $$$$$ *2A Canton Rd. (p 120)*

Best **Waterside Rooms**
★★★ InterContinental Hong Kong $$$$ *18 Salisbury Rd. (p 121)*

Best **East Meets West**
★★★ Mandarin Oriental $$$$ *5 Connaught Rd. (p 123)*

Best **Bar-Hopping Location**
★ Hotel LKF $$ *33 Wyndham St. (p 120)*

Best **Value**
★ The Salisbury YMCA $ *41 Salisbury Rd. (p 126)*

Most **Spacious Rooms**
★★★ Landmark Mandarin Oriental $$$$ *15 Queen's Rd. (p 122)*

Most **Child-Friendly Hotel**
★★ JW Marriott Hong Kong $$$$ *88 Queensway (p 121)*

Rooms at the Landmark Mandarin Oriental were made bigger after renovations.

Kowloon Lodging

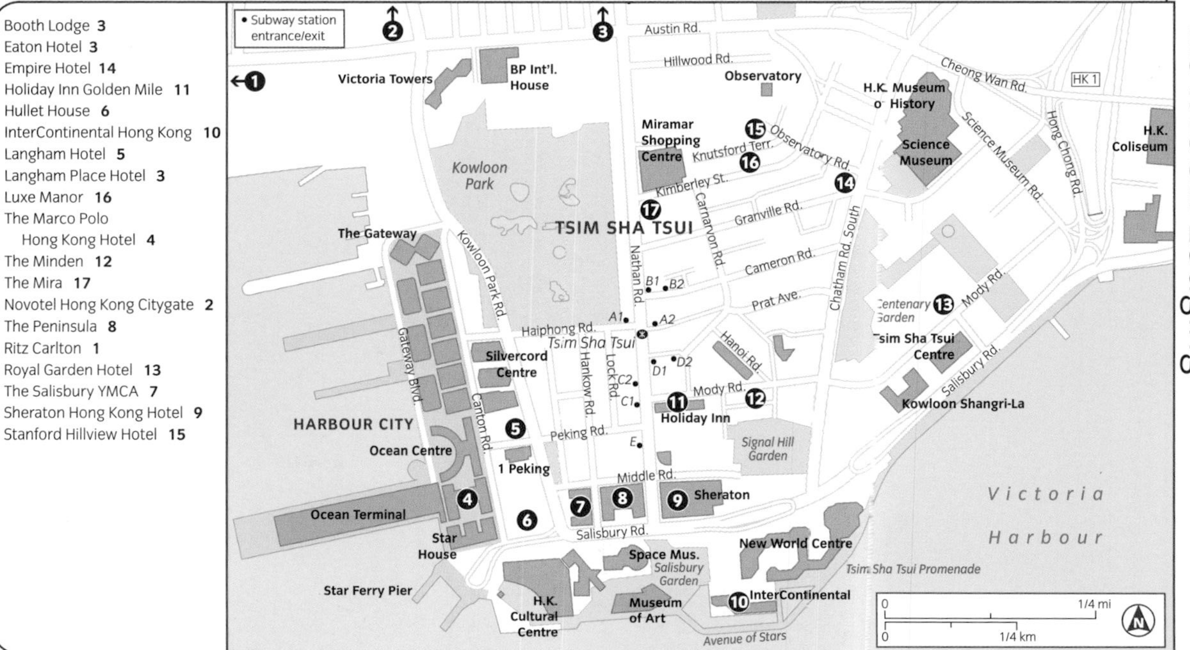

Page 113: The InterContinental offers a room with a panoramic view of Victoria Harbour.

Central Lodging

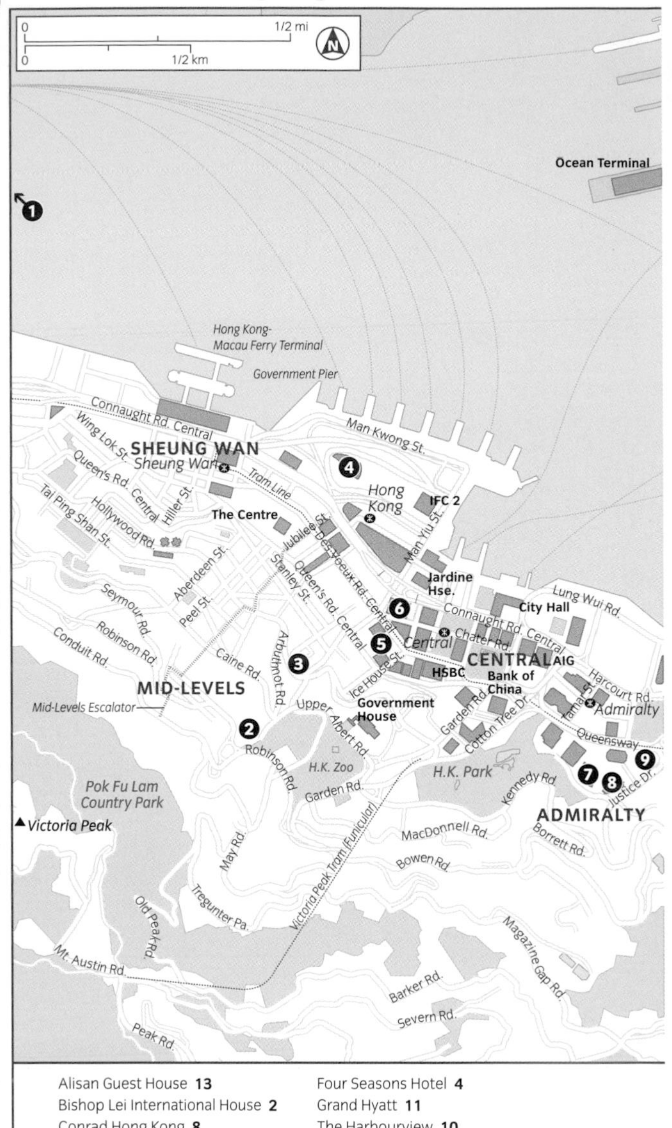

Alisan Guest House **13**
Bishop Lei International House **2**
Conrad Hong Kong **8**
The Excelsior **14**
Four Seasons Hotel **4**
Grand Hyatt **11**
The Harbourview **10**
Hong Kong Bank Foundation SG Davis Hotel **1**

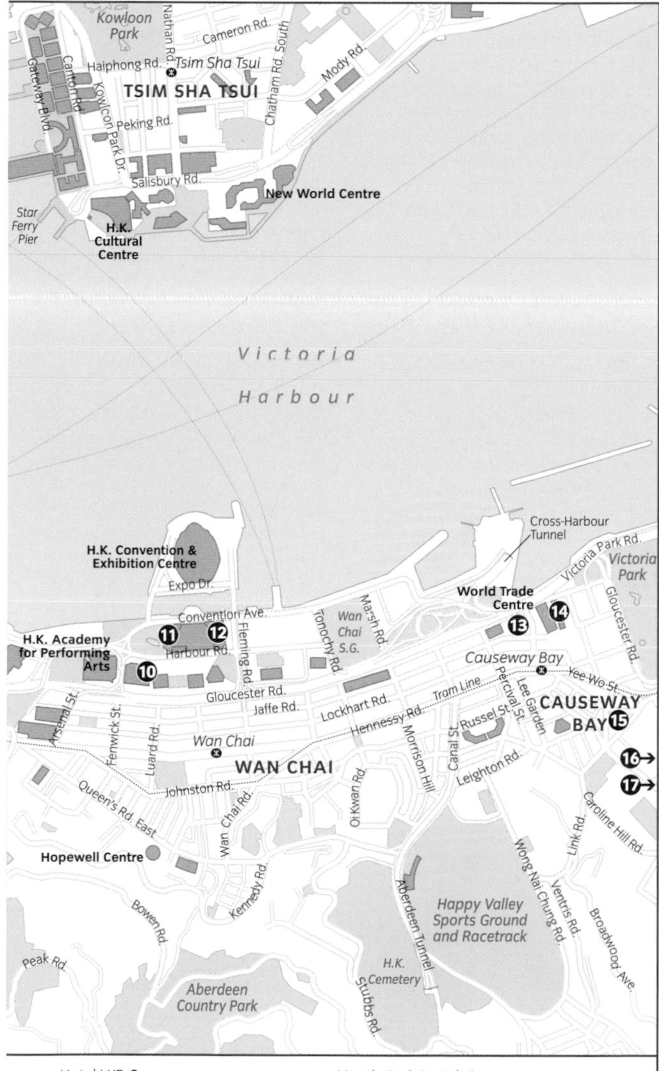

Hotel LKF **3**
Island Shangri-La **7**
JIA **15**
JW Marriott Hong Kong **9**
Landmark Mandarin Oriental **5**
Mandarin Oriental **6**
Metropark Hotel **17**
Renaissance Harbour View Hotel **12**
Rosedale on the Park **16**

Lodging A to Z

Alisan Guest House CAUSEWAY BAY This spot has some of the cheapest rates for harbor-view rooms in the city. The rooms here may be sparsely furnished, but the English-speaking manager offers great advice for getting around Hong Kong. *275 Gloucester Rd. (enter on Cannon St.), 5/F. ☎ 852/2838-0762. http://home.hkstar.com/~alisangh. 30 units. Doubles $HK320. No credit cards. MTR: Causeway Bay, exit D1. Map p 116.*

★ **Bishop Lei International House** MID-LEVELS Some of the rooms at this conveniently located hotel are tiny (welcome to Hong Kong), but they're comfortable and several have kitchenettes and/or harbor views. There's free WiFi throughout the hotel. *4 Robinson Rd. ☎ 852/2868-0828. www.bishopleihtl.com.hk. 227 units. Doubles $HK650–$HK815. AE, MC, V. Bus: 3B, 12, 12M, 23, 23A, or 40 to Robinson Rd. Map p 116.*

★★ kids **Booth Lodge** YAU MA TEI The Booth Lodge may not offer luxury, but it does offer large rooms that are spotlessly clean and well maintained at very reasonable rates. It's very conveniently located if you're planning to spend time in Tsim Sha Tsui and Yau Ma Tei. Some of the rooms are a bit noisy, so ask for one facing the hills if you want complete quiet. *11 Wing Sing Lane. ☎ 852/2771-9266. http://boothlodge.salvation.org.hk. 53 units. Doubles $HK420 and up. AE, MC, V. MTR: Yau Ma Tei. Map p 115.*

The Bishop Lei International House offers a free shuttle to Central, Admiralty, and Wan Chai.

★★ **Conrad International Hong Kong** ADMIRALTY Located above shopping haven Pacific Place, this elegant spot is a sea of calm in the center of the city. The rooms are simply done in soothing earth tones, and the lobby has a surprisingly homey feel, with wood paneling and polished granite. *88 Queensway, Pacific Place. ☎ 852/2521-3838; 800/CONRADS (266-7237) in the U.S. and Canada. www.conrad.com.hk. 513 units. Doubles $HK3,000–$HK3,400. AE, DC, MC, V. MTR: Admiralty, exit F. Map p 116.*

★★ **Eaton Hotel** YAU MA TEI This 460-room hotel is accessible by a four-story escalator that leads from chaotic Nathan Road to a peaceful lobby (where there's free Wi-Fi). The rooms are not big, but the nicest have floor-to-ceiling windows with views of the harbor. The staff is efficient and helpful. *380 Nathan Rd. ☎ 852/2782-1818; 800/223-5652 in the U.S. and Canada. www.eaton-hotel.com. 460 units. Single or double $HK1,300–$HK1,850. AE, DC, MC, V. MTR: Jordan, exit B1. Map p 115.*

★ **Empire Hotel Kowloon** TSIM SHA TSUI The rooms located between the 8th and 26th floors of this glass tower have floor-to-ceiling windows, with those above the 17th floor offering views of the harbor in the distance. The glass motif continues throughout the hotel's design, extending to desktops, tables, and bathrooms. The pool is, unfortunately, located on the bottom floor, but with prices far below five-star hotels, it's a minor detraction from this modern hotel with reasonable rates. *62 Kimberley Rd. ☎ 852/3692-2222. www.empirehotel.com.hk. 343 units. Doubles $HK1,600. AE, DC, MC, V. MTR: Tsim Sha Tsui. Map p 115.*

★★ **The Excelsior** CAUSEWAY BAY With harbor-view rooms, top-notch Chinese and Italian restaurants, and the breathtaking ToTT's roof bar, it's no wonder the Mandarin Oriental's Excelsior is always packed. The rooms have clever design touches, like couches that are built into the walls to maximize space. You'll also have access to a rooftop tennis court. *281 Gloucester Rd. ☎ 852/2894-8888; 800/526-6566 in the U.S. and Canada. www.excelsiorhongkong.com. 864 units. Doubles $HK2,180–$HK2,880. AE, DC, MC, V. MTR: Causeway Bay, exit D1. Map p 116.*

★★★ **Four Seasons Hotel** CENTRAL The rather lordly Four Seasons brand gets a funky overhaul at this sleek waterside hotel. There is Chinese artwork on the walls, marble fittings in the bathrooms, and comfy leather chairs and couches throughout. The hotel is attached to the IFC, which can make it feel a bit informal, but things are suitably exclusive at the stunning rooftop pool. Lung King Heen (p 86) is the only three-Michelin-star restaurant in Hong Kong. *8 Finance St. ☎ 852/3196-8888; 800/233-1234 in the U.S. and Canada. www.fourseasons.com/hongkong. 399 units. Doubles $HK4,200. AE, DC, MC, V. MTR: Central, exit A. Map p 116.*

You can relax after a day of sightseeing at the stunning rooftop pool at the Grand Hyatt.

★★★ **Grand Hyatt** CENTRAL The lobby alone makes this hotel worth a look: an enormous atrium with black marble floors, glass chandeliers, and curving staircases leading to a restaurant with water views.

A sitting room at the chic Four Seasons.

The lobby bar at the InterContinental offers amazing city views.

The rooms are less elegant, but the outdoor pool, with a bubbling fountain, green ferns, and lounge chairs more comfortable than some hotel beds, is a big plus. *1 Harbour Rd. ☎ 852/2588-1234. www.hongkong.hyatt.com. 572 units. Doubles $HK3,000–$HK3,600. AE, DC, MC, V. MTR: Wan Chai, exit A5. Map p 116.*

★ The Harbourview WAN CHAI The big draw at this former YMCA is the fact that more than half of the rooms face the water. Granted, the rooms are teeny—all have either twin or double beds—but they're clean and well maintained. The location, in the heart of Wan Chai and right next to the Hong Kong Arts Centre, is convenient, and the prices (even for rooms with harbor views) are often well below advertised rates. *4 Harbour Rd. ☎ 852/2802-0111. www.theharbourview.com.hk. 320 units. $HK1,600–$HK2,000. AE, DC, MC, V. MTR: Wan Chai, exit A5. Map p 116.*

Those who stay at JIA get the VIP treatment, including special access to local clubs.

★ kids Holiday Inn Golden Mile TSIM SHA TSUI While the Holiday Inn's decor includes bland colors and ubiquitous hotel art, its rooms are spacious and the staff is helpful. The hotel also offers some surprisingly good eating and entertainment options: Child-friendly Avenue Restaurant has floor-to-ceiling windows overlooking Nathan and Mody roads, and Hari's at Golden Mile Bar has live music every night. *50 Nathan Rd. ☎ 852/2369-3111; 800/465-4329 in the U.S. and Canada. www.goldenmile-hk.holiday-inn.com. 609 units. Doubles $HK1,520–$HK1,760. AE, DC, MC, V. MTR: Tsim Sha Tsui, exit G. Map p 115.*

★ Hong Kong Bank Foundation SG Davis Hostel LANTAU The main reason to stay at this spotless and very inexpensive hostel is its proximity to the top of Lantau Peak. Located far from both the bustle of Hong Kong's urban centers and the residential areas on Lantau, this place is perfect if you want to hike Lantau Peak in time to watch the sunrise. *Ngong Ping. ☎ 852/2985-5610. www.yha.org.hk. 38 beds and 2 doubles. Double room $HK30–$HK45. MC, V accepted if booking online. Bus: 2 from Mui Wo. Map p 116.*

★ Hotel LKF CENTRAL Lan Kwai Fong is party central, but this elegant hotel is pleasantly subdued. The lobby, with its curved walls and dangling silver disks, is space-age cool. Though rooms aren't enormous, space is maximized with flatscreen TVs and built-in shelves. The bathrooms are huge, perfect for primping for an evening out. The final touch is the illy espresso machine in every room. *33 Wyndham St. ☎ 852/3518-9688. www.hotel-lkf.com.hk. 95 units. Doubles $HK2,088–$HK2,688. AE, DC, MC, V. MTR: Central, exit D2. Map p 116.*

★★★ **Hullett House** TSIM SHA TSUI Opened in 2010, this all-suite boutique hotel takes up the top two floors of the former Marine Police Headquarters building, the lynchpin of the 1881 Heritage development beside Kowloon's Star Ferry pier. The spacious suites are beautifully designed, catering to traditional, eccentric, and artsy sensibilities. Each comes with its own balcony, though water views are blocked by the Hong Kong Culture Centre. The rates are extraordinarily high but the experience really is unique. *2A Canton Rd. ☎ 852/3988-0000. www.hulletthouse.com. 10 units. Doubles from $HK9,000–$HK12,000. AE, DC, MC, V. MTR: Tsim Sha Tsui, exit F. Map p 115.*

★★★ kids **InterContinental Hong Kong** TSIM SHA TSUI You'll be impressed the minute you enter this hotel's modern lobby, which has a glass wall revealing Hong Kong's skyline. Rooms are tastefully designed, with silk bedspreads, Asian artwork, and sunken bathtubs, and most have harbor views. Even for nonguests, it's worth visiting for the dining options, among them the famous French-fusion eatery Spoon. *18 Salisbury Rd. ☎ 852/2721-1211. www.hongkong-ic.intercontinental.com. 495 units. Doubles $HK2,100–$HK3,200. AE, DC, MC, V. MTR: Tsim Sha Tsui, exit F. Map p 115.*

★★★ **Island Shangri-La** ADMIRALTY The Island is all about ostentatious luxury. A massive painting created by 40 Beijing artists hangs in the 17-story atrium while Viennese chandeliers illuminate the lobby and many of the rooms. The large rooms feature marble-topped desks, Chinese lacquerware cabinets, and silk bedspreads. There's a similar sister hotel on Mody Road in Kowloon. *Pacific Place, Supreme Court Rd. ☎ 852/2877-3838; 866/565-5050 in the U.S. www.shangri-la.com. 565 units. Doubles from $HK3,600. AE, DC, MC, V. MTR: Admiralty, exit F. Map p 116.*

★★ **JIA** CAUSEWAY BAY This Philippe Starck–designed hotel is a modernist's dream. The huge rooms have sitting areas separated from sleeping areas by gauzy curtains and marble bathrooms with glass showers and bowl-shaped tubs. The

Rooms at the JW Marriott are designed with right-angle "sawtooth" windows to maximize views.

rooms also feature flat-panel TVs, DVD players, and surround sound. *1–5 Irving St.* ☎ *852/3196-9000. www.jiahongkong.com. 57 units. Doubles $HK1,850–$HK2,150. AE, DC, MC, V. MTR: Causeway Bay, exit F. Map p 116.*

★★ kids **JW Marriott Hong Kong** ADMIRALTY A great place for families, as the rooms are comfortably spacious, and you can rent video game consoles at the front desk. The outdoor pool, with views up toward the Peak, is also a treat. *88 Queensway.* ☎ *852/2810-8366; 888/236-2427 in the U.S. and Canada. www.marriotthotels.com. 602 units. Doubles $HK3,600–$HK4,000. AE, DC, MC, V. MTR: Admiralty, exit F. Map p 116.*

★★★ **Landmark Mandarin Oriental** CENTRAL The trendiest of Mandarin Oriental's three Hong Kong offerings, this hotel features sleek curves and gleaming black marble and metal. The rooms are huge by Hong Kong standards, and use design innovations like floating walls to separate sleeping and sitting areas. Its fine-dining restaurant, Amber, has two Michelin stars (p 83). *15 Queen's Rd.* ☎ *852/2132-0188; 800/526-6566 in the U.S. and Canada. www.mandarinoriental.com/landmark. 113 units. Doubles $HK3,000–$HK4,100. AE, DC, MC, V. MTR: Central, exit G. Map p 116.*

★★★ **Langham Hotel** TSIM SHA TSUI The only Leading Hotels of the World member in Hong Kong, the Langham exudes easy elegance, with a rooftop pool and hand-painted lobby dome. The rooms are a bit on the small side but are well appointed, with gold-plated bathrooms. The hotel is a quick walk from the Star Ferry. *8 Peking Rd.* ☎ *852/2375-1133; 800/223-6800 in the U.S. and Canada. www.langhamhotels.com. 490 units. Single or double $HK2,350–$HK3,800. AE, DC, MC, V. MTR: Tsim Sha Tsui, exit C1. Map p 115.*

★★★ **Langham Place Hotel** MONG KOK Like the mall attached to it, this innovative and modern hotel (not to be confused with the Langham Hotel) stands out in run-down Mong Kok. Standard rooms are stylish, and spa rooms feature Jacuzzi tubs and futon beds. The hotel's best feature may be the views of the teeming streets below. *555 Shanghai St.* ☎ *852/3552-3388. http://hongkong.langhamplacehotels.com. 665 units. Doubles $HK1,400–$HK4,000. AE, DC, MC, V. MTR: Mong Kok, exit C3. Map p 115.*

Bedside control panels allow guests at the Langham to operate everything from the TV to the air-conditioning.

Guests can enjoy the neoclassical charm of the pool at the Mandarin Oriental.

★★ Luxe Manor TSIM SHA TSUI From the moment the medieval wooden swing doors open onto a spangled lobby, you know you're entering an alternative realm. The glam "manor house" style is sprinkled throughout the 159 rooms and, true to its name, the hotel goes into "luxe" overdrive with the six top-floor suites. Travelers overwhelmed by Hong Kong's urbanity will appreciate the Safari Suite, with its rustic wooden floorboards and ceiling lights that twinkle like stars. *39 Kimberley Rd. ☎ 852/3763-8888. www.theluxemanor.com. 159 units. Doubles from $HK1,500. AE, DC, MC, V. MTR: Tsim Sha Tsui, exit B1. Map p 115.*

★★★ Mandarin Oriental CENTRAL This famously posh hotel is the Hong Kong Island equivalent of the Peninsula. Opened in 1963 and fully renovated in 2006, it's nothing much to look at from the outside but has some of the most luxurious rooms in Hong Kong—beds piled high with silk pillows, Chinese lacquer furniture, and flatscreen TVs. With superior service, this is a place for the luxury-loving traditionalist. *5 Connaught Rd. ☎ 852/2522-0111; 800/526-6566 in the U.S. and Canada. www.mandarinoriental.com. 502 units. Doubles $HK2,950–$HK4,200. AE, DC, MC, V. MTR: Central, exit F. Map p 116.*

★ Marco Polo Hong Kong Hotel TSIM SHA TSUI Connected to the Harbour City mall by a walkway, the Marco Polo boasts a great location at the tip of TST. Rooms are subdued but stylish, with large desks, walk-in closets, and generous sitting areas. If you splurge on a luxury harbor view, you're literally on top of the water—ocean liners dock right next to your window. *3 Canton Rd., Harbour City. ☎ 852/2113-0088; 800/448-8355 in the U.S. and Canada. www.marcopolohotels.com. 664 units. Doubles $HK2,050–$HK3,650. AE, DC, MC, V. MTR: Tsim Sha Tsui, exit A1. Map p 115.*

★★ Metropark Hotel CAUSEWAY BAY If you're looking for the conveniences of a modern hotel but want to avoid the thick of the urban jungle, the Metropark is for you. The design is modern and bright with plenty of natural sunlight throughout. Though the rooms are small, they're well designed, with separate sitting and sleeping areas. Ask for a room overlooking Victoria Park. *148 Tung Lo Wan Rd. ☎ 852/2600-1000; 800/223-5652 in the U.S. and Canada. www.metroparkhotel.com. 266 units. Doubles $HK1,260–$HK2,300. AE, DC, MC, V. MTR: Tin Hau, exit B. Map p 116.*

★ The Minden TSIM SHA TSUI Set within a trendy bar enclave, the Minden is somewhere between no-frills and boutique. The tiny lobby is sparsely decked out, while the small rooms display thoughtful touches, like cushy beds and fresh flowers. There's also a funky bar and restaurant. *7 Minden Ave. ☎ 852/2739-7777. www.theminden.com. 64 units. Doubles $HK900–$HK1,200. AE, MC, V. MTR: Tsim Sha Tsui, exit G. Map p 115.*

★★ The Mira TSIM SHA TSUI In itself a major destination for drinkers and diners, the Mira offers a pared-down luxe experience. The striking designer "egg chairs" set the tone in room design, and are complemented by a host of techy touches like Bose iPhone ports, Web-wired radio, and Blu-ray DVD player. *118 Nathan Rd.* ☎ *852/2315-5606. www.themirahotel.com. 492 units. Doubles $HK1,600–$HK1,900. AE, DC, MC, V. MTR: Tsim Sha Tsui, exit B1. Map p 115.*

★★ **Novotel Hong Kong Citygate** LANTAU It's not quite as close to the airport as the older Regal, but this fantastically modern hotel is my pick if you're flying in late or leaving early. Rooms are cleverly designed to create a sense of space and have wonderful views of the new hives of Tung Chung. With regular free shuttle buses making the 5-minute journey to the terminals, it's both comfy and convenient. Given the quality, the room rates are really very reasonable. *50 Man Tung Rd., Tung Chung.* ☎ *852/3602-8888. www.novotel.com. 440 units. Doubles $HK1,000–$HK1,400. AE, DC, MC, V. MTR: Tung Chung, exit C. Map p 115.*

★★★ **The Peninsula** TSIM SHA TSUI The Peninsula lives up to its reputation as one of the best hotels in Asia. Built in the 1920s, it has maintained a classic feel while completely modernizing. The lobby is ornate, as are the rooms, which have dark-wood furnishings, Chinese art, and controls for the TV and radio inlaid into panels by the bed. There's also a stunning indoor pool. It's pricey, but you won't wonder why. *Salisbury Rd.* ☎ *852/2920-2888; 800/462-7899 in the U.S. and Canada. www.peninsula.com. 300 units. Doubles $HK4,200–$HK5,800. AE, DC, MC, V. MTR: Tsim Sha Tsui, exit F. Map p 115.*

★★ kids **Renaissance Harbour View Hotel** WAN CHAI This hotel has a spacious lobby with a lounge and bar overlooking the harbor. The rooms are havens of quiet, with plenty of space to spread out, and even if you don't score a harbor view, you'll overlook lush gardens. There's also an outdoor pool that looks out at the surrounding skyscrapers. Prices are not cheap but tend to comfortably undercut those at the adjacent Grand Hyatt. *1 Harbour Rd.* ☎ *852/2802-8888; 800/228-9290 in the U.S. and Canada. www.renaissancehotels.com. 861 units. $HK2,000–$HK3,700. AE, DC, MC, V. MTR: Wan Chai, exit A5. Map p 116.*

Even the bathrooms at the Peninsula have great views of the city.

The Novotel Hong Kong Citygate features a beautiful outdoor pool and deck.

★★★ **The Ritz-Carlton** WEST KOWLOON Ensconced in the top stories of Hong Kong's tallest building, the Ritz-Carlton takes advantage of its status as the world's highest hotel with floor-to-ceiling windows. As always, Ritz-Carlton delivers spectacular service, but this hotel has to be regarded as a bit special on account of the staggering views. Even the spa, on the 116th floor, takes full advantage. Don't expect to do much relaxing if you have vertigo. *102–118/F, International Commerce Centre, 1 Austin Rd.* ☎ *852/2864-8000; 800/542-8680 in the U.S. and Canada. www.ritzcarlton.com. 312 units. Contact hotel for prices. AE, DC, MC, V. MTR: Kowloon, exit C1. Map p 115.*

★ **Rosedale on the Park** CAUSEWAY BAY The Rosedale is easily the cheapest of the upmarket hotels in Causeway Bay. There's free WiFi in the rooms, free drinks in the fridge when you check in, and even in-house mobile phones that allow you to get calls when you're not in your room. Some rooms have kitchenettes and dining tables, making them feel more like apartments. *8 Shelter St.* ☎ *852/2127-8888; 800/521-5200 in the U.S. and Canada. www.rosedale.com.hk. 274 units. Doubles $HK848–$HK1,248. AE, DC, MC, V. MTR: Causeway Bay, exit F. Map p 116.*

★★ **Royal Garden** TSIM SHA TSUI This small hotel has one of the cooler interiors in Hong Kong. Rooms open onto a 15-story inner atrium modeled after traditional Chinese inner gardens. The rooms are great, too, though you won't get much of a view of the nearby harbor. You will get a mix of modern and colonial furniture, a plasma TV, and a chilled purified water tap in the bathroom. *69 Mody Rd.* ☎ *852/2721-5215; 800/448-8355 in the U.S. www.rghk.com.hk. 419*

Chinese art decorates the walls of the Renaissance Harbour View's lobby.

The inner atrium is one of the big draws at the Royal Garden.

units. Doubles $HK2,300–$HK2,900. AE, DC, MC, V. MTR: Tsim Sha Tsui East, exit P2. Map p 115.

★ kids The Salisbury YMCA TSIM SHA TSUI Don't want to spring for the Peninsula, but envy its location? The Salisbury's simple but spotless rooms are the answer. With a pool, a restaurant, and even a climbing wall, it's good value—and great if you have kids, as you can get larger rooms for less. It's also one of the few hotels in Hong Kong to offer single bedrooms. *41 Salisbury Rd. ☎ 852/2268-7000. www.ymcahk.org.hk. 363 units. Doubles $HK850–$HK1,100. AE, DC, MC, V. MTR: Tsim Sha Tsui, exit F. Map p 115.*

★★★ Sheraton Hong Kong Hotel TSIM SHA TSUI The modern rooms here feature marble bathrooms and plush bedding, and extras include a year-round, rooftop swimming pool. The Sheraton doesn't have the history of the Peninsula or the fun surprises of the InterContinental, but it's a bit cheaper and still offers luxury and convenience. *20 Nathan Rd. ☎ 852/2369-1111; 800/462-7899 in the U.S. and Canada. www.sheraton.com/hongkong. 782 units. Doubles $HK2,300–$HK2,900. AE, DC, MC, V. MTR: Tsim Sha Tsui, exit F. Map p 115.*

★ Stanford Hillview Hotel TSIM SHA TSUI This intimate hotel manages to provide the best of both worlds in terms of location. It's in the heart of bustling Tsim Sha Tsui, but it stands slightly apart, under some banyan trees in a quiet spot on a hill next to the Royal Observatory. The rooms are small and basic—most have twin beds—but the staff is friendly and the vibe here is far more laid-back than elsewhere in this increasingly posh neighborhood. There's a small kitchen for guests to use. Prices are often easier to negotiate than at the internationally branded establishments. *13–17 Observatory Rd. ☎ 852/2722-7822. www.stanfordhillview.com. 177 units. $HK1,480–$HK2,080. AE, DC, MC, V. MTR: Tsim Sha Tsui, exit B2. Map p 115.* ●

10 The Best Day Trips & Excursions

Macau

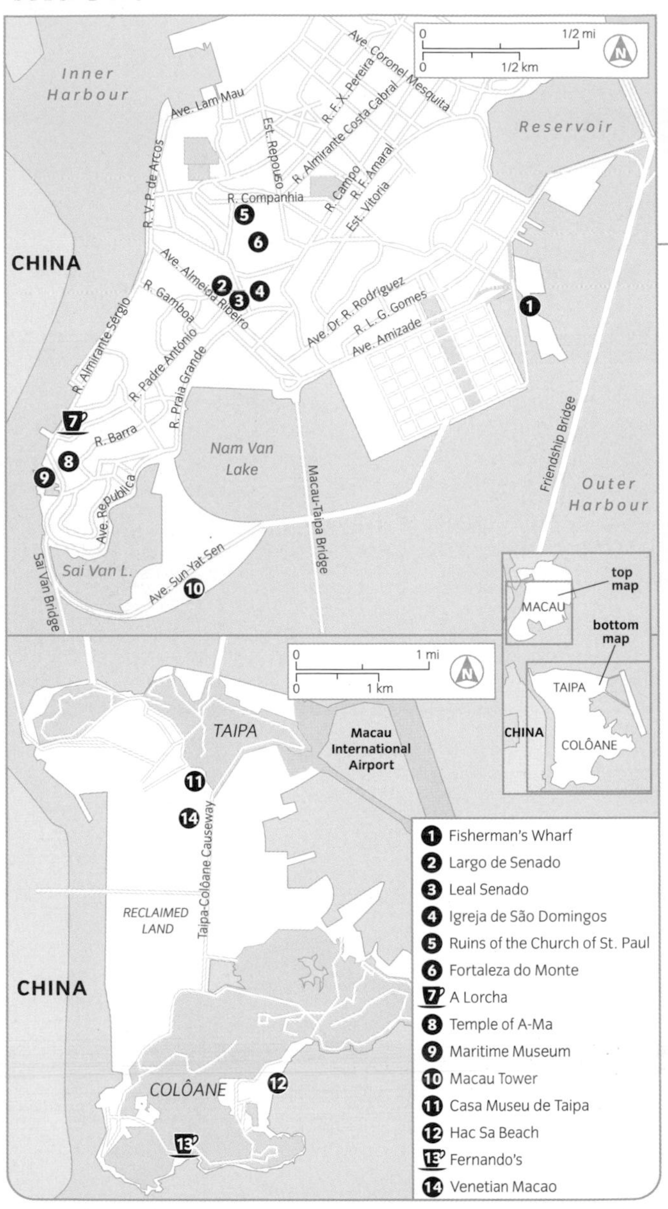

Previous page: Buddha, as carved into a rock wall in Shenzhen.

Macau's turbocharged development has transformed this pocket-size peninsula into the world's biggest gambling den. More money changes hands here than in Las Vegas, but there is more to this tiny area than supersized casinos. Portugal ruled the roost until 1999 and this colonial heritage is seen in Macao's architecture and excellent food. There are nice beaches on the conjoined "islands" of Taipa and Coloane. Macau is less than an hour away from Hong Kong by ferry, which means you can spend a full day and evening here and be back home before bedtime. **START: Macau Ferry Pier, Central.**

1 ★ kids Fisherman's Wharf. Located right beside the ferry terminal, this multimillion-dollar theme park features a giant Ferris wheel, roller coasters, a 40m-tall (131-ft.) flame-erupting volcano, and, of course, a casino. The "culture" comes in the form of the replica architecture, drawn from four continents, which houses restaurants and brand stores. Consider skipping if you haven't got kids. ⌚ *2 hr. Avenida Dr., Sun Yat-Sen. www.fishermanswharf.com.mo. Free admission; rides ticketed individually. Daily 24 hr. Bus: 1A, 3, 3A, 8, 10, 10A, 10B, 17, 28A, 28B, 28BX, 28C, or 32.*

2 ★★★ Largo de Senado (Senate Square). Florid 18th-century colonial buildings now house Western outlets like Starbucks

The vibrantly colored buildings in Macau's Largo de Senado are a remnant of the Portuguese influence here.

Getting There

Even though Macau is part of China, you must have your passport with you to buy a ticket. Two ferry terminals service Macau in Hong Kong: one in Sheung Wan and the other in Tsim Sha Tsui. Sheung Wan (200 Connaught Rd.) is most convenient, with ferries leaving every 15 minutes during the day and at slightly longer intervals throughout the night. I suggest taking the TurboJET, which takes only 55 minutes (☎ 852/2859-3333; www.turbojet.com.hk; one-way fares Mon–Fri $HK236 for super class, $HK134 for economy class; Sat–Sun $HK252 and $HK146; both fares rise on weekends and during the night).

Pedicabs, like this one parked outside the Leal Senado, were a common form of transportation in Macau until the 1980s.

and the Body Shop in Macau's central square. Though distracting, the multinationals don't completely spoil the delightful architectural mélange. There's also a useful information booth for visitors. ⌚ *45 min. Avenida de Almedia Ribeiro. Bus: 3, 3A, 4, 5, 7, 8, 10, 10A, 10B, 11, 21, 21A, 26, 26A, or 33.*

❸ ★ **Leal Senado (Loyal Senate).** Built in the 1780s beside the Largo de Senado, the Leal Senado was the seat of the Portuguese colonial government. Today it houses the offices of the mayor. Inside is an art gallery with historical paintings of Macau, as well as the ornately furnished Senate Library. The garden at the back is small but beautifully landscaped, with a bronze bust of Luis de Camoes, the 14th-century Portuguese poet. ⌚ *30 min. 163 Avenida de Almedia Ribeiro. Free admission. Gallery Tues–Sun 9am–9pm; library Mon–Sat 1–7pm. Bus: 3, 3A, 4, 5,7, 8, 10, 10A, 10B, 11, 21, 21A, 26, 26A, or 33.*

❹ ★ **Igreja de São Domingos (Church of St. Dominic).** This striking yellow church dates back to the 17th century. Serried pews face a majestic altar where a crucifix hangs. The upper floors house the Tesouraria de Arte Sacra (Treasury of Sacred Art), which has religious paraphernalia from the start of the missionary era, including clerical vestments, bronze church bells, and statues of saints. Downstairs an exhibit details the construction of the church. ⌚ *30 min. Largo de São Domingos.* ☎ *853/2836-7706. Church daily 8am–6pm; Tesouraria de Arte Sacra daily 10am–6pm. Bus: 3, 3A, 4, 5, 7, 8, 10, 10A, 10B, 11, 21, 21A, 26, 26A, or 33.*

❺ ★★★ **Ruins of the Church of St. Paul.** Although only the facade of this late-17th-century baroque cathedral remains, it remains the grandest sight in Macau, sitting atop a large stone staircase and overlooking the city below. Designed by an Italian Jesuit and constructed by exiled Japanese Christians, it was the largest Catholic Church in Asia before being decimated by a typhoon in 1835. ⌚ *20 min. Rua de São Paulo.* ☎ *853/2835-8444. Museum daily 9am–6pm. Bus: 8A, 17, 18, 19, or 26.*

A detail from the facade of the Igreja de São Domingos (Church of St. Dominic).

The front wall is all that remains standing of the Church of St. Paul.

❻ ★★ **Fortaleza do Monte (Monte Forte).** The walls of this fort formed the boundaries of the original Portuguese settlement in Macau in the early 1600s. The colonial government's military was based here until 1966. Today, the fort offers wonderful views of Macau from behind old cannons and parapets. It also houses the Macau Museum, which gives a detailed history of the territory in slides and photographs. ⌚ *45 min. 112 Praceta do Museu de Macau.* ☎ *853/2835-7911. www.macaumuseum.gov.mo. Admission $HK15 adults, $HK8 kids. Tues–Sun 10am–6pm. Bus: 8A, 17, 18, 19, or 26.*

7 ★★ **A Lorcha.** The Portuguese food at this small, whitewashed restaurant is superb, with dishes such as codfish in a cream sauce, baked minced beef potato pie, and chargrilled king prawns. Its name refers to a Portuguese junk or sailboat, which is fitting considering its proximity to the ocean. *289A Rua do Almirante Sergio.* ☎ *853/2831-3193. $$.*

❽ ★★ **Temple of A-Ma.** This is Macau's oldest Chinese temple, with some parts dating back more than 600 years. It is dedicated to A-Ma, the Chinese goddess of seafarers, and has a large boulder in front with a colored relief of a *lorcha,* a traditional sailing junk. Midway up the stone steps you'll find an altar for burning incense and praying to A-Ma. ⌚ *45 min. Rua de Sao Tiago da Barra. Daily 6:30am–6pm. Bus: 1, 1A, 2, 5, 6, 7, 9, 10, 10A, 11, 18, 21, 21A, 28B, or 34.*

❾ ★★ **Maritime Museum.** This museum showcases Macau's long relationship with the sea. You'll find an exhibit using replicas of boats to show how fishermen worked and lived and a maritime history section that illustrates the routes explorers took to reach Macau. ⌚ *45 min. Rua de Sao Tiago da Barra.* ☎ *853/2859-9548. Admission $HK10 adults, $HK5 kids 10–17, free for children 9 and under. Tues–Sat 10:30am–5:30pm.*

❿ ★★ **Macau Tower.** There's a strong Kiwi connection at this 338m-high (1,109-ft.) landmark. It was designed by the same team behind

Fireworks hang at the Temple of A-Ma.

Diners dig in at Fernando's, which sits right on the beach at Hac Sa.

Auckland's Sky Tower and there are also a variety of heart-stopping sky walks and bungee rope–assisted rides by New Zealand's most famous son, thrill-seeker extraordinaire A. J. Hackett. Two observation decks offer fine views across low-rise Macau. ⌚ ***90 min. Largo da Torre de Macau.*** ☎ ***853/2893-3339. Admission to 58/F Observation Lounge $HK100 adults, $HK50 kids 10–17, free for children 9 and under. Bus: 9A, 23, or 32.***

⑪ ★★ Casa Museu da Taipa (Taipa Houses Museum). Built in the early 1920s for several wealthy Macanese families, this collection of colonial-style buildings is now a museum that offers real insight into Macau's colonial past. There are period paintings, furniture, and personal artifacts on display. ⌚ ***30 min. Avenida da Praia, Taipa.*** ☎ ***853/2882-7088. Admission $HK5. Tues–Sun 10am–6pm. Bus: 11, 22, 28A, 30, 33, or 34.***

⑫ ★ Hac Sa Beach. A small black-sand beach beside the South China Sea, Hac Sa is a great place for a break. There's a recreation center with a swimming pool, minigolf, badminton courts, and jet skis for hire. ⌚ ***2 hr. Coloane Village. Bus: 21A or 26A.***

13 ★★★ Fernando's. This unpretentious seaside eatery does fantastic Portuguese fare: Try the charcoal-grilled chicken or the Portuguese chorizo, codfish, and mussels. The bread comes from the restaurant's own bakery and the vegetables are from its garden across the border in China. ***9 Praia de Hac Sa, Coloane.*** ☎ ***853/2888-2264. $$.***

An altar at a temple in Taipa, a formerly sleepy island recently transformed by development.

If you're looking for the ultimate gambling experience, head to the Venetian Macao.

⑭ ★★★ **Venetian Macao.** The biggest casino in the world takes Vegas glitz to a whole new level. There are 3,000 suites, 800 gaming tables spread over four zones, a huge concert hall, and a life-size canal right in the middle of the building. Macau's other 27 casinos are not exactly small, but in terms of in-your-face ostentation, this takes the prize. 🕘 *2 hr. Estrada da Baía de N. Senhora da Esperança, Taipa.* ☎ *853/2882-8888. www.venetianmacao.com.*

Where to Stay

★★ Hotel Guia MACAU PENINSULA If you're looking for a quiet retreat at a reasonable price, this lovely hotel is it. Surrounded by traditional colonial architecture, the Hotel Guia sits on the slope of Guia Hill, below the Guia Fort and Lighthouse. The staff is warm and helpful and the rooms are spotless (ask for a room with a view of the lighthouse and harbor). You're a bit far from the roar of Macau's nightlife, but that's not necessarily a bad thing. *Estrada do Engenheiro Trigo, 1–5.* ☎ *853/2851-3888. www.hotelguia-macau.com. 90 units. Doubles $HK880–$HK1,080. Bus: 28C.*

★★ Pousada de Sao Tiago MACAU PENINSULA Built around the ruins of the Portuguese Fortress da Barra, which dates to 1629, this dramatic beach hotel has a secluded, romantic feel. Little wonder, then, that's it's such a popular wedding destination. The rooms are filled with ornately carved Portuguese furniture, and almost all have balconies overlooking the sea. *Avenida Da Republica, Fortaleza de Sao Tiago da Barra.* ☎ *853/2837-8111. www.saotiago.com.mo. 24 units. Doubles $HK2,600–$HK3,200. Bus: 28B.*

★★★ Pousada de Mong Ha MACAU PENINSULA This is a wonderful hotel for the price. Run by the Instituto de Formacao Turistica (Institute for Tourism Studies), the setting is pleasant and quiet, the staff attentive, and the rooms cozy. *Colina de Mong Ha.* ☎ *853/2851-5222. www.ift.edu.mo/pousada/eng/enchantment.htm. 20 units. Doubles $HK600–$HK800. Bus: 12.*

Shenzhen

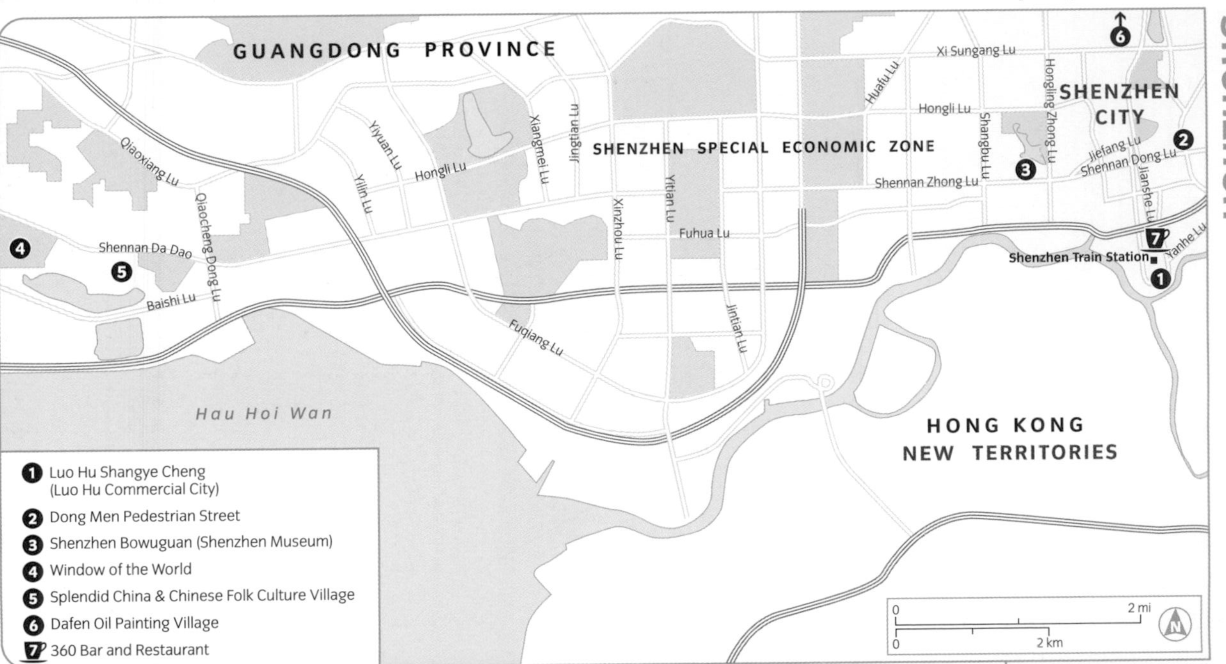
GUANGDONG PROVINCE
SHENZHEN CITY
SHENZHEN SPECIAL ECONOMIC ZONE
HONG KONG NEW TERRITORIES
Hau Hoi Wan
Xi Sungang Lu
Huafu Lu
Hongli Lu
Hongling Zhong Lu
Shangbu Lu
Jiefang Lu
Shennan Dong Lu
Jianshe Lu
Yanhe Lu
Shennan Zhong Lu
Shenzhen Train Station
Jingtian Lu
Xiangmei Lu
Yiyuan Lu
Yilin Lu
Xinzhou Lu
Yitian Lu
Fuhua Lu
Jintian Lu
Fuqiang Lu
Qiaoxiang Lu
Qiaocheng Dong Lu
Shennan Da Dao
Baishi Lu
0
2 mi
0
2 km
1 Luo Hu Shangye Cheng (Luo Hu Commercial City)
2 Dong Men Pedestrian Street
3 Shenzhen Bowuguan (Shenzhen Museum)
4 Window of the World
5 Splendid China & Chinese Folk Culture Village
6 Dafen Oil Painting Village
7 360 Bar and Restaurant

For communist China, Shenzhen was the capitalist test-tube experiment that rather outgrew the lab. It's almost impossible to believe that in the early 1980s this sea of glittering high-rises was a down-and-out border town. China's richest city is now a major destination for Hong Kong tourists who want to get a taste of mainland China, and do some discount (or counterfeit) shopping. Bear in mind you'll need a visa and you must change your Hong Kong dollars for Chinese yuan (see "Getting There," below). **START: Lo We Border Crossing.**

❶ ★★ Luo Hu Shangye Cheng (Luo Hu Commercial City). This multilevel shopping center, located just beside the border control building, is loaded with stalls and shops selling everything from purses to massages to pirated DVDs. There are some great deals to be had but steel yourself before you go in, as sellers can be aggressive. Unlike Hong Kong, every price is negotiable. 🕘 *1 hr. Metro: Luoho, exit A. Daily 8:30am–11:30pm.*

❷ ★★ Dong Men Pedestrian Street. The heart of "old" Shenzhen is now a frenetic shopping zone where history takes a firm backseat to the relentless pursuit of profit. Retail here is sport, with haggling merchants and tailors competing for your cash. Always try on clothing before buying, as Chinese cuts often mean short sleeves for men and tiny waists for women. 🕘 *2 hr. North of Shennan Dong Lu, Luohu District. Metro: Luojie.*

❸ Shenzhen Bowuguan (Shenzhen Museum). While it can't compete with China's more famous museums, Shenzhen Museum has a fascinating—if slightly politicized—exhibition of Shenzhen's development from crumbling backwater to mighty metropolis on the third floor. Check out the pair of before-and-after shots in Exhibition Room 8, which prove that, as always, McDonald's got there first. 🕘 *30 min. Lizhi Gongyuan, Futian District (entrance off Shennan Zhong Lu). ☎ 755/8210-1044. Free admission. Tues–Sun 9am–5pm. Metro: Ke Xue Guan.*

Not an inch of advertising space is wasted at Luo Hu Shangye Cheng.

A miniature Taj Mahal is just one of the oddities found at Window of the World.

4 Window of the World. This park is worth visiting not so much for its intended purpose—to wow you with its replicas of the world's great tourist sites—but as a revealing look at China tourism's love of kitsch. You'll find a 108m-tall (354-ft.) Eiffel Tower, an Egyptian pyramid, and the Taj Mahal. Live shows throughout the day celebrate various world cultures. ⏱ *1 hr. Overseas Chinese Town, Nanshan District.* ☎ *755/2660-8000. Adults $HK120. Mon–Fri 9am–9pm; Sat–Sun 9am–10:30pm. Metro: Shi Ji Zhi Chuang. Bus: 20, 21, 26, 204, 209, 210, 222, 223, 101, 105, 113, 301, 310, 311, 320, 324, 328, 329, or 370.*

5 Splendid China & Chinese Folk Culture Village. This park is designed to show that Han-dominated China respects its

Getting There

You'll need a visa to visit Shenzhen. For the cheapest deal, go directly to the China visa office (7/F, 26 Harbour Rd., Wan Chai; ☎ 852/3413-2424). You'll need to queue and allow 3 days for processing. You can speed things up with an express service, or pay any number of agents to do the job for you (well worth the premium if time is tight). The China Travel Service (C.T.S. House, 78–83 Connaught Rd., Central; ☎ 852/2853-3888; www.ctshk.com/english/index.htm) offers a number of organized tours, though getting to Shenzhen by yourself is incredibly easy on the MTR. Simply head to Lo Wu and follow the crowds. This is the world's busiest border crossing so expect to spend some time waiting in line. Once in Shenzhen, you'll need to use mainland China's currency, the Renminbi, known colloquially as the yuan. It's worth around 10% more than the Hong Kong dollar. There are money exchanges at the border as well as ATMs.

large population of ethnic minority groups despite evidence the feeling is not always mutual (there were notable uprisings in Tibet in 2008 and in Xinjiang in 2009). The exhibits tend to caricature these "simple, honest" minorities. Still, you'll get some idea of China's varied population, with exhibits showing the wardrobes, rituals, and songs of 56 different ethnic groups. *1 hr. Overseas Chinese Town, Nanshan District. 755/2692-6808. Adults $HK120. Mon–Fri 10am–10:30pm; Sat–Sun 10am–8pm. Metro: Shi Ji Zhi Chuang. Bus: 20, 21, 26, 204, 209, 210, 222, 223, 101, 105, 113, 301, 310, 311, 320, 324, 328, 329, or 370.*

Models of China's famous terra-cotta warriors are on display at Splendid China & Chinese Folk Culture Village.

5 Dafen Oil Painting Village. If you think copying movies is wrong, you'll want to skip Dafen, where hundreds of artists duplicate classic Western paintings ranging from works by van Gogh to Miró. Luckily, they also do some original work that is worth checking out. *2 hr. B-930, ZhenYe Building, Bao'an Lu, Longgang District. 755/2586-3235. www.chinae.com.cn. Taxi.*

6 ★★ 360 Bar and Restaurant. The views from the top of this luxury hotel are top-notch, ditto for the cuisine, to say nothing of the wine list and traditional decor. The restaurant serves a wide variety of food, mainly European but with a few Asian specialties on the menu. *31–32/F, Shangri-la Shenzhen, 1002 Jianshe Lu, Luohu District. 755/8396-1380. $$$.*

An artist is hard at work on a copy of a Miró painting at the Dafen Oil Painting Village.

Lamma

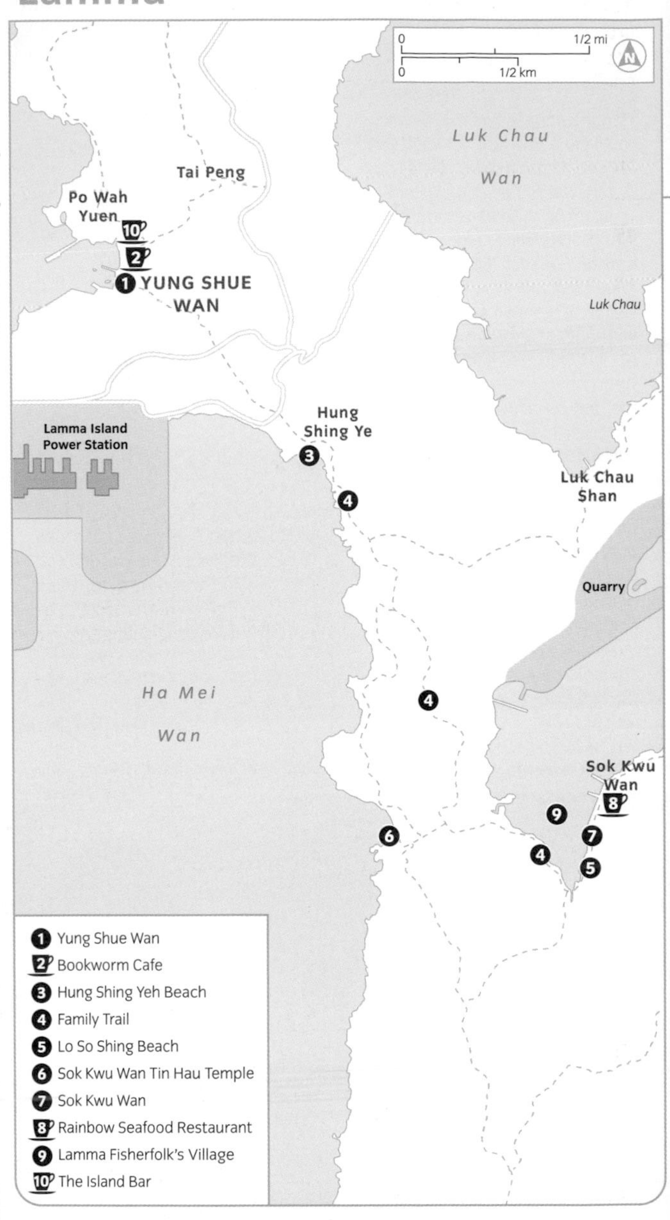
0
1/2 mi
0
1/2 km
N
Luk Chau
Wan
Tai Peng
Po Wah
Yuen
YUNG SHUE
WAN
Luk Chau
Hung
Shing Ye
Lamma Island
Power Station
Luk Chau
Shan
Quarry
Ha Mei
Wan
Sok Kwu
Wan
1 Yung Shue Wan
2 Bookworm Cafe
3 Hung Shing Yeh Beach
4 Family Trail
5 Lo So Shing Beach
6 Sok Kwu Wan Tin Hau Temple
7 Sok Kwu Wan
8 Rainbow Seafood Restaurant
9 Lamma Fisherfolk's Village
10 The Island Bar

Lamma, one of the largest but least populated of Hong Kong's 260 islands, feels light years away from the hubbub of urban life. Lamma is largely undeveloped (there are no cars on the island), but there are two main villages, connected by a lovely 90-minute hike. Slow- and high-speed ferries stop at both villages, so I suggest heading to Yung Shue Wan and then walking to Sok Kwu Wan for dinner before catching a ride back to Hong Kong. **START: Yung Shue Wan Pier.**

1 Yung Shue Wan. The most inhabited part of Lamma, Yung Shue Wan, or "Banyan Tree Bay," has a cluster of shops, restaurants, bars, and a few small hotels, all catering to tourists. There's a laid-back vibe here—a pleasing reminder that Hong Kong is not all banks and skyscrapers. Stroll the winding streets and enjoy the shops before heading to tiny Tin Hau Temple, on the water's edge. Tin Hau is the goddess of the sea. This temple was built more than 150 years ago, and it is still used for prayer by locals. *2 hr. www.lamma.com.hk. Ferry: Pier 4 from Central; fast and slow ferries run all day.*

The **2 Bookworm Cafe** is a real find. Located beyond the more touristy seafood places, this vegetarian restaurant is the informal meeting place for the island's large expat community. It's easy to see why: A range of books and magazines lines the walls of the small dining room, the menu is eclectic (everything from pancakes to vegetarian lasagna), and there's even an outdoor terrace. *79 Main St. ☎ 852/2982-4838. $$.*

3 Hung Shing Yeh Beach. This is Lamma's most popular beach, thanks mostly to its proximity to town. Though the island's power station smokestacks do intrude on the otherwise stunning view of the ocean and surrounding hills, the beach has a lot to offer. It's broad enough to accommodate the crowds that gather here on hot days, and it's kept spotlessly clean. A nearby beach resort offers drinks, and there are free showers and changing rooms. *1 hr.*

4 Family Trail. At the far end of Hung Shing Yeh Beach, you'll see a modern pagoda overlooking the South China Sea. That's the entrance to the slightly hilly, paved trail that will take you to the other side of the island. The walk takes about 90 minutes, and along the way, you'll climb to the top of a barren hill before descending through

Fishing boats dominate the sleepy harbor at Yung Shue Wan on Lamma.

Worshipers light thick sticks of incense at the Sok Kwu Wan Temple.

lush banana groves. You'll get some excellent views of the island and gorgeous glimpses of the ocean. The hike is not particularly strenuous but can be trying on a hot day, so bring water. *90 min.*

5 Lo So Shing Beach. This beach is truly a gem. It's one of the least populated beaches around—enjoy the solitude while you can. The beach is small, but there are lifeguards and changing rooms. If you want a break from the sun, head for the back of the beach, where the surrounding trees provide plenty of cooling shade. *2 hr.*

6 Sok Kwu Wan Tin Hau Temple. Near the end of Family Trail, you'll come to the 150-year-old Sok Kwu Wan Tin Hau Temple—yet another temple dedicated to the goddess of the sea. Locals often gather out front to play mahjong or Chinese chess. The original building was destroyed by a fire in 2004, but it has since been reconstructed. The new building contains a bell and altar from the original. *20 min.*

7 Sok Kwu Wan. This long pier is crammed with open-air restaurants serving fresh fish, abalone, and shrimp and lobsters caught in local waters. The seafood is typically prepared Cantonese style—meaning lots of garlic and ginger, and accompanying bowls of steamed rice. Prepare a few polite refusals for the touts who will inevitably try to entice you into their restaurants, though feel free to have a peek at tanks of live seafood. *30 min.*

8 Rainbow Seafood Restaurant. The largest open-air restaurant on Sok Kwu Kan's waterfront also happens to have one of the best views of the harbor. There's an English-language menu with plenty of pictures of its main dishes, and the food is excellent—specialties include grilled lobster and fried crab with ginger and scallions. Best of all, the restaurant offers a free ferry service back to Central and Tsim Sha Tsui—be sure you make a reservation. To locate it, look for the whirling ceiling fans and red lanterns out front. *23–25 1st St., Sok Kwu Wan.* ☎ *852/2982-8100. www.rainbowrest.com.hk. $$.*

Seafood doesn't get any fresher than at the markets and restaurants along the piers at Sok Kwu Wan.

❾ **Lamma Fisherfolk's Village.** Sok Kwu Wan's harbor is home to Hong Kong's largest fleet of fish-breeding rafts, some of which also support family homes. This floating "village," reached by shuttle from the public pier, consists of moorings, fish-breeding rafts, and displays relating to local fisherfolk culture. There's even a 60-year-old junk you can explore. 🕘 *90 min. Sok Kwu Wan Harbor.* ☎ *852/2982-8585. www.fisherfolks.com.hk. Admission, including shuttle, $HK40 (for 2 hr.).*

10 The Island Bar. To hang out with Lamma locals, head to this longtime bar and gweilo (foreign) hangout. It's located next to Man Fung Restaurant on the waterfront, about a minute's walk from the ferry pier. Owned by expats living in Yung Shue Wan, it's a cozy place to play darts while you wait for the ferry out. *6 Yung Shue Wan Main St., Yung Shue Wan.* ☎ *852/2982-1376.*

Lamma's gorgeous coastline offers views stretching to Hung Shing Yeh Beach.

Peng Chau

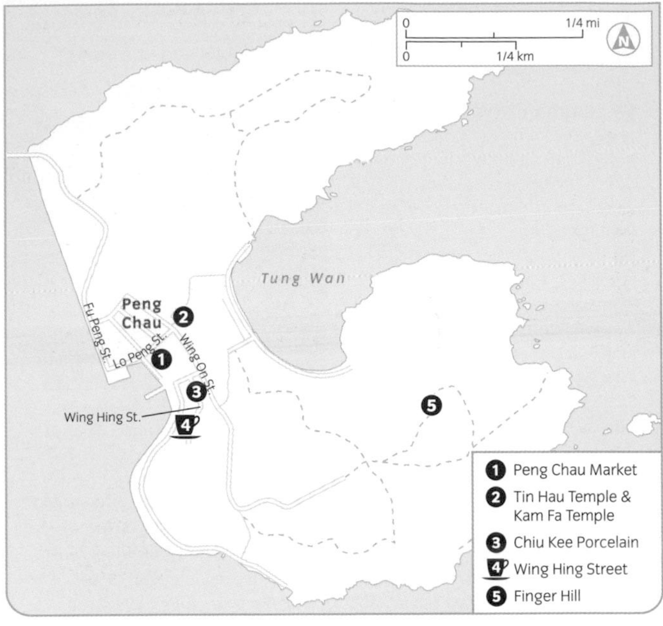

Peng Chau is a tiny island that draws only modest numbers of visitors. What it lacks in standout tourist attractions it makes up for in cheap seafood restaurants and a get-away-from-it-all atmosphere. That isn't to say it's completely quiet: As always in Hong Kong, the fish markets are lively and the clatter of mahjong tiles will likely guide you back to civilization if ever you get lost. **START: Peng Chau Pier.**

1 ★ Peng Chau Market. You've likely already visited a wet market during your time in Hong Kong, but the proximity of the sea makes this one feel more authentic than anything back in the city proper. In addition to the live fish, you can find fresh fruits and vegetables, and plenty of cooking spices and herbs. ⏱ *1 hr. Ferry: Pier 5 from Central; fast and slow ferries run all day.*

2 ★★ Tin Hau Temple and Kam Fa Temple. The Tin Hau Temple was built in 1792 and is, like most such places in Hong Kong, an active place for prayer. But this pretty little temple has something the others don't: a 2m (6½-ft.) whale bone, blackened by incense smoke, which serves as an offering to the gods in return for keeping the island's inhabitants safe and prosperous. Nearby is the smaller, less

A traditional Chinese junk is moored in Peng Chau's harbor.

colorful Kam Fa Temple. Kam Fa is a goddess who is said to have learned kung fu in order to steal from the rich and give to the poor. *45 min.*

3 Chiu Kee Porcelain. Chiu Kee Porcelain is said to be the only hand-painted porcelain factory left in Hong Kong (the porcelain industry once dominated this region, but it is now based on the mainland). The owner, Lam Hon-chiu, came here from mainland China during the Communist purges of 1957, and though he no longer paints the teapots, cups, and plates for sale here himself, his wife continues the tradition. *45 min. Shop 7, Wing Hing St. ☎ 852/2983-0917.*

The lack of tourists means there aren't all that many eating options on Peng Chau. The small main village contains a number of small, unpretentious restaurants. Wander along waterfront **4 Wing Hing Street,** or Wing On Street, which runs through the middle of the village, and take your pick. Whether or not you're food hunting, it's worth exploring these streets and soaking up the local atmosphere.

5 ★★★ Finger Hill. At 95m (312 ft.), this is the highest point on the island. A trail takes you to the top, where a small pavilion offers a place to sit and admire the views. You'll see the ocean, the island, and the western edge of Hong Kong Island. *2 hr.*

A Chinese fisherwoman carries her bundles the old-fashioned way as she walks up a wooden gangplank.

Cheung Chau

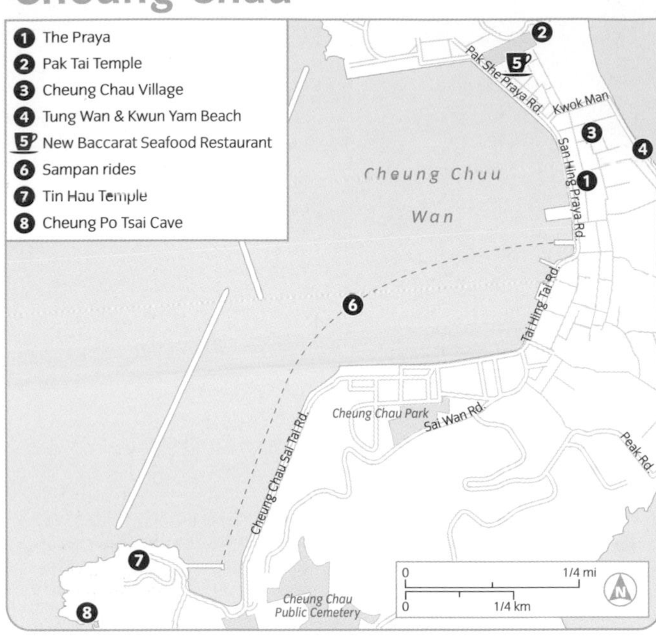

Once a refuge for pirates, Cheung Chau is now a favorite getaway for both city day-trippers and tourists. The main village is a warren of narrow lanes where you'll get a real feel for rural Cantonese life. There are no cars, but the island is easy to walk or bike around. **START: Cheung Chau Ferry Pier.**

1 The Praya. Alarm bells may ring as you exit the ferry to be greeted by McDonald's and big-brand convenience stores, but relax. The Praya, a harborside promenade, is the only place on Cheung Chau with this kind of Western atmosphere. It's also the best spot to rent bikes. Wander north and enjoy the views of the busy fishing harbor. *1 hr. 852/2131-8181. www.cheungchau.org. Ferry: Pier 5 from Central; fast and slow ferries run all day.*

2 Pak Tai Temple. Built in 1783, this large temple is the focus of the Bun Festival in late April or May, which features a 15m-high (49-ft.) tower of steamed buns. The temple is dedicated to Pak Tai, Taoist god of the sea and "Supreme Emperor of the Dark Heaven." He's actually a peace-loving god and not nearly as scary as he sounds. Inside is a 1,000-year-old iron sword nearly 2m (6½ ft.) long found by local fishermen. Statues of generals Thousand Miles Eye and Favorable Wind Ear,

Sticks of incense burn in a stone urn outside the Pak Tai Temple.

whose combined powers are said to be able to guard against any attack, stand at the altar. ⌚ *30 min. Pak She St.*

❸ **Cheung Chau Village.** The narrow, winding streets of this village are filled with shops selling medicinal herbs, fish, and other local goods. Watch for homes with small altars open to the street—families leave offerings to their ancestors in exchange (they hope) for good luck. My advice is to just wander for a bit, mingling with locals and enjoying a scene very different from that of downtown Hong Kong. ⌚ *1 hr.*

❹ **Tung Wan and Kwun Yam Wan Beaches.** Cheung Chau's main beach at Tung Wan is easily accessible from the village. Beyond the landmark Warwick Hotel is another, smaller beach, Kwun Yam Wan, which is a prime windsurfing spot. If you want to give it a try, the Cheung Chau Windsurfing Centre rents boards and offers lessons. Lee Lai-shan, Hong Kong's first Olympic gold medalist, learned the sport here. ⌚ *2 hr. Cheung Chau Windsurfing Centre.* ☎ *852/2981-8316. Rentals start at $HK110 for 2 hr.*

❺ **New Baccarat Seafood Restaurant.** This open-air restaurant sits at the end of the Praya and has a view of the harbor. It's run by a fishing family and has tanks of live sea creatures on display, so you know the fish is fresh. Try the steamed fish or the garlic prawns. *9A Pak She Praya Rd.* ☎ *852/2981-0606. $$.*

Paper lanterns for sale in Cheung Chau Village.

6 Sampan Ride. Though it's easily walkable, the best way to visit the southwestern corner of the island is by taking a *kai do,* or water taxi. The trip usually lasts 10 minutes or so and costs only $HK5. Departures are from Cheung Chau Ferry Pier. If you want a longer ride or you'd like to see some of the fishing junks up close, negotiate a price with your driver. ***30 min. Praya St.***

7 Tin Hau Temple. This temple, located just off the ferry pier, isn't much different from the many temples around Hong Kong dedicated to Tin Hau, goddess of the sea and protector of fishermen and women, but it's a lovely place to absorb the island's quiet calm. ***15 min. Tsan Tuen Rd.***

8 Cheung Po Tsai Cave. Legend has it that 19th-century pirate Cheung Po Tsai once commanded 600 junks and a gang of 4,000 men. He terrorized the seas until 1810, when he surrendered to the Chinese government and became (what else?) an official. But he first hid his treasure, perhaps near this cave that he used as a hiding place. If you're interested in spelunking, consider that the cave requires patience and a lack of claustrophobia as you inch your way through its very tight spaces. Bring a flashlight and be careful as the rocks can be slippery. ***45 min. Cheung Po Tsai Rd.***

There are no cars on Cheung Chau, so bikes are the main mode of transportation.

The
Savvy Traveler

Before You Go

Government Tourist Offices

IN THE U.S.: 115 E. 54th St., 2/F, New York, NY 10022-4512 (☎ 212/421-3382); 5670 Wilshire Blvd., Ste. 1230, Los Angeles, CA 90036 (☎ 323/938-4582). **IN CANADA:** 9 Temperance St., G/F, Toronto, Ontario M5H 1Y6 (☎ 416/366-2389). **IN THE UK:** 6 Grafton St., London W1S 4EQ (☎ 020/7533-7100). **IN AUSTRALIA:** Hong Kong House, Level 4, 80 Druitt St., Sydney, NSW 2000 (☎ 02/9283-3083).

The Best Times to Go

It's best to visit Hong Kong in the autumn or spring when temperatures are warm but rarely extreme. Summers are hot, humid, and quite uncomfortable, though air-conditioning is ubiquitous. It's wise to book ahead no matter when you go as conferences and mainland Chinese tourists keep the city busy year-round. If you can, avoid dates around May Day, National Day (Oct 1), and Chinese New Year (Jan or Feb) when the SAR floods with mainland tourists.

Festivals & Special Events

SPRING. The **Hong Kong Rugby World Cup Sevens** (☎ 852/2504-8311; www.hksevens.com.hk) is a major expat event—and a major excuse for beer drinking. Teams (and their supporters) come from around the world to play. The **Man Hong Kong International Literary Festival** (www.festival.org.hk) is one of the biggest literary events in Asia (though it's still not all that big). Novelists, short-story writers, and poets from around the world give talks and readings. During the 1-night-only **Hong Kong ArtWalk** (☎ 852/2854-1018; www.hongkongartwalk.com), more than 60 galleries are open to the public. The **Ching Ming Festival** (☎ 852/2508-1234; www.discoverhongkong.com) in March or April is a time to honor one's ancestors by ritually sweeping graves and picnicking. The **Hong Kong International Film Festival** (☎ 852/2970-3300; www.hkiff.org.hk) is held in March and/or April and lures a plethora of local and international films (and film stars) to the city. The **Birthday of Tin Hau** honors the patroness of sailors at the many Tin Hau temples in Hong Kong and takes place in April or May (☎ 852/2508-1234; www.discoverhongkong.com). The **Cheung Chau Bun Festival** is held in late April or May on Cheung Chau, and culminates with an extraordinary race up a tall tower of steamed buns (☎ 852/2508-1234; www.discoverhongkong.com). Though you won't see that many signs of the **Birthday of Lord Buddha** in May, there are some interesting rituals and festivities around the Po Lin Monastery on Lantau (☎ 852/2508-1234; www.discoverhongkong.com).

SUMMER. In June you can see (and even join) teams racing long "dragon boats" in the waters around Hong Kong during the **Dragon Boat Races,** part of the **Tuen Ng Festival** (☎ 852/2508-1234; www.discoverhongkong.com). The final race is held in Stanley. During the 2-week-long **Yue Laan Festival**—the Festival of the Hungry Ghost—in July or August, you'll see people burning paper money and votives in the shapes of things like cars and houses. These offerings are to appease restless spirits who are

Previous page: Bank of China and Queensgate Road at night.

said to be allowed to walk the earth during the event (☎ 852/2508-1234; www.discoverhongkong.com). If you're around in July, you can check out **Hong Kong Fashion Week** (☎ 852/1830-668; www.hkfashionweekss.tdctrade.com), though it's primarily a trade event.

FALL. The **Mid-Autumn Festival** (☎ 852/2508-1234; www.discoverhongkong.com), in September or early October, celebrates Hong Kong's harvest and the brightest moon of the year. It's tradition to light (or turn on battery-charged) lanterns of all shapes and sizes and eat "moon cakes." The **Chung Yueng Festival** (☎ 852/2508-1234; www.discoverhongkong.com), also in September or October, is the second time of the year when ancestral graves are ritually swept and offerings made to the deceased.

WINTER. Chinese New Year, in January or February, is the most important holiday on the calendar. Many shops close as staff head off to spend time with their families. There are celebratory parades and Chinese fireworks but the sheer number of people who visit make it an uncomfortable time to be in Hong Kong. The **Hong Kong Arts Festival** (☎ 852/2824-2430; www.hk.artsfestival.org) is a month of music, performing arts, and exhibitions from local and international artists. It's held in February and March.

The Weather

Spring and fall are warm and sticky but relatively mild. Summers, on the other hand, are oppressively humid (the ubiquitous air-conditioning helps make it bearable) and punctuated by deluges of rain. Though hardly a winter sun destination, Hong Kong is often mild and pleasant in winter, though things can occasionally turn chilly.

Useful Websites

www.discoverhongkong.com: This is the best resource for travelers headed to Hong Kong, and for those considering a visit, with maps, major attractions, a calendar of events, hotels, restaurants, tours, and even definitions of Chinese terms and holidays.

www.epd-asg.gov.hk/eindex.php: This is the Environmental Protection Department's pollution index—sadly worth checking out in a city where poor air quality is an issue.

www.hkoutdoors.com: The most comprehensive site if you plan on hiking or trail running on your trip.

Cellphones (Mobile Phones)

If your phone is on a **GSM (Global System for Mobiles) Wireless Network** (GSM 900, PCS 1800, or CDMA), you will be able to make and receive calls in Hong Kong.

A cheaper option is to buy a local SIM card. **CSL** (☎ 852/2888-1010; www.hkcsl.com) sells prepaid

HONG KONG'S AVERAGE DAILY TEMPERATURE & RAINFALL

	JAN	FEB	MAR	APR	MAY	JUNE
Daily Temp. (°F)	61	61	64	72	77	80
Daily Temp. (°C)	16	16	18	22	25	27
Rainfall (in.)	5.6	8.9	10.1	11.1	14.9	14.2

	JULY	AUG	SEPT	OCT	NOV	DEC
Daily Temp. (°F)	84	84	80	77	70	64
Daily Temp. (°C)	29	29	27	25	21	18
Rainfall (in.)	17.5	17.3	14.4	8.6	5.9	3.9

SIM cards for as little as $HK48. They also rent phones for $HK35 per day, with rechargeable SIM chips costing $HK180 to $HK280 for 293 to 600 minutes. Top-up cards cost $HK100 to $HK500. Other places that sell SIM cards and rent phones include **SmarTone** (☎ 852/2880-2688; www.smartone-vodafone.com), and **3 Hong Kong** (☎ 852/3162-8888; www.three.com.hk); both have shops all over town.

Car Rentals

Given that Hong Kong is a small city with a world-class public transport network, renting a car will likely be an unnecessary expense and hassle. If you need to have a car at your disposal, book one before you leave home—and remember that companies often offer better prices online. Try **Hertz** (www.hertz.com) or **Avis** (www.avis.com.hk). There is also a multitude of chauffeur services. **Ace Hire Car** (www.acehirecar.com.hk) is but one of the options.

Getting **There**

By Plane

Hong Kong International Airport is consistently ranked one of the best airports in the world (☎ 852/2181-8888; www.hongkongairport.com). Major airlines that fly to Hong Kong from North America, Europe, and Australia include Air Canada (☎ 888/247-2262; www.aircanada.com); British Airways (☎ 0870/850-9850; www.britishairways.com); Hong Kong's home carrier Cathay Pacific (☎ 800/233-2742; www.cathaypacific.com); Continental Airlines (☎ 800/231-0856; www.continental.com); Qantas (☎ 02/9691-3636; www.qantas.com); and Singapore Airlines (☎ 800/742-3333; www.singaporeair.com).

From Hong Kong International Airport: Once you collect your baggage, you'll have a chance to withdraw money from international ATMs and collect maps and tourist information from the Hong Kong Tourism Board booths.

Once you're set, there are a number of ways to get into the city. The quickest and easiest is the **Airport Express** (☎ 852/2881-8888; www.mtr.com.hk). This high-speed train stops in Kowloon ($HK90) and Hong Kong Island ($HK100). Trains run every 12 minutes between approximately 6am and 1am, and it takes 24 minutes to get to Central. When returning to the airport, note that both the Kowloon and Hong Kong Island stations offer downtown airport check-in services. Free shuttle buses take passengers to and from most major hotels (www.mtr.com.hk).

A slightly cheaper way to get into the city is the **Cityflyer Airbus** (☎ 852/2873-0818; www.citybus.com.hk). Of the five routes, the most useful is the A21, which goes through Mong Kok, Yau Ma Tei, Jordan, and down Nathan Road through Tsim Sha Tsui; and the A11, which goes to Hong Kong Island. Buses depart every 10 to 30 minutes. It's $HK33 to Kowloon and $HK40 to the island.

For those who prefer the ease of a **taxi,** note that only red cabs are allowed to travel to Kowloon and Hong Kong Island, so be sure you opt for the right rank. Prices vary depending on where you are going, but expect to pay up to $HK300 for a ride to Central. There is an additional $HK20 levy on each bag stored in the trunk. It will take around 45 minutes to reach Central.

By Train

The MTR corporation (www.mtr.com.hk) runs three intercity routes into mainland China. The long-distance Beijing and Shanghai through-trains (23½ hr. and 18½ hr. respectively) run on alternate days. Tickets cost $HK601/$HK934 for hard/soft sleeper seats to Beijing, and $HK530/$HK825 to Shanghai. The third route covers the neighboring province of Guangdong and extends out as far as Zhaoqing in the west of the Pearl River Delta. There are regular fast trains to Guangzhou, which take just under 2 hours. Tickets cost $HK190 and can be booked through the Intercity Passenger Service Hotline (☎ 852/2947-7888).

On Foot

Everyone crossing the border with the mainland at Lo Wu, the world's busiest customs point, must board the MTR's **East Rail Line.** It runs as far as Hung Hom station, in Tsim Sha Tsui, where it's easy to connect to the rest of the MTR network. The fare is $HK33 and the journey takes exactly 43 minutes.

By Bus

A number of bus companies offer routes to and from cities in Guangdong at competitive rates. Some options are **CTS Express Coach** (☎ 852/2365-0118; http://ctsbus.hkcts.com); **Eternal East** (☎ 852/3412-6677; www.eebus.com); **Gogobus** (☎ 852/2375-0099; www.gogobus.com); and the **Motor Transport Company of Guangdong & Hong Kong** (☎ 852/2375-2991; www.gdhkmtc.cn).

Boat

Boats run to and from Shenzhen, Macau, and several Pearl River Delta cities. **TurboJET** (☎ 852/2859-3333; www.turbojet.com.hk) and **New World First Ferry** (☎ 852/2131-8181; www.nwff.com.hk) serve Macau and Shenzhen, while the **Chu Kong Passenger Transport Company** (☎ 852/2858-3876; www.cksp.com.hk) covers other mainland routes.

Getting **Around**

Note that for all the following public transport options, fares rise slightly on Sundays.

By Subway

The **Mass Transit Railway** (**MTR;** ☎ 852/2881-8888; www.mtr.com.hk) is the fastest way to get around the city, though there are a few long walks required at major connecting stations. All stations have self-service ticket machines and prices range from $HK4 to $HK33. However, I highly recommend getting a prepaid Octopus card, available from customer service centers at all MTR stations. A $HK50 deposit is required ($HK7 of which is nonrefundable if you return the card within 3 months) but because Octopus journeys are marginally cheaper, you'll save both time and money. Each time you swipe your card you'll get a readout of how much credit you have left, and you can easily top-up in $HK50 or $HK100 bursts. Importantly, Octopus cards also work for buses, ferries, and at places like grocery stores, movie theaters—even horse-racing tracks.

The MTR network has expanded rapidly, absorbing the former Kowloon-Canton Railway (KCR) in 2007, and continues to grow. There are currently nine regular lines, covering 168km (104 miles) of track and 80 stations. Additionally, the MTR also runs the Airport Express line and 36km (22 miles) worth of light-rail lines in the New Territories. It also provides the through-train services to mainland China.

By Tram

Hong Kong's **double-decker trams** are an option for traveling along the busy northern shore of Hong Kong Island. The trams are slow, but fun and cheap—a ride costs $HK2. Trams operate from 6am to 12:30am and cover six routes: Kennedy Town to Western Market, Kennedy Town to Causeway Bay, Kennedy Town to Happy Valley, Sai Ying Pun (Whitty St.) to North Point, Sheung Wan (Western Market) to Shau Kei Wan, and Happy Valley to Shau Kei Wan.

By Bus

Hong Kong's **Citybus** (www.citybus.com.hk) is fairly easy to use if you have a map and a little patience. Its routes cover nearly the whole of Hong Kong and run day and night. Fares range from $HK2.40 to $HK45 depending on where you're going and at what time of day. The major bus terminus in Central is located below Exchange Square and has routes to Aberdeen, Repulse Bay, and Stanley. In Tsim Sha Tsui, the bus terminal is located next to the Star Ferry Pier. Signs at bus stops give a detailed breakdown of fare information and bus stop locations. All buses with an M stop at MTR stations and those with an X are express and sometimes take the highways, so be careful you don't overshoot your stop if taking them.

Citybus also runs the **Rickshaw Sightseeing Bus.** Specially decorated in a rickshaw livery, the bus offers a daylong $HK50 hop-on, hop-off service from Central, tailored to tourists. The "Metropolitan" route runs east out towards Admiralty and Wan Chai, while the "Heritage" route covers the Chinese heart of Hong Kong.

Minibuses also cover the entirety of Hong Kong but the difficulty of communicating with drivers, few of whom speak English, makes them hard for casual visitors to use. Green minibuses run set routes with designated stops, while the red variety operate flexible routes and allow passengers to alight at any point. Minibuses will generally not stop unless someone asks to get off, difficult to do if you don't speak any Cantonese (or Mandarin).

By Ferry

There are four **Star Ferry** (www.starferry.com.hk) routes between the island and the peninsula. The routes run from Central to Tsim Sha Tsui, Central to Hung Hom, Wan Chai to Tsim Sha Tsui, and Wan Chai to Hung Hom. A number of other ferries go to outlying islands like Lantau, Cheung Chau, and Lamma. You can catch these ferries from one of the Central piers.

By Car

Driving is not recommended because taxis are cheap and the crowded, often steep roads take some getting used to. Frequent traffic jams are also a deterrent. If you do drive, having GPS will likely be essential.

Fast **Facts**

APARTMENT RENTALS There are a number of serviced apartments available for long-term stays in Hong Kong. They range from the very expensive to the quite expensive. **Four Seasons Place Hong Kong** (☎ 852/3196-8228; www.fsphk.com) is on the former end, **W Studios** (☎ 852/9866-8333; www.wstudios.com.hk) on the latter. Check this website for a list: http://hongkong.asiaxpat.com/property/serviced.asp.

ATMS/CASHPOINTS You can withdraw funds from home checking and savings accounts if you have a card that's part of the **Cirrus** or **PLUS** network. There are many ATMs scattered around the city. Most banks charge a fee for international withdrawals, so check before you leave home.

BABYSITTING A reliable place to get part-time sitters or longer-term nannies is **The Nanny Experts** (☎ 852/2335-1127; www.thenannyexperts.com).

BIKE RENTALS I wouldn't bother renting bikes to explore Kowloon or Hong Kong Island. Their crowded sidewalks and steep, winding roads make riding a serious challenge. Bicycles are better suited to Cheung Chau, where rental shops can easily be found.

BUSINESS HOURS Hong Kong is a late-rising city. Official business hours are 9am to 5:30 or 6pm, Monday to Friday, and 9am to noon on Saturday. However, many shops will not open until 10am or even 11am but stay open well after dark. While banks and post offices will close on public holidays, attractions and shops will generally stay open.

CONSULATES & EMBASSIES **American Consulate,** 26 Garden Rd., Central (☎ 852/2523-9011; http://hongkong.usconsulate.gov); **Canadian Consulate,** 12–14/F, 1 Exchange Square, 8 Connaught Place, Central (☎ 852/3719-4700; www.hongkong.gc.ca); **British Consulate,** 1 Supreme Court Rd., Central (☎ 852/2901-3000; www.britishconsulate.org.hk); **Australian Consulate,** 23/F Harbour Centre, 25 Harbour Rd., Wan Chai (☎ 852/2827-8881; www.hongkong.china.embassy.gov.au).

CREDIT CARDS Most major credit cards are accepted in large shops, restaurants, hotels, and ticket booths. Your best bet is to have a Visa, MasterCard, or American Express, though Diners Club and JCB are sometimes taken. Bring your banking and credit card details in case you need to call to cancel anything or have trouble withdrawing funds.

CURRENCY EXCHANGE You can cash traveler's checks or exchange money at banks or foreign exchange offices around the city, including those in hotels and at the airport.

CUSTOMS When entering Hong Kong, those 18 and older can bring in duty free a 1-liter (34-oz.) bottle of alcohol and 60 cigarettes, 15 cigars, or 75 grams (2⅔ oz.) of tobacco. To see what you can take home, check the website of your country's Customs and border protection department.

DENTISTS & DOCTORS There are 41 public hospitals in Hong Kong. Two reliable options are **Queen Mary Hospital,** 102 Pokfulam Rd., Sai Ying Pun (☎ 852/2255-3838), and **Queen Elizabeth Hospital,** 30 Gascoigne Rd., Jordan (☎ 852/2958-8888). Most first-class hotels in Hong Kong actually have in-house medical clinics with registered nurses and doctors on call in case of emergencies. The U.S. consulate also provides a list of English-speaking doctors.

ELECTRICITY The standard voltage is 220 volts, 50 hertz AC. Most outlets are designed to accommodate the British three square pins. Buy an adapter before you leave home or pick one up at a shop in the Hong Kong airport terminal or around the city.

EMERGENCIES To call for an ambulance or the police, or in case of a fire, dial ☎ **999.**

EVENT LISTINGS ***HK Magazine, BC Magazine,*** and ***Time Out Hong Kong,*** as well as local newspapers, all list events in the city. The tourist board website **www.discoverhongkong.com** also has an excellent event calendar.

FAMILY TRAVEL Hong Kong is a great place to travel with older children, since there's so much to see and do (notably Ocean Park and Hong Kong Disneyland). There are also many discounts available for kids on everything from shows to public transportation. Traveling with small kids is a bit trickier; many places are crowded and noisy. If you're traveling with an infant or toddler, be prepared for lots of tight spaces and steep steps—your stroller may not fit.

GAY & LESBIAN TRAVELERS There is a vibrant gay and lesbian community in Hong Kong. Discrimination is not a serious issue here though you may encounter some less-than-open-minded types. There are a limited number of gay bars and clubs, but many places have designated gay or lesbian nights.

HOLIDAYS The dates of many public holidays change from year to year, based on the lunar calendar. Check out www.gov.hk/en/about/abouthk/holiday/index.htm for details. In general, public holidays are: New Year's Day on January 1, 3 days for Lunar New Year in January or February, Ching Ming Festival in April, Labour Day in May, Tuen Ng Festival in May or June, Establishment Day of the Special Administrative Region on July 1, the day following the Mid-Autumn Festival in September or October, National Day on October 1, and Christmas Day on December 25.

INSURANCE Although Hong Kong is a safe travel destination, if you want to insure your tickets, belongings, or health, go to **InsureMyTrip.com** for estimates on travel insurance. For trip cancellation insurance, try **Travel Guard International** (☎ 800/826-4919; www.travelguard.com). For medical insurance, **Travel Assistance International** (☎ 800/821-2828; www.travelassistance.com) offers plans that cover you while you're on the road. For lost luggage insurance, check with your airline.

INTERNET ACCESS Free Internet is becoming the norm in Hong Kong. There's free WiFi available across Hong Kong International Airport. The MTR Corporation has installed six free Web terminals at Central station. Free Internet access is now common in hotels, but some still charge. There are an increasing number of government-provided free wireless hotspots around the city—look out for the signs. All of Hong Kong's public libraries (including the huge **Central Library** in Causeway Bay) offer free Internet services. More ubiquitous are outlets of **Pacific Coffee Company** (www.pacificcoffee.com), which have terminals where customers can surf for free. The Internet cafes that do exist are often not streetside and generally cater to teenage gamers rather than tourists.

LIQUOR LAWS The drinking (and smoking) age in Hong Kong is 18. Beer and wine can be found at convenience stores around the city, and liquor is also sold at department stores and supermarkets. Bar hours vary, but some stay open until dawn.

LOST PROPERTY To report lost or stolen property, call the police hotline at ☎ 852/2527-7177. Information on police stations is available at www.police.gov.hk.

MAIL The postal service in Hong Kong is safe and reliable, and most post offices are open Monday to Friday from 9:30am to 5pm and Saturday from 9:30am to 1pm. Postal workers generally speak some English, so you shouldn't have trouble getting the correct stamps and postage fees. Airmail letters take about 5 to 7 days to reach their destination in the U.S. and Europe. The main post office is on Hong Kong Island (2 Connaught Place, Central; ☎ 852/2921-2222). For other locations check out www.hongkongpost.com.

MONEY The local currency is the Hong Kong dollar ($HK), which is pegged to the U.S. dollar at a rate of around US$1 to $HK7.80. The Hong Kong dollar is divided into denominations of $10, $20, $50, $100, $500, and $1,000. There are coins of 10 cents, 20 cents, 50 cents, $1, $2, $5, and $10.

NEWSPAPERS & MAGAZINES The best local English-language daily newspaper is the *South China Morning Post* (www.scmp.com), which sells for $HK7. The *Hong Kong Standard* (www.thestandard.com.hk) focuses on business and costs $HK6 (Mon–Sat). The *China Daily* is a state-run newspaper out of Beijing that brings news from the mainland as well as reports on Hong Kong from a mainland perspective; it sells for $HK6. International titles are available in airports, hotels, and bookstores, and include the *Wall Street Journal Asia, USA Today,* the *International Herald Tribune,* and the *Financial Times*.

There are three city magazines that have articles and listings that may be useful for tourists: *HK Magazine, BC Magazine,* and *Time Out Hong Kong*. There are also local editions of international magazines, such as *Hong Kong Tatler* (www.hktatler.com) and *Time Asia*.

PASSES You can buy a $HK30 museum pass that allows a week of unlimited access to seven of Hong Kong's most popular museums. It can be bought from the participating museums. A prepaid Octopus card, available at all MTR stations, will allow you to swipe on and off all major public transportation and can be used like a debit card at many shops around the city.

PASSPORTS If your passport is lost or stolen, contact your consulate or embassy. It's smart to have photocopies of all your important documents with you.

PHARMACIES There are no 24-hour drugstores in Hong Kong, so if you're in desperate need of a prescription, contact a hospital or the police. One of the best-known pharmacy chains is Watson's—there are more than 100 around the city and they're open from 9am to 10pm daily. You can also buy medication at small Chinese drugstores.

POLICE Dial ☎ 999 in an emergency. Otherwise, you can call the police via a crime hotline at ☎ 852/2527-7177. The Rape Crisis Line is ☎ 852/2375-5322.

QUALITY TOURISM SERVICES The Quality Tourism Services (QTS) Scheme gives a seal of approval to a variety of shops, restaurants, and guesthouses operating at the lower end of the market. QTS notes price clarity and high standards of customer service, reliability, and hygiene. It's particularly reassuring for those looking to buy, eat, or stay cheaply. Look out for the sign.

RESTROOMS There are free public restrooms all around Hong Kong. Most are clean, with Western-style toilets, though I highly recommend carrying your own tissues. Be warned that there are no public bathrooms inside MTR stations.

SAFETY Hong Kong is a very safe city for tourists. The official crime rate is low and there's very little menace when wandering around the streets, even at night. There have been rare cases of hikers being robbed, though heat stroke is a bigger danger.

SENIOR TRAVELERS Seniors receive discounts to many museums, shows, public transportation options, and activities in Hong Kong; bring along identification that clearly states your age. Some discounts are available for those 60 and over, while others are only open to those 66 and over, so be sure to ask. Be aware that many activities in Hong Kong involve walking—though with a little extra planning, you can minimize how much time you spend on your feet. Also, the heat in the summer can be stifling, an issue for both young and old.

SMOKING Since 2007 smoking has been banned in virtually all public indoor areas in Hong Kong, including bars and restaurants. Many venues have designated outdoor smoking zones. There are generally smoking rooms available in hotels but nonsmoking has become the norm in recent years.

STAYING HEALTHY The two biggest health scares in Hong Kong in the past decade have been bird flu and SARS, leading to major changes in policy. All travelers to Hong Kong now have their temperature checked on arrival, and strict rules on housing and slaughtering livestock in markets have been introduced. Hong Kongers are exceedingly conscious of health issues—expect to get dirty looks if you do not properly muffle coughs or sneezes on the MTR—and the city is as safe for a short stay as any developed country (though in the long term, the air pollution may be detrimental to your health). Generally, you can dine without worry anywhere in the city, including roadside eateries. It's safe to drink water in the city center, including ice in restaurants, but stick to bottled water if traveling to rural Hong Kong or mainland China.

TAXES Hotels will add a 10% service charge and a 3% government tax to your bill. Restaurants and bars will add a 10% service charge, but there is no tax. There's an airport departure tax of $HK120 that will generally be included in your ticket price. There is no tax for purchasing electronics, which is why buying those items here is often such a steal.

TELEPHONES The international country code for Hong Kong is 852. All local calls in Hong Kong are free except at public pay phones, where they cost $HK1 for every 5 minutes. International direct-dial (IDD) calls can be made from public phones with a phone card or from hotels. Phone cards are sold at 7-Elevens, Circle Ks, and other convenience stores around the city. To make **international calls** from Hong Kong dial ☎ 001 and then the country code (**U.S.** or **Canada** 1; **UK** 44; **Ireland** 353; **Australia** 61; **New Zealand** 64). For **directory assistance in English** call ☎ 1081.

TELEVISION & RADIO The two English-language stations in Hong Kong are TVB Pearl and ATV World. English-language radio includes RTHK Radio 3 (567AM, 1584AM, 97.9FM, and 106.8FM). RTHK Radio 4 (97.6FM–98.9FM), RTHK Radio 6 (675AM), AM 864 (864AM), and Metro Plus (1044AM).

TICKETS You can get tickets at any of the 34 URBTIX outlets around the city or online at www.urbtix.hk.

TIME Hong Kong standard time is 8 hours ahead of Greenwich Mean Time; there is no daylight saving time.

TIPPING There isn't a tipping culture in Hong Kong. Cabdrivers only expect you to round up to the nearest dollar, and hotel bellboys will be happy with $HK10 to $HK20. Most restaurants and some bars add a 10% service charge. Anything additional is discretionary.

TOURIST OFFICES The **Hong Kong Tourism Board** (☎ 852/2508-1234; www.discoverhongkong.com) is extremely active in promoting Hong Kong and offers a multitude of services (see "Tours," below). There are branches at Hong Kong International Airport, the Star Ferry Concourse in Tsim Sha Tsui, the Peak Piazza on Hong Kong Island, and the Lo Wu border crossing, though the website is a treasure-trove of useful information.

TOURS The **Hong Kong Tourism Board** (☎ 852/2508-1234; www.discoverhongkong.com) organizes a variety of tours, courses, and events, everything from tea appreciation classes to architectural walks, many of which are free. See the "Things to Do" section of the website. The efficiency and reach of the HKTB makes a lot of tours offered by private operators rather redundant, though **Splendid Tours & Travel** (☎ 852/2316-2151; www.splendidtours.com) and **Sky Bird Travel** (☎ 852/2369-9628; www.skybird.com.hk) are among the more established independent companies. You can go dolphin spotting with **Hong Kong Dolphinwatch** (☎ 852/2984-1414; www.hkdolphinwatch.com), and get outdoors with **Kayak and Hike** (☎ 852/9300-5197; www.kayak-and-hike.com). **Walk the Talk** (☎ 852/2380-7756; www.walkthetalk.hk) provides a useful audio guide to major attractions, downloadable to Smart Phone or iPhone.

TRAVELERS WITH DISABILITIES Hong Kong tries, but often fails, to be a friendly city to those with disabilities. If you're planning a trip, be aware that while MTR stops have escalators and elevators, there are often very long distances in between the entrances and exits and the train. There are also huge crowds to contend with. Many buses are now wheelchair accessible, though English may be a problem with some bus drivers. Taxis are generally easy to find in any major part of the city, and nearly all buildings have elevators. Public toilets are generally wheelchair accessible, crosswalks are equipped with sound sensors for crossing, and there are textured lines on major streets for the visually impaired. For information contact the **Transport Department** (☎ 852/2804-2660; www.td.gov.hk) or the **Joint Council for the Physically and Mentally Disabled** (☎ 852/2864-2931; www.hkcss.org.hk).

VISAS Citizens of Australia, Canada, Japan, New Zealand, and the USA can enter Hong Kong for 90 days without a visa. People from South Africa have 30 days, and people from the UK and other European Union countries have 180 days. If coming from any other region, please check visa regulations at www.immd.gov.hk/ehtml/hkvisas_4.htm. If you're traveling to mainland China, you will need a visa. There are hundreds of agents offering mainland visa services but the cheapest method is to apply in person at China's Foreign Ministry office in Wan Chai. See www.fmcoprc.gov.hk for more details and the office's location.

Hong Kong: **A Brief History**

4000–1500 B.C. Early settlers of Asian Mongoloid background settle throughout southern China, including Hong Kong. They leave behind tools and burial grounds.

221–206 B.C. Hong Kong is incorporated into China under the Qin dynasty.

A.D.618–907 Under the Tang dynasty, the Guangdong region becomes a major trading center. Tuen Mun, in what is now Hong Kong's New Territories, was a naval base, salt production center, and base for pearl trading.

960–1500s Pirates roam the seas around Hong Kong.

1276 During the Mongol invasion, the Southern Song dynasty court moved to Lantau Island, and then to Kowloon City. Hong Kong also saw its first population boom thanks to Chinese refugees during this period.

1514 Portuguese traders establish a base in nearby Macau.

1839 The Chinese emperor destroys the British opium stockpile in a desperate attempt to quell the growing opium trade, which is draining China's wealth. The British Royal Navy retaliates by firing on Chinese war junks, starting the First Opium War.

1842 The Treaty of Nanking is signed by China and Britain, putting an end to the First Opium War. The treaty cedes Hong Kong Island to Britain. Sir Henry Pottinger is the territory's first governor.

1860 Under the Peking Convention of 1860, following the Second Opium War, China cedes the Kowloon area to Britain.

1865 The Hongkong and Shanghai Banking Corporation (HSBC) is founded.

1888 The Peak Tram makes its first run up Victoria Peak, reducing the travel time from 3 hours to 8 minutes.

1898 Under the Second Peking Convention, Britain and China agree on a 99-year lease on the New Territories, including surrounding islands. The British, who fear Hong Kong will be vulnerable to Chinese attack without the added land, pay nothing. Had the British not settled on a lease, it's possible they would not have had to hand Hong Kong back to China in 1997. The first major wave of Chinese immigrants arrives in Hong Kong, fleeing civil war.

1900 Hong Kong's population is 263,000.

1912 The University of Hong Kong opens.

1904 The tram system is constructed along the waterfront on Hong Kong Island.

1910 The Kowloon Railway is completed, linking Hong Kong with China.

1911 The Manchu dynasty is overthrown by Sun Yat-sen's Nationalist revolution, and a second wave of Chinese refugees arrives in Hong Kong.

1925 Hong Kong's first and only general strike occurs. Nationalists and Communists join in a united front, organizing antiforeign strikes and boycotts in China that spread to Hong Kong. The economy is paralyzed.

1941–45 Japan invades and occupies Hong Kong during World War II. After the war ends in 1945, Britain resumes control of Hong Kong.

1949 China's Communists defeat the Nationalists and win control of China. The war drives many to Hong Kong, where squatter villages begin to develop on the city's outskirts.

1960–70s Hong Kong residents begin to clash with the colonial government and police, some under the rubric of Communism akin to that on the mainland. Officials in Hong Kong step up anti-Communist purges and close pro-Beijing newspapers. But as the city's economy takes off thanks to manufacturing and international trade, economics wins out over rebellion.

1976 Mao Zedong, the all-powerful Chinese Communist Party chairman, dies and Deng Xiaoping emerges as the country's leader, calling for opening and reform. Britain asks for a renewal on its 99-year lease of the New Territories, but Deng refuses and calls for the return of all of Hong Kong to China.

1979 The MTR transportation system is founded.

1984 British Prime Minister Margaret Thatcher and China Premier Zhao Ziyang sign the Joint Declaration requiring Britain to transfer sovereignty of Hong Kong to China at midnight on June 30, 1997. China vows to give Hong Kong a "high degree of autonomy" and permits it to retain its capitalist system for 50 years after 1997.

1989 After Beijing's military crackdown on protestors in Tiananmen Square, more than one million people in Hong Kong take to the streets in protest.

1992–95 The British governor, Christopher Patten, announces democratic reforms for the 1994 local and 1995 legislative elections. Critics see it as a belated effort to bring democracy to Hong Kong after years of colonial rule. Relations between China and Britain grow strained, and many Hong Kong residents apply for British and Canadian citizenship.

JULY 1, 1997 Hong Kong is officially ceded to China and becomes a Special Autonomous Region (SAR). Beijing strikes down many of the last-minute rules and liberties Patten put in place before he left, and institutes an interim legislature. Port tycoon Tung Chee-hwa, viewed by many as Beijing's handpicked choice, becomes chief executive of the SAR.

OCTOBER 23, 1997 The Hong Kong stock market crashes after interest rates are raised to protect the Hong Kong dollar from currency speculators. Millions of dollars are lost overnight and the property market goes into a slump.

1998 The SAR has its first legislative election under Chinese rule. Pro-democracy politicians win 60% of the popular vote but only 20 seats in the 60-seat legislature. In the first major protest since Tiananmen Square in 1989, 40,000 people commemorate the anniversary of that incident. Hong Kong International Airport opens.

FEBRUARY 19, 2002 Hong Kong's chief executive, Tung Chee-hwa, secures a second 5-year term in office without an election.

JUNE 24, 2002 Tung announces a new cabinet of ministers that marks the biggest shake-up in the territory's governance since it ceased to be a colony.

2003 Severe Acute Respiratory Syndrome (SARS) rocks the territory and bruises the economy.

JUNE 21, 2005 Donald Tsang takes over as chief executive of Hong Kong after the resignation of Tung Chee-hwa, who had been criticized by the public for bungling leadership of the territory.

The **People**

Hong Kong is a city of just over seven million people on a land area of approximately 1,100 sq. km (425 sq. miles, or half the size of Rhode Island in the U.S.). Though the long years of British colonial rule make it like no other city in China, it's still 95% ethnically Chinese, with over half of those residents born in Hong Kong.

Most Chinese in Hong Kong come from the neighboring province of Guangdong (Canton), thus the establishment of Cantonese instead of Mandarin as the primary official language.

Influence from mainland China is becoming more and more evident, particularly in terms of a focus on national issues, and the increased numbers of mainland visitors and residents. Long a beacon of money and upward mobility to mainland Chinese, people still flock to Hong Kong if they can afford it and can find the necessary permits (Hong Kong is not open to the vast majority of Chinese people). About 54,000 mainland Chinese come to try to make it in Hong Kong every year, offsetting one of the world's lowest birth rates.

Because of its dense population, limited land space, and 16,000 people per square mile, Hong Kong has long been plagued with housing shortages. In 1953, a huge fire left more than 50,000 people homeless. Since then, Hong Kong has implemented a housing scheme to try and provide every family with a home.

By 1993, more than half of Hong Kong's population lived in government-subsidized public housing. A typical apartment in such living areas is about 23 sq. m (248 sq. ft.), with a single window. It has a living room/bedroom, small cooking area, and bathroom, and is often shared by a couple with one or two children. While space may be tight, the standards of living are decent. According to the government, every household in Hong Kong has at least one television, more than enough food, and access to public transportation and recreation in public facilities.

Useful Phrases & Menu Terms

Cantonese and English are Hong Kong's two official languages, with Cantonese being used by some 94% of the population. English is the primary language of the legal, professional, and business sectors, and even outside these environments, most people speak at least a little English though many worry that standards have slipped since 1997. Though it's not yet an official language, Mandarin has rapidly gained in importance in Hong Kong, a trend that has become more pronounced given the increasingly intimate relationship Hong Kong enjoys with the mainland. All signs are in both Chinese and English. Knowing some basic words in Cantonese is an advantage, though it is a difficult language to learn and few locals will expect a foreigner to speak it. There are nine different tones, though you can make do with six. This means that a word pronounced "yow," depending on the tone, can mean thin, have, friend, to worry, or to rest. If you really want to learn Chinese, I recommend attending classes or hiring a tutor—it's impossible for books to convey how to pronounce tone. But for now, just trying some of these words will endear you to locals and get you, at worst, an uncomprehending smile.

Accommodations

ENGLISH	CANTONESE
I'm looking for . . .	Ngo yiu wan . . .
Guesthouse	Jiu doi so
Hotel	Jau dim
Do you have any rooms available?	Yau mo fong a?
I'd like a (single/double) room.	Ngo seung yiu yat gaan (daan yan/seung yan) fong.
How much is it per night?	Yiu gei do cin yat maan a?

Shopping

ENGLISH	CANTONESE
How much does this cost?	Ni go gei do chin a?
That's too much.	Taai gwai loa.
I want to buy . . .	Ngo seung maai . . .
Do you accept credit cards?	Nei dei sau m sau sun yung kaat a?
I'm just looking.	Ngo sin tai yat tai.
More	Do di
Less	Siu di
Bigger	Daai di
Smaller	Sai di

Greetings

ENGLISH	CANTONESE
Hello, how are you?	Nei ho ma?
Goodbye.	Baai baai/joi gin.
Yes	Hai
No	M hai
I'm fine.	Ngo gei ho.
Excuse me.	M goi.
Thank you (for a gift).	Do je.
Thank you (for service).	M goi.
Do you speak English?	Nei sik m sik gong ying man a?
I don't understand.	Ngo m ming.

ENGLISH	CANTONESE
What's your surname?	Cheng man gwai sing?
My surname is . . .	Siu sing . . .
My name is . . .	Ngo giu . . .
Can you please repeat that?	Cheng joi gong yat chi?

Emergencies

ENGLISH	CANTONESE
I'm sick.	Ngo yau beng.
Call the police!	Giu ging chaat!
Call an ambulance!	Giu gau seung che!
Call a doctor!	Giu yi sang!
Help!	Gau meng a!
Where's the police station?	Ging chue hai bin do a?

Health

ENGLISH	CANTONESE
Where's the nearest . . . , please?	Cheng man jui kan ge . . . bin do a?
Chemist/pharmacy	Yeuk fong
Doctor	Yi sang
Dentist	Nga yi sang
Hospital	Yi yuen
I'm sick.	Ngo yau beng.
I need a doctor.	Ngo yiu tai yi sang.
Asthma	Yau haau chuen.
Diarrhea	To ngo
Fever	Yau faat siu
Headache	Tau tung
Pain	Tung

Questions

ENGLISH	CANTONESE
Who?	Bin go a?
What?	Mat ye a?
When?	Gei si a?
Where?	Bin do a?
How?	Dim yeung a?

Restaurants & Food

ENGLISH	CANTONESE
Bring the check please.	M goi, maai daan.
I'm a vegetarian.	Ngo hai sik jaai ge.
That was delicious.	Jan ho mei.
Breakfast	Jo chaan
Dim sum	Dim sam
Lunch	Ng chaan

ENGLISH	CANTONESE
Dinner	Maan chaan
Can you recommend a . . . ?	Ho m ho yi gai siu gaan . . . ?
Bar	Jau ba
Restaurant	Chaan teng
Roast pork	Char siu
Barbecued pork with rice	Char siu fan
Roast duck	Char siu ngap
Fried rice	Chau fan
Fried noodles	Chau min
Braised mixed vegetables	Lo hong tsai

Time

ENGLISH	CANTONESE
Today	Gam yat
Tomorrow	Ting yat
Yesterday	Kam yat
Monday	Sing kei yat
Tuesday	Sing kei yi
Wednesday	Sing kei saam
Thursday	Sing kei sei
Friday	Sing kei ng
Saturday	Sing kei luk
Sunday	Sing kei yat

Numbers

ENGLISH	CANTONESE
0	Ling
1	Yat
2	Yi (Leung for pair)
3	Saam
4	Sei
5	Ng
6	Luk
7	Chat
8	Baat
9	Gau
10	Sap
11	Sap yat
12	Sap yi
20	Yi sap
30	Saam sap
40	Sei sap
50	Ng sap
100	Yat baak
1,000	Yat chin

Toll-Free Numbers & Websites

From the U.S. & Canada

AIR CANADA
☎ *888/247-2262*
www.aircanada.com

CATHAY PACIFIC AIRWAYS
☎ *800/233-2742*
www.cathaypacific.com

CONTINENTAL AIRLINES
☎ *800/231-0856*
www.continental.com

DELTA AIRLINES
☎ *800/221-1212*
www.delta.com

JAPAN AIRLINES
☎ *800/525-3663*
www.jal.com

KOREAN AIR
☎ *800/438-5000*
www.koreanair.com

PHILIPPINE AIRLINES
☎ *800/435-9725*
www.philippineairlines.com

SINGAPORE AIRLINES
☎ *800/742-3333*
www.singaporeair.com

UNITED AIRLINES
☎ *800/538-2929*
www.united.com

From the UK

BRITISH AIRWAYS
☎ *0870/850-9850*
www.britishairways.com

CATHAY PACIFIC
☎ *020/8834-8888*
www.cathaypacific.com

VIRGIN ATLANTIC AIRWAYS
☎ *0870/380-2007*
www.virgin-atlantic.com

From Australia

CATHAY PACIFIC
☎ *131747*
www.cathaypacific.com

QANTAS
☎ *131313*
www.qantas.com.au

From New Zealand

CATHAY PACIFIC
☎ *0508/800454*
www.cathaypacific.com

Discount Airfare Websites

www.orbitz.com
www.bing.com
www.cheapflights.com
www.kayak.com
www.opodo.co.uk
www.priceline.com
www.sidestep.com

Discount Hotel Websites

www.hotels.com
www.quikbook.com
www.agoda.com
www.tripadvisor.com
www.asiatravel.com
www.asiahotels.com

Index

See also Accommodations and Restaurant indexes, below.

Accommodations

Restaurants

Photo **Credits**

p viii: © Fumio Okada/Getty Images; p 3, bottom: © icpix_hk/Alamy Images; p 4, top: © Walter Bibikow/Getty Images; p 4, bottom: © Ulana Switucha/Alamy Images; p 5: © Jon Bower/Alamy; p 7, bottom: © Andrew Burke/Lonely Planet Images; p 8, bottom: © Timothy O'Rourke; p 9, top: © Timothy O'Rourke; p 11, top: © Dbimages/Alamy; p 11, bottom: © Lyndon Giffard Images/Alamy Images; p 12, bottom: © Charles Bowman/Alamy Images; p 13, top: © Timothy O'Rourke; p 13, bottom: © Jon Arnold Images/Alamy; p 15, top: © islandspics HK/Alamy; p 15, bottom: © Greg Elms/Lonely Planet Images; p 16, bottom: © Steve Allen Travel Photography/Alamy; p 17, top: © Dbimages/Alamy; p 18, top: © Paul Springett/Alamy; p 18, bottom: © Timothy O'Rourke; p 19: © Timothy O'Rourke; p 21, top: © Timothy O'Rourke; p 21, bottom: © Timothy O'Rourke; p 22, top: © Picturamic/Alamy; p 22, bottom: © Dallas Stribley/Lonely Planet Images; p 23, bottom: © Phil Weymouth/ Lonely Planet Images; p 25, bottom: © travelstock 44/Alamy; p 26, top: © Peter Bowater/ Alamy; p 26, middle: © Timothy O'Rourke; p 26, bottom: © Gisela Damm/eStock Photo; p 27, top: © Greg Elms/Lonely Planet Images; p 27, bottom: © Reuters/CORBIS; p 30, top: © Dallas Stribley/Lonely Planet Images; p 30, bottom: © BOBBY YIP/Reuters/Corbis; p 31, top: © Derek M. Allan, Travel Ink/Corbis; p 31, bottom: © Steve Vidler/eStock Photo; p 32, top: © Reuters/CORBIS; p 32, bottom:Courtesy of The Pawn; p 33, top: © Greg Elms/Lonely Planet Images; p 36, top: © Prisma/SuperStock, Inc.; p 37, top: © Tristan Deschamps/AGE Fotostock, Inc./SuperStock, Inc.; p 37, bottom: © Alan Howden - Hong Kong Stock Photography/Alamy Images; p 38, top: © Greg Elms/Lonely Planet Images; p 38, bottom: © Phil Weymouth/Lonely Planet Images; p 39: © Miles Ertman/Masterfile; p 41, top: © Ron Stroud/ Masterfile; p 41, bottom: © Rough Guides/Alamy; p 42, bottom: © Timothy O'Rourke; p 43, top: © Timothy O'Rourke; p 43, bottom: © Timothy O'Rourke; p 45, top: © Michele Falzone/ Alamy; p 45, bottom: © AW Photography/Alamy; p 46, bottom: © Doug Houghton/Alamy; p 47, top: © Gareth Jones/Jupiterimages; p 49, top: © Greg Elms/Lonely Planet Images; p 49, bottom: © Steve Vidler/AGE Fotostock, Inc; p 50, top: © Timothy O'Rourke; p 51, middle: © Timothy O'Rourke; p 51, bottom: © Timothy O'Rourke; p 52, top: © Robert Harding Picture Library Ltd/Alamy; p 52, bottom: © Timothy O'Rourke; p 53: © Timothy O'Rourke; p 54, bottom: © Timothy O'Rourke; p 58, top: © Timothy O'Rourke; p 58, bottom: © Timothy O'Rourke; p 59, top: © Timothy O'Rourke; p 60, top: © Timothy O'Rourke; p 60, bottom: © Timothy O'Rourke; p 61, top: © Guillaume Jioux/AGE Fotostock; p 61, bottom: © Timothy O'Rourke; p 62, top: © Timothy O'Rourke; p 62, bottom: © Timothy O'Rourke; p 63, top: © Timothy O'Rourke; p 64, top: © Timothy O'Rourke; p 64, bottom: © Werner Otto/AGE Fotostock; p 65, top: © Timothy O'Rourke; p 65, bottom: © islandspics HK/Alamy; p 66, bottom: © Timothy O'Rourke; p 67: © ArkReligion.com/Alamy; p 70, top: © Doug Houghton; p 71, bottom: © James Marshall/Corbis; p 74, top: © Timothy O'Rourke; p 75, top: © Timothy O'Rourke; p 75, bottom: © Dbimages/Alamy; p 76, bottom: © Doug Houghton/Alamy Images; p 77: © Timothy O'Rourke; p 78, bottom: Courtesy of Isola; p 83, bottom: © Timothy O'Rourke; p 84, bottom: © Rough Guides/Alamy; p 85, top: © Steve Vidler/eStock Photo; p 86, top: © Rough Guides/Alamy; p 86, bottom: © Timothy O'Rourke; p 87, top: © JTB Photo Communications, Inc./Alamy; p 87, bottom: © Jeff Greenberg; p 88, bottom: © James Marshall/ Corbis; p 89, top: © Justin Guariglia/Corbis; p 89, bottom: © Joey Nigh/Corbis; p 90, top: © Timothy O'Rourke; p 91: © Arcaid/Alamy; p 92, bottom: © Timothy O'Rourke; p 96, top: © Timothy O'Rourke; p 97, top: © Timothy O'Rourke; p 97, bottom: © Timothy O'Rourke; p 98, top: © Timothy O'Rourke; p 99, top: © Timothy O'Rourke; p 99, bottom: © Timothy O'Rourke; p 100, bottom: © Larry Lilac/Alamy; p 101, bottom: Courtesy of Dusk til Dawn; p 102, top: © Timothy O'Rourke; p 103: © Timothy O'Rourke; p 104, bottom: © Timothy O'Rourke; p 107, top: © Paul Hilton/epa/Corbis; p 107, bottom: © Atlantide Phototravel/ Corbis; p 108, top: © Greg Elms/Lonely Planet Images; p 108, bottom: © Terry Whittaker/ Alamy; p 109, top: © Timothy O'Rourke; p 110, bottom: © Melvyn Longhurst/Alamy; p 111, top: Courtesy of Peel Fresco; p 112, bottom: © Timothy O'Rourke; p 113: © Timothy O'Rourke; p 114, bottom: © Timothy O'Rourke; p 118, bottom: © Timothy O'Rourke; p 119, top: © Timothy O'Rourke; p 119, bottom: © Timothy O'Rourke; p 120, top: © Jochen Tack/ Alamy; p 120, bottom: © Greg Elms/Lonely Planet Images; p 121, bottom: © Timothy O'Rourke; p 122, bottom: © Timothy O'Rourke; p 123, top: © Massimo Pacifico/AGE Fotostock; p 124, bottom: © Rough Guides/Alamy; p 125, top: Courtesy of Novotel; p 125, bottom: © Timothy O'Rourke; p 126, top: © Michael Kemp/Alamy; p 127: © JTB Photo Communications, Inc./Alamy; p 129, middle: © Thomas Lehne/Alamy; p 130, top: © Iain Masterton/Alamy; p 130, bottom: © Melvyn Longhurst/Alamy; p 131, top: © P. Narayan/ AGE Fotostock; p 131, bottom: © Macduff Everton/Corbis; p 132, top: © Timothy O'Rourke; p 132, bottom: © K. Westermann/Corbis; p 133, top: © Prisma/SuperStock, Inc.; p 135, bottom: © Bill Wassman/Corbis; p 136, top: © imagebroker/Alamy; p 137, top: © SCPhotos/ Alamy; p 137, bottom: © Jean Pierre Amet/BelOmbra/Corbis; p 139, bottom: © Ian Trower/ Alamy; p 140, top: © Timothy O'Rourke; p 141, top: © Timothy O'Rourke; p 141, bottom: © Travel Library Limited/SuperStock, Inc.; p 143, top: © Derek M. Allan; Travel Ink/Corbis; p 143, bottom: © James Davis Photography/Alamy; p 145, top: © Melvyn Longhurst/Alamy; p 145, bottom: © Andrew Burke/Lonely Planet Images; p 146, bottom: © Karen McCunnall PCL/SuperStock, Inc.; p 147: © Alan Novelli/Alamy Images